Principles
of
Reinsurance
Volume II

Principles
of
Reinsurance
Volume II

BERNARD L. WEBB, CPCU, FCAS, MAAA
Professor Emeritus of Actuarial Science and Insurance
Georgia State University

HOWARD N. ANDERSON, CPCU, AIM
Vice President
Skandia America Group

JOHN A. COOKMAN
Vice President, Claims
Seneca Insurance Company

PETER R. KENSICKI, D.B.A., CPCU, CLU, FLMI
Professor of Insurance and Chairholder of Insurance Studies
Eastern Kentucky University

First Edition • 1990

INSURANCE INSTITUTE OF AMERICA
720 Providence Road, Malvern, Pennsylvania 19355-0770

First Edition • June 1990 • Second Printing

Library of Congress Catalog Number 90-80135
International Standard Book Number 0-89462-052-5

Printed in the United States of America

Table of Contents

Chapter 12—Financial Analysis 127

Accounting Methods ~ *Liquidating Versus Continuity Concept; Statutory Accounting Principles Versus GAAP; Realization Concepts; Tax Accounting*

Ratio Analysis ~ *Operating Ratios; Return on Equity*

Factors Affecting Surplus and Statutory Ratios ~ *Changes in Premium Volume; Changes in Loss Reserves; Changes in Investment Values; Reinsurance Transactions; Statutory Accounting Effects; GAAP Effects; Effects on the Reinsurer*

Summary

Chapter 13—Financial Security 155

Information Sources ~ *Insurance Regulatory Authorities; Securities and Exchange Commission (SEC); Informal; Reinsurance Association of America (RAA); A. M. Best; Insurance Solvency International; Standard & Poor's*

Regulation ~ *Aspects of Regulation; Compliance Tools; Future of Reinsurance Regulation*

Ratings of Reinsurers ~ *A. M. Best Company; Insurance Solvency International; Standard and Poor's Corporation; Comparisons; National Association of Insurance Commissioners*

Managing Reinsurance Security ~ *Selecting Reinsurers; Establishing Criteria for Evaluating Security of Reinsurers; Limiting the Amount of Reinsurance Exposure with Selected Reinsurers; Backup Security; Monitoring Reinsurers; Documentation*

Summary

CHAPTER 8

Principles of Loss Reserving

Losses are the amounts an insurer is obligated to pay to claimants as a result of the occurrence of insured events under insurance contracts issued by the insurer. Losses do not include loss adjustment expenses, but only the amounts paid directly to claimants. Loss reserves are established to reflect the legal obligation of the insurer to pay for covered losses that have already happened but have not yet been paid. Loss adjustment expense reserves are established to reflect both the future cost of adjusting covered losses and the expense to defend either groundless claims or claims where the legal obligation of the insurer has yet to be established. Both loss and loss adjustment expense reserves are necessary to give a proper indication of an insurer's financial condition at any given point in time.

Loss reserves are the largest liability for most property-liability insurers. Exhibit 8-1 shows the aggregate for the property-liability insurance business for policyholders' surplus, aggregate loss and loss expense reserves, and the ratio of the reserves to policyholders surplus for the twenty two years 1967 through 1988. It reveals a significant trend in the relationship between loss and loss adjustment expense reserves and policyholders surplus. In 1967, policyholders' surplus exceeded reserves by a slight margin, but in 1988 reserves more than doubled surplus. This changing relationship resulted from three underlying trends: (1) the gradual change from a predominately property insurance business to a predominately liability insurance business; (2) a substantial lengthening of the average period (the "tail") between the occurrence of a liability loss and the settlement of that loss; and (3) a slight increase in the ratio of net written premiums to policyholders' surplus from 1.59 in 1967 to 1.71 in 1988.

Failure to establish adequate loss and loss adjustment expense reserves causes the insurer's financial condition to appear stronger

1

Exhibit 8-1

Property-Liability Insurer Policyholders' Surplus and Loss and
Loss Expense Reserves, 1967-1988 (000,000 omitted)*

(1) Year	(2) Policyholders' Surplus	(3) Loss and Loss Expense Reserves	(4) Ratio of Reserves to Surplus (3)÷(2)
1967	$14,802	$ 13,987	0.94
1968	16,192	15,747	0.97
1969	13,964	18,027	1.29
1970	15,499	20,256	1.31
1971	19,065	22,927	1.20
1972	23,812	26,609	1.12
1973	21,389	30,394	1.42
1974	16,270	34,574	2.13
1975	19,712	39,513	2.00
1976	24,631	47,105	1.91
1977	29,300	56,970	1.94
1978	35,379	68,787	1.94
1979	42,395	81,113	1.91
1980	52,174	92,493	1.77
1981	53,805	102,422	1.90
1982	60,395	111,959	1.85
1983	65,606	122,715	1.87
1984	63,809	134,926	2.11
1985	75,511	154,425	2.05
1986	94,288	184,577	1.96
1987	103,996	217.646	2.09
1988	118,195	241,692	2.04

*Based on data from *Best's Aggregates & Averages* (Property/Casualty
Insurance Edition), 1989, p. 86.

than it actually is. At the 1988 ratio of reserves to policyholders'
surplus, an error of 10 percent in estimating loss reserves would cause
an error of about 20 percent in the stated policyholders' surplus.

Some weak insurers intentionally understate loss reserves to
conceal their financial weakness. Insurers have concealed insolvency by
this method until management succeeded in returning their companies
to solvency. However, this practice appears to have been exceptional.
Chronically inadequate loss and expense reserves usually are a
warning that an insurer is nearing insolvency.

Loss and loss adjustment expense reserves are required for all
lines of property-liability insurance. However, the reserves for property

insurance are relatively smaller and easier to estimate. Consequently, most of this chapter is devoted to the much more complex problem of estimating liability loss and loss adjustment expense reserves. The methods used for reserving for property losses are very similar to those used for liability losses.

Loss and loss adjustment expense reserves may be categorized under several headings:

- Loss Reserves:
  - Losses adjusted but not yet paid
  - Losses in course of adjustment
  - Losses incurred but not reported
- Loss Adjustment Expense Reserves:
  - Allocated loss adjustment expenses
  - Unallocated loss adjustment expenses

The reserve for losses adjusted but not yet paid is the easiest part of the loss reserve to calculate. Since the amount of the payment has already been agreed upon, the calculation of that part of the reserve is simply a matter of adding up the agreed settlement amounts for all claims in that category. The estimation of the other reserves is more complex.

Allocated loss adjustment expenses (ALAE) are those loss adjustment expenses that relate to a specific claim. Examples include fees for defense attorneys, fees for expert witnesses, and court costs. Unallocated loss adjustment expenses (ULAE) are the adjustment expenses not directly charged to a specific claim. Examples include the cost of office space occupied by the claims department, the salary of the claims vice president and other high officials, and similar expenses. The term "loss adjustment expenses" (LAE), without a modifier, includes both ALAE and ULAE for primary insurers. However, in reinsurance agreements, LAE usually includes only allocated loss adjustment expenses.

CASE RESERVES

Most insurers establish a claim file for each reported claim. It is customary for the claims department to include in each file an estimate of the amount that will ultimately be paid to the claimant or claimants. Some insurers establish a separate claim file for each claimant, while others include all claimants from a single event, such as a traffic accident, in a single file. The claims department estimate of ultimate payments, less any payments already made, constitutes the case reserve for the file. A similar estimate is made by the claims department for allocated loss adjustment expenses. Unallocated loss adjustment expenses cannot be allocated directly to individual files, so they must be estimated for all claims (in bulk) by formula.

Case Loss Reserves

Case loss reserves may be established by any of several methods. Three standard methods are (1) the judgment method, (2) the average or factor method, and (3) the tabular method; but other methods or combinations of these methods may be used in some cases.

Judgment Method. In the judgment method, an adjuster, claims examiner, or other claims person estimates the value of the claim based largely on intuition and judgment. This method does not involve any special statistical analysis, although the reserve is influenced generally by past experience with similar claims. A technique based almost entirely on judgment is not susceptible to detailed explanation.

The judgment method of establishing loss reserves suffers from the same weaknesses as the judgment method of doing most things. The accuracy of the existing reserves depends on the quality of the judgment of the person who estimates them. Two people estimating reserves for the same losses may vary rather widely in the amount of the reserves established. Even reserves established by the same person may vary randomly from time to time. Also, it is difficult to explain how a particular reserve figure was derived, or to pass on the skill from one person to another.

Average or Factor Method. The second method of setting case reserves is more mathematical. It is sometimes referred to as the "factor method" or "average method." The reserve for each case is set at an average figure. Preferably, the average figure used should be based on an analysis of past claims and adjusted for inflation, law changes, changes in amounts insured, or other factors that might cause future payments to differ from past payments. When used alone, the average method is most suitable for lines of insurance in which claims are relatively frequent and are not subject to extreme variations. Automobile physical damage coverage is a good example of such a line.

The average method does not yield an accurate reserve for most individual claims. It is inherent in the method that the reserves for many individual claims are inadequate, while the reserves for others are excessive. However, from an accounting standpoint, the goal of the loss reserving process is to arrive at an aggregate loss reserve that accurately indicates the obligations of the insurer to pay outstanding claims. The average method may well achieve this goal, especially if

(1) there is little variation in the amounts of individual claims and (2) claims are reported and paid promptly.

The average method, if used alone, may produce inadequate reserves for some liability lines. This result is especially likely for liability lines with a wide variation in individual claim amounts and long delays in settlements. Medical malpractice insurance and product liability are examples of such lines. In these lines, the small cases usually are settled first, and the large cases remain open longer. Thus, the average amount for open claims, the ones on reserve, would be higher than the average of all claims.

The average method and the judgment method sometimes are used together to cope with this problem. In such combined systems, the average value is assigned to each claim as soon as it is reported. For example, every auto bodily injury claim may be initially reserved at an average value of $7,500. This average reserve may be used for no more than sixty days. The reserve is then adjusted upward or downward by judgment in sixty days or as soon as additional information becomes available. This combination method is used frequently for lines of insurance for which the average method alone is not suitable because of substantial variation in the amounts of individual claims.

Tabular Method. The third, and final, method of setting individual case reserves is the tabular method. It is most useful in calculating reserves for long-term disability insurance, income loss benefits for workers compensation insurance, and structured settlements under liability insurance. A *structured settlement* is an agreement under which at least a part of the claim amount is paid out in installments over an agreed period of years or over the lifetime of the claimant.

Under the tabular method, an interest rate and factors from one or more actuarial tables are combined to calculate the present value of future payments, which becomes the reserve for those payments. Tables that may be used include the following:

1. *Morbidity tables*, showing the probability that a disabled person will recover
2. *Mortality tables*, showing the probability of death
3. *Remarriage tables*, showing the probability that a widow or widower will remarry

The remarriage table is used only if the benefits are terminated on remarriage.

For example, suppose a workers compensation benefit of $300 per week for life is payable to a fifty-year-old permanently disabled male worker. By calculating the probabilities that a fifty-year-old male will live exactly one year, exactly two years, and so forth, and by calculating present value factors at a selected interest rate, the actuaries can calculate the present value factor for an annual annuity of $1 payable to this worker for life. Assume this present value factor is 16.118. The indicated tabular reserve is $300 per week × 52 weeks × 16.118, or $251,441. Such calculations are more involved for an excess of loss reinsurance. Assume such a reinsurer has an excess of loss contract with a $100,000 per loss retention for the reinsured. The reserve of the reinsurer is not simply $251,441 minus $100,000, or $151,441. Instead the reinsurer must consider the probability that the claimant may die before the reinsurance retention is pierced. These calculations are beyond the scope of this text.

Each case reserve calculated by the tabular method can be viewed as an average reserve for all claims with the same characteristics (for example, claimants with the same age, health, and marital status). Consequently, the method is likely to yield an appropriate aggregate reserve if a large number of individual claims exists. However, the reserve for any given claim may vary substantially from the amount ultimately paid.

Other Methods. Because of the stated limitations of the judgment method, many people have experimented with various mathematical methods for setting loss reserves. However, none of the mathematical methods (other than the tabular method) has achieved widespread acceptance. Elaborate formulas for liability claims have been developed to reflect the kind of injury, the economic status of the claimant, the age of the claimant, and other relevant factors.

More recently, expert systems technology, a branch of the science of artificial intelligence, has been used with some success in loss reserving. However, it is too early to evaluate the effectiveness of this technique. An explanation of expert systems is beyond the scope of this chapter, but a brief summary may be useful.

A typical expert system consists of (1) a knowledge base and (2) a computer program. The knowledge base consists of a series of if-then rules, perhaps several thousand of them. A somewhat simplified and hypothetical if-then rule for auto liability claims might read:

> If the insured failed to stop for a traffic signal, and if the plaintiff is thirty-five years old, and if the plaintiff is a neurosurgeon, and if the plaintiff is permanently and totally disabled, and if the case will be tried in Dade County, then the reserve should be $1 million.

The computer program searches the knowledge base for the rule that most closely matches the case to be reserved. The if-then rules might be based on the judgment of a person who has demonstrated unusual accuracy in setting loss reserves. They also could be based on an analysis of closed claims, if the insurance company has a sufficient number of closed files. Expert systems for loss reserving are still experimental, but show substantial promise.

Loss Adjustment Expenses

The case reserves for allocated loss adjustment expenses are established either by judgment or as a percentage of the loss reserve. The judgment method of establishing the ALAE reserve suffers from the same weaknesses as the judgment system for establishing loss reserves. If the ALAE reserve is established as a percentage of a judgment loss reserve, the same weaknesses exist.

If the percentage method is used on a case-by-case basis, the percentage factor is multiplied by the case loss reserve. The percentage factor is derived from an analysis of the historical data of the insurance company showing the relationship between loss payments and loss adjustment expenses. The percentage factor so derived should be adjusted to reflect any known factors that might cause the relationship to change over time. Also, some recognition should be given to the possibility that ALAE is likely to be a higher percentage for large claims than it is for small claims. The percentage method is more likely to be used for calculating bulk ALAE reserves than for case reserves.

The reserve for ULAE is almost always calculated as a percentage. The percentage usually is applied to loss reserves plus ALAE reserves or to earned premiums.

Additional Case Reserves

Sometimes case reserves "develop," or are subsequently found to be inadequate. Two courses of action are available to meet this problem. First, a bulk amount of reserves, not allocated to individual claim files, can be added so that the total loss reserves are adequate even though the reserves specified in individual claim files are not. This common practice is satisfactory, since the goal is adequate aggregate reserves rather than accurate individual case reserves. This method is discussed elsewhere in this chapter and in Chapter 9.

The second method for correcting inadequate case reserves is to increase the reserve in each individual claim file. The simplest way of doing this is to add the same percentage increase to each file. However, this is a temporary expedient. It will most likely result in the reserves for some files becoming overstated or redundant while others remain inadequate. As claims are settled, the files with redundant reserves tend to be closed sooner, and closing those files eliminates the redundant reserves. The total reserve again becomes inadequate, requiring further adjustment.

Another, but more expensive, approach is to review each open claim file individually, increasing only those reserves that appear inadequate. This approach assumes that the reviewers possess greater skill in loss reserving than those who established the original reserves or that more information has become available, but corresponding reserve changes have not been posted. Also, care must be taken to see that the total amount added is appropriate. This is the approach used in reinsurance where the claims personnel of the reinsurer review the reported case reserves of the reinsured and, if they believe a more conservative (larger) case reserve is needed, an additional case reserve is added. The reported case reserve plus the additional case reserve make up the total case reserve for a reinsurer.

BULK RESERVES

Case reserves are the basis for the loss and loss adjustment expense reserves shown in the NAIC Annual Statement. However, case reserves seldom, if ever, enter the Annual Statement without amendment. On some occasions, the case reserves may be so redundant that they are reduced for Annual Statement purposes. However, the amendments usually consist of adding one or more kinds of bulk reserves to the case reserves. The term *bulk reserves* indicates reserves that are actuarially determined and are not allocated to specific claim files or cases. Bulk reserves are added to:

1. comply with minimum reserve requirements for some lines of insurance,
2. adjust for inadequate case reserves,
3. provide for losses that have been incurred but have not yet been reported to the insurer, and
4. for workers compensation, to allow for the reopening of claims that have previously been settled and closed.

The last three items listed above usually are included within the general category of losses "incurred but not reported" (IBNR). All four of the items are discussed below.

Statutory Minimum Reserves

The statutes of the various states require that minimum reserves be established for auto liability, medical malpractice liability, other liability (also known as general liability), and workers compensation.

Minimum reserves are required for these lines because of the long delays in reporting and settling losses and the consequent potential for errors in reserving.

The minimum reserves apply only to the most recent three years. The method of calculating the statutory reserve is specified in the NAIC Annual Statement instructions for Schedule P:

> The percentage to be used is based on the company's actual loss ratios in the five years immediately prior to the most recent three, provided that at least three of the five years have at least $1 million in net earned premium. Use the lowest ratio of losses and loss expenses incurred for these years using only years which have at least $1 million in net earned premium. If the lowest qualifying ratio is less than 60%, then use 60% (65% for workers' compensation). If the lowest qualifying ratio is more than 75%, then use 75%. If at least three of the five years do not have at least $1 million in net earned premium, use 60% (65% for workers' compensation). Round percentages to the nearest tenth of one percent.[1]

For auto liability insurance, for example, the statutory reserve is calculated by (1) multiplying the earned premium for each of the last three years by either (a) 60 percent or (b) the lowest loss ratio greater than 60 percent incurred by the company in any one of the five years immediately preceding the latest three years, whichever is greatest; (2) from the amount calculated in (1), claims paid for losses incurred in the year in question are deducted. Regardless of the loss ratios reported for the five-year experience period, the percentage used in the foregoing formula cannot be less than 60 percent or more than 75 percent. Only the ratios for years with earned premiums of $1 million or more for auto liability are considered. Loss ratios are rounded to the nearest one-tenth of one percent in these calculations.

The hypothetical data in Exhibit 8-2 illustrate this process. The object of Exhibit 8-2 is to calculate the statutory minimum reserve for the years 19X6, 19X7, and 19X8, the most recent three years of the company. Consequently, the minimum incurred loss percentage will be the greater of 60 percent or the lowest loss ratio (Column 12) for any of the years 19X1 through 19X5, except that 19X1 will be ignored because the earned premiums in that year were less than $1 million. Therefore, the minimum incurred loss percentage will be 68.5 percent, the loss ratio (including LAE) for 19X2.

Exhibit 8-3 shows the calculation of the statutory minimum reserve for years 19X6, 19X7, and 19X8 using the data from Exhibit 8-2.

Exhibit 8-4 shows the calculation of the excess of statutory reserves over statement reserves. The total of Column 4 of Exhibit 8-4 is the total excess of statutory reserves over statement reserves. This

Exhibit 8-2
Calculation of Statutory Minimum Reserve
Automobile Liability Insurance—Hypothetical Data

(1) Year*	(2) Premiums Earned	(5) Loss and Loss Expense Payments	(11) Total Loss and Loss Expenses Incurred	(12) Loss Ratio (11) ÷ (2)
19X1	$ 950,000	$ 520,000	$ 622,250	65.5
19X2	1,500,000	850,000	1,027,500	68.5
19X3	2,500,000	1,050,000	1,752,500	70.1
19X4	3,000,000	1,080,000	2,082,000	69.4
19X5	3,500,000	1,210,000	2,418,500	69.1
19X6	4,000,000	1,280,000	2,652,000	66.3
19X7	5,000,000	1,410,000	3,205,000	64.1
19X8	5,500,000	860,000	3,426,500	62.3

*Year in which premiums were earned and losses were incurred.

Exhibit 8-3
Calculation of Statutory Minimum Reserve from Hypothetical Data
in Exhibit 8-2

(1) Year[1]	(2) Premiums Earned[2]	(3) Statutory Minimum Loss Ratio[3]	(4) Minimum Incurred Losses[4]	(5) Loss and Loss Expense Payments[5]	(6) Statutory Minimum Reserve[6]
19X6	$4,000,000	68.5	$2,740,000	$1,280,000	$1,460,000
19X7	5,000,000	68.5	3,425,000	1,410,000	2,015,000
19X8	5,500,000	68.5	3,767,500	860,000	2,907,500

1. Year in which premiums were earned and losses were incurred
2. From Exhibit 8-2, Column (2)
3. From Exhibit 8-2, Column (12), for 19X2
4. [(3) x (2)] ÷ 100
5. From Exhibit 8-2, Column (5) (payments already made)
6. (4) − (5)

Exhibit 8-4

Excess of Statutory Reserves over Statement Reserves from
Hypothetical Data in Exhibits 8-2 and 8-3

(1)	(2)	(3)	(4)
Year	Statutory Minimum Reserve[1]	Statement Reserve[2]	Excess of Statutory Reserves over Statement Reserves[3]
19X6	$1,460,000	$1,372,000	$ 88,000
19X7	2,015,000	1,795,000	220,000
19X8	2,907,500	2,566,500	341,000
Totals	$6,382,500	$5,733,500	$649,000

1. From Exhibit 8-3, Column (6)
2. Calculated from Exhibit 8-2, Column (11) − Column (5)
3. (4) = (2) − (3)

amount appears on line 15 of the liability section of the balance sheet in
the NAIC Annual Statement blank.

The objective of this calculation is to assure that the three most
recent accident years are reserved at least at a minimum and realistic
loss ratio, based on the assumption that the reserves of the insurer are
not reliable until they have matured for at least three years. However,
based on the results of the insurance business during the soft pricing
and underwriting segment of an underwriting cycle, a minimum loss
ratio of between 60 and 75 percent may be unrealistically low and may
fail the intended purpose at times.

The statutory ratios for all other affected lines are calculated in the
same manner. However, for workers compensation, 65 percent is
required in lieu of the 60 percent shown in the examples. If the
statutory reserve, as calculated above, exceeds the statement reserves
for the same year, the excess for each year and line is shown in the
Schedule P Interrogatories of the Annual Statement, and the total for
all lines and years is shown on the balance sheet as a liability on page 3,
line 15, of the Annual Statement.

IBNR Reserves

At any given time, the insurer has a liability for losses that have
already happened, even though they are not known to the insurer.

A method similar to that outlined above is used sometimes to calculate IBNR reserves for the so-called "long-tail" lines, which often involve a long delay in the reporting and settlement of claims. The reserves labeled IBNR actually encompass three kinds of reserves:

1. Reserves for losses that have been incurred but not yet reported on the statement date (the true IBNR reserves)
2. For workers compensation, a reserve for the reopening of claims that have already been settled and closed
3. Bulk reserves to compensate for the inadequacy, if any, of reported case reserves

These three parts of the IBNR reserves are not shown separately in the Annual Statement, but as a single lump sum. Most insurance companies do not calculate items (1) and (3) separately even for internal purposes. An exception may be when a claims department of a reinsurer establishes additional case reserves believed necessary on certain individual claim files. In this case, the aggregate amount of the additional case reserves is factored into any IBNR established by the actuarial department or consultant to the reinsurer.

There are several methods for estimating the IBNR reserves, some of them relatively complex. Most of the estimation methods use reported losses as a base for estimating IBNR. Earned premiums also may be used as a base. Methods using reported losses as a base are not satisfactory in the early stages of development for extremely long-tail lines, such as medical malpractice liability insurance written on an occurrence basis. For that line, approximately 1 percent of losses incurred in a given year are reported within the year in which they are incurred, leaving approximately 99 percent of the losses for the year for IBNR. These reported losses are not an adequate base for the accurate estimation of incurred but not reported losses. Two relatively simple methods are discussed here: the loss ratio method and the percentage method.

Loss Ratio Method. One approach to estimating IBNR for the first year or two for the long-tail lines is to assume that the ultimate loss ratio will equal the permissible loss ratio used in calculating rates. Thus, if the rates assumed a loss ratio of 80 percent, the ultimate dollar losses are assumed to equal 80 percent of earned premiums. Deduction of reported losses from that amount yields the IBNR reserves. However, this method is not responsive to changing circumstances. Furthermore, if the premium rates charged were inadequate, the expectation is that the permissible loss ratio will be lower than the ultimate loss ratio. A reinsurer needs to recognize any rate inadequacy in both the subject premium of the reinsured and the rates charged the reinsured to develop an ultimate loss ratio. If used at all, the loss ratio method should be used only for the first year or two of development. More sophisticated and responsive methods should be used as soon as reported losses provide an adequate basis for projection.

Percentage Method. If reported losses provide an adequate basis for projection, IBNR losses may be assumed to be some percentage of reported losses. The percentage usually is derived from past experience. To use this method, a company must be able to tabulate losses by reporting date. Thus, in estimating IBNR for the Annual Statement, all losses incurred during the statement and prior years but reported after December 31 of the statement year would be IBNR losses. For example, if, over a period of years, the IBNR losses calculated in that manner were 30 percent of total incurred losses, the IBNR losses for the statement year would be assumed to be 30 percent of incurred losses for that year. If there is a measurable trend (upward or downward) in the percentage of IBNR losses, the percentage should be adjusted to reflect it. A separate percentage would be used for each year of development. That is, the IBNR percentage would be lower at twenty-four months of development than at twelve months, and so forth.

The percentage method, as outlined here, contemplates only pure IBNR loss reserves. It does not provide any amount to compensate for the possible underestimation of case reserves.

The reserve for reopened workers compensation claims may be calculated by a similar method. The number and amounts of such claims reopened in the past are tabulated to arrive at the appropriate percentage.

The percentage method is reasonably satisfactory for all lines except those with very long delays in reporting and settlement of losses, such as medical malpractice and product liability. For the long-tail lines, more complex methods of estimation are used. These methods are discussed in Chapter 9. (The methods discussed in Chapter 9 can be used for any line of property-liability insurance, if desired.) Those methods provide a bulk reserve amount for the possible underestimation of reported cases as well as reserves for pure IBNR and reopened cases. Exhibit 8-5 summarizes the methods discussed and the kinds of reserves to which they are applicable.

Loss Adjustment Expense Reserves

The reserve for loss adjustment expenses usually is divided into two segments for purposes of estimation: (1) allocated loss expenses and (2) unallocated loss expenses. Bulk reserves for allocated loss

Exhibit 8-5

Methods of Estimating Loss and Loss Expense Reserves

Kind of Reserve	Estimation Methods Applicable	Case or Bulk
Losses		
Adjusted but not paid	Add agreed amounts	Case
In course of adjustment	Judgment	Case
	Average or factor	Case
	Tabular	Case
	Expert system	Case
	Percentage	Bulk
	Loss triangles	Bulk
IBNR	Percentage	Bulk
	Loss ratio	Bulk
	Loss triangles	Bulk
Statutory minimum	Percentage	Bulk
Loss adjustment expenses		
Allocated	Judgment	Case
	Percentage	Bulk
	Loss triangles	Bulk
Unallocated	Percentage	Bulk

adjustment expenses can be estimated by applying a percentage multiplier to either earned premiums or the reserve for open claims. The percentage factor is determined by an analysis of the past experience of the insurance company for the line of insurance under consideration. If experience has shown that allocated loss adjustment expenses averaged 25 percent of incurred losses, then that percentage is applied to the current reserve for outstanding losses to estimate the current reserve for allocated loss expenses. A weakness of this method is that this simple calculation assumes that there have been no changes that will affect the loss adjustment expense percentage. If such changes have occurred, some adjustment must be made for them.

Another weakness of this method results from the manner in which losses usually are settled. Small losses, especially those settled without payment, usually are settled more quickly than large losses. Consequently, the loss reserves at any given time are likely to include a larger share of large losses, when compared to incurred (known) losses. Since large losses usually involve proportionately more allocated loss adjustment expense, the simple percentage calculation outlined may understate the allocated loss adjustment expense reserve. Loss development triangles, discussed in Chapter 9, may be used to overcome this problem.

Unallocated loss adjustment expenses, by definition, cannot be attributed to specific claims. Consequently, the reserve for such expenses must be estimated on a bulk basis. The reserve for unallocated loss adjustment expenses usually is estimated as a percentage of the sum of incurred losses and allocated loss adjustment expenses. The percentage factor is based on the experience of the insurer.

Unallocated loss expenses consist of budgetable items, such as salaries, office expenses, and similar items. Therefore, the total amount of such expenses to be paid in a given year is known with substantial accuracy at the beginning of the year. However, some of the unallocated loss expenses paid in a given year will be related to losses incurred during that year, and some will be related to losses incurred in earlier years. This presents a serious allocation problem for the long-tail lines of insurance. The regulatory authorities have solved this allocation problem by including the following guideline as an interrogatory for Schedule P of the Annual Statement:

> The unallocated loss expense payments paid during the most recent calendar year should be distributed to the various years in which losses were incurred as follows: (1) 45% to the most recent year, (2) 5% to the next most recent year, and (3) the balance to all years, including the most recent year, in proportion to the amount of loss payments paid for each year during the most recent calendar year. If the distribution in (1) and (2) produces an accumulated distribution to such year in excess of 10% of the premiums earned for such year, disregarding all distributions under (3), such accumulated distribution should be limited to 10% of premiums earned and the balance distributed in accordance with (3).

This distribution rule is largely judgmental and arbitrary, but it provides an officially approved method for solving a difficult problem.

SALVAGE AND SUBROGATION

Additional items considered in establishing an insurer's loss reserves are salvage and subrogation. These items may reduce the loss reserves when they are liquidated.

Salvage

In the process of settling claims, an insurer sometimes takes title and possession of property, usually a part of the property insured. For example, an insurer might pay a total loss on a stolen automobile. If the car is recovered after the loss is paid, the insurer takes title to it and possession of it. Property taken under such circumstances is called salvage.

Salvage is not considered as an asset, and does not appear on the statutory balance sheet of the insurer. Also, loss reserves are not reduced to reflect actual or potential salvage in the NAIC balance sheet. When the salvage is liquidated, the money received for it does appear as an asset. Incurred losses for that year are reduced to reflect the money received, even though the salvage may have resulted from a loss incurred in an earlier year.[2]

Subrogation

When an insurer pays a claim, especially a property claim, it may take over any right the claimant has to collect the loss from a third party. For example, an insurer that pays a collision damage claim on a car it insures may be entitled to collect from the driver of another vehicle if that driver's negligence caused the damage to the insured vehicle. This process is known as subrogation.

Potential subrogation recoveries are not shown as an asset or used to reduce loss reserves on statutory financial statements. Proceeds of subrogation, when received, are shown as an asset and are used to reduce incurred losses in the year received.[3]

REPORTING BASES AND THEIR USES

Insurers and reinsurers report loss and other policy statistics on several bases, depending on the purpose for which they will be used. The most common bases for primary insurance are calendar year, accident year, and policy year. Reinsurance statistics are generally reported on either an underwriting year or a treaty year basis.

Reporting Bases for Primary Insurance

Reporting bases for primary insurance are determined largely by accounting and ratemaking needs.

Calendar-Year Statistics. Calendar-year statistics are taken directly from accounting records. They reflect transactions that take place during a calendar year, January 1 through December 31. Calendar-year statistics have the advantage of being fast and easy to obtain because they are compiled in the normal accounting process. Calendar-year statistics are required for statutory accounting purposes, but they are inadequate for ratemaking except for certain insurance lines, like auto physical damage, for which losses are reported and paid promptly.

Accurate ratemaking, especially for the long-tail lines, requires a close matching of losses with the premiums that paid for them. Earned premiums and incurred losses are needed for ratemaking purposes but are not recorded directly in the accounting records. They are calculated (or rather estimated) from written premiums and paid losses by the following formulas:

- Earned premiums = first of year unearned premium reserve + written premiums − end of year unearned premium reserve
- Incurred losses = end of year loss reserve + paid losses − first of year loss reserve

The earned premiums formula provides a reasonably accurate estimate of earned premiums for the year. However, the incurred loss formula has a serious flaw. If a reserve for an outstanding loss is changed, either increased or decreased, the change affects incurred losses for the current year, even though the actual loss occurred several years in the past. The same effect results if an old claim is settled for more or less than the reserve established for it at the beginning of the year. The accident-year method of reporting statistics was developed to overcome this problem of loss reserve development.

Accident-Year Statistics. Accident-year incurred losses are calculated by adding up all claim amounts, *both paid and reserved*, arising from insured events that occurred during the year. Because they are not affected by changes in outstanding loss reserves for prior years, accident year statistics are more accurate for ratemaking purposes than are calendar year statistics. They are slightly more expensive to obtain, since they require additional records that are not needed for accounting purposes. Accident-year statistics are used for ratemaking in most lines of property and liability insurance (policy-year statistics are used for a few lines that are politically sensitive).

Policy-Year Statistics. Policy-year statistics are more accurate for ratemaking purposes than either calendar-year or accident-year statistics because they tie the policy year incurred losses directly to the premiums that were intended to pay for them. A policy year consists of data from all policies issued during a given year. All premiums for those policies are credited to that policy year, and all losses under those policies are charged to that policy year. Thus the losses are compared directly to their associated premiums.

The policy-year statistical system has two serious disadvantages. First, a policy-year (assuming only annual policies are issued) extends over two calendar years. The last policy in the policy year is issued on

Exhibit 8-6
Loss and Reserve Data

Claim Number	Policy Number	Date of Accident	Reserve on 12-31-19X1	Reserve on 12-31-19X2	Reserve on 12-31-19X3
1	53	8-15-19X1	$ 75,000	$100,000	$100,000
2	104	11-17-19X1	25,000	75,000	75,000
3	130	1-23-19X2	—	50,000	50,000
4	135	4-07-19X2	—	25,000	25,000
5	247	9-03-19X2	—	40,000	40,000
6	376	12-11-19X2	—	90,000	90,000
7	414	3-04-19X3	—	—	120,000
8	463	4-15-19X3	—	—	40,000
			$100,000	$380,000	$540,000

December 31 and does not expire until December 31 of the following year. Premium adjustments for audits and retrospective rating plans may come in even later, and claims may be reported several years later. Consequently, policy-year statistics are available at a much later date than calendar- and accident-year statistics. Also, policy-year statistics are more expensive to obtain, since they require extensive records not needed for accounting purposes.

A Comparison. A simplified example may help to clarify the differences among these three reporting bases. Assume that Quaking Casualty Company started business in 19X1 and wrote the following policies, all with one-year terms and all written on July 1 of the respective years:

Year	Policy Numbers	Total Premium
19X1	1 to 200	$300,000
19X2	201 to 500	450,000

Also assume that only the following losses were incurred, that no losses were paid in either 19X1, 19X2, or 19X3 and that all loss files were still open on December 31, 19X3. Exhibit 8-6 shows the pattern of accidents and reserves, while Exhibit 8-7 shows the summary of loss data by reporting base.

Exhibit 8-7
Summary of Loss Data by Reporting Bases

Calendar Year		19X1 100,000	19X2 280,000	19X3 160,000
Accident year	19X1	100,000	175,000	175,000
	19X2	0	205,000	205,000
	19X3	0	0	160,000
Policy year	19X1	100,000	250,000	250,000
	19X2	0	130,000	290,000

Following is the formula to determine losses for a reporting period:

$$\text{Losses} = \frac{\text{Ending}}{\text{Reserves}} + \frac{\text{Paid}}{\text{Losses}} - \frac{\text{Beginning}}{\text{Reserves}}$$

Calendar-year incurred losses for 19X2 = $380,000 + 0 − 100,000 = $280,000. This includes the reserve increases for claims 1 and 2, even though those claims arose from occurrences in 19X1.

The accident year incurred losses for 19X2 would be $205,000, the sum of claims 3, 4, 5, and 6, the only claims that were incurred in 19X2.

The policy-year incurred losses for 19X2 as of 12-31-19X3 would be $290,000 (the sum of claims 5 through 8). All of those claims were covered by policies issued in 19X2, although two accidents occurred in 19X3.

The unearned premium reserve at the end of 19X1 was $150,000. It was $225,000 for the end of 19X2. The earned premiums for calendar year 19X2 and accident year 19X2 were:

$$\text{Earned premiums} = \$150,000 + 450,000 - 225,000 = \$375,000$$

The policy year earned premiums for 19X2 will be $450,000 when the policy year is completed, assuming no premium changes in any of the policies issued in 19X2. Thus depending on the reporting base used, the ratios of incurred losses to earned premiums for 19X2 are:

$$\text{Calendar year} = \frac{\$280,000}{\$375,000} \times 100\% = 74.7\%$$

$$\text{Accident year} = \frac{\$205,000}{\$375,000} \times 100\% = 54.7\%$$

$$\text{Policy year} = \frac{\$290,000}{\$450,000} \times 100\% = 64.4\%$$

Reporting of Reinsurance Statistics

Reporting statistics are generally reported by underwriting year although treaty-year statistics are required in some situations.

Underwriting-Year Statistics. Policy-year statistics are used for direct insurance. Reinsurers use a similar concept known as underwriting year statistics. An underwriting year consists of all reinsurance agreements executed during a given year. An underwriting year extends over three calendar years, assuming all the reinsurance agreements and all the reinsured policies are for one-year terms. The last agreement of underwriting year 19X1 would be issued on December 31, 19X1, and the last direct insurance policy reinsured under that agreement would become effective on December 31, 19X2, and would expire on December 31, 19X3, three years after the first agreement in underwriting year 19X1 was issued. Underwriting year statistics mature very slowly.

Exhibit 8-8 is the result of an excess of loss casualty reinsurance agreement cast in terms of the 19X5 underwriting year for the Amann Reinsurance Company. For illustration purposes, only one agreement is shown—for the Crowley Fire and Marine Insurance Company. The agreement is for a first casualty excess of loss covering $400,000 excess of $100,000 per occurrence. The premium rate is 10 percent of the subject underlying primary premium with a $100,000 minimum and deposit premium. Brokerage commissions are 10 percent of the reinsurance premium. Amann Re allocates internal overhead at the rate of 2 percent of subject premium.

Results for calendar year 19X5 show an underwriting gain of $58,000 based on reported losses of $30,000 falling under the agreement. In calendar 19X6, an additional premium of $37,500 is paid to Amann Re. No additional losses were reported, and in fact, outstanding losses were reduced $5,000 after a $15,000 payment. Calendar year 19X6 showed a $38,000 underwriting profit.

In calendar year 19X7, $17,500 of premium was returned to Crowley Fire and Marine based on an audit of the agreement. The return premium could have arisen because of cancellations of primary contracts, other business improperly coded to this agreement, or other reasons. Return commissions and internal expenses are also shown. Later developing losses of $70,000 more than offset the $5,000 saved over 19X6 outstanding losses, and an underwriting loss for the calendar year 19X7 of $80,400 was incurred.

No new premium was received under the treaty for calendar 19X8, but an additional $50,000 in losses was reported, generating an underwriting loss for the calendar year 19X8 of $50,000.

Exhibit 8-8

Amann Reinsurance Company 19X5 Underwriting-Year Experience as of December 31, 19X8*

Treaty: CXL 09371
Reinsured: Crowley Fire & Marine

Rate: 10 percent net subject earned premium, minimum and deposit $100,000
Cover: 1st casualty excess of loss 400 x 100 per occurrence

	Calendar 19X5	Calendar 19X6	Calendar 19X7	Calendar 19X8	Inception to Date
Premiums	$100,000	$37,500	($17,500)	0	$120,000
Commissions and brokerage	10,000	3,750	(1,750)	0	12,000
Internal expense	2,000	750	(350)	0	2,400
Paid losses and LAE	0	15,000	5,000	20,000	40,000
Beginning outstanding losses	0	30,000	10,000	70,000	100,000
Ending outstanding losses	30,000	10,000	70,000	100,000	0
Total incurred losses	30,000	(5,000)	65,000	50,000	140,000
Underwriting gain (loss)	$ 58,000	$38,000	($80,400)	($50,000)	($34,400)

Expense ratio	12.0%
Loss ratio	116.7%
Combined ratio	128.7%

*Used with permission of Charles E. Erickson, Executive Vice President, Signet Reinsurance.

The "treaty-year 19X5" for this reinsurance is summarized in the "Inception to Date" column. Overall, the agreement generated a 19X5 underwriting year loss of $34,400, with an expense ratio of 12 percent, a loss ratio of 116.7 percent, and a resulting combined ratio of 128.7 percent.

The exhibit reveals that any given underwriting year has associated with it calendar years that may generate statutory underwriting profit or loss. For reinsurance management purposes, the summary by underwriting year is more meaningful than any given calendar year because of the slow reporting of losses under reinsurance agreements.

Treaty-Year Statistics. The term "treaty year" is used less commonly now than in the past. The term was used in connection with reinsurance treaty rating plans that extended over a period of several years. The treaty year indicates the number of years that the treaty has been in force. For example, assume that a treaty became effective on January 1, 19X1, so that 19X1 would be the underwriting year. Then 19X1 would also be treaty year one, 19X2 would be treaty year two, 19X3 would be treaty year three, and so forth as long as the treaty remains in force.

SUMMARY

Loss and loss adjustment expense reserves are the largest liability of most property-liability insurers. Consequently, it is imperative that such reserves be estimated as accurately as possible. Case reserves are established by adding the best estimates of the ultimate loss payments and loss expenses for each individual claim and updating them as necessary. Bulk reserves do not relate to individual claims, but they must be included in the total loss reserve to allow for statutory minimum reserves, IBNR losses, and unallocated loss adjustment expenses. Loss reserves in the statutory Annual Statement are not reduced for potential salvage or subrogation recoveries. Under statutory accounting, both salvage and subrogation are accounted for on a cash basis and are applied to reduce incurred losses (but not reserves) in the year cash is received.

Loss statistics (and other policy statistics) may be reported in a variety of ways, depending on the use. Statutory accounting requires insurers to report premiums, losses, and statistics on a calendar-year basis. Accident-year statistics are more accurate for ratemaking purposes. Policy-year statistics are even more accurate, but they involve greater expense and longer delays. Reinsurers generally use the similar concept of underwriting-year statistics, although treaty-year statistics are required in some situations. Thus the evaluation of loss statistics can vary according to the reporting basis used.

Chapter 9 discusses loss development triangles and other more advanced methods for estimating loss and LAE reserves, as well as the strengths and weaknesses of the various methods.

Chapter Notes

1. National Association of Insurance Commissioners, *Annual Statement Instructions: Property and Casualty*, p. 82-1.
2. For GAAP accounting purposes, the fair market value of unliquidated salvage on hand may be shown as an asset or applied to reduce incurred losses. These and other differences are explained in Chapter 12.
3. Under GAAP accounting, a reasonable estimate of the value of subrogation rights can be shown as an asset or applied to reduce incurred losses.

CHAPTER 9

Evaluation of Loss Reserves

Chapter 8 introduced loss reserving techniques used in estimating case reserves, bulk reserves, and salvage and subrogation. This chapter describes an essential tool in loss reserving, especially for the long-tail lines: the loss triangle. It also extends the discussion into more complex techniques and discusses the special problems of excess of loss reserving.

LOSS TRIANGLES

A loss triangle is a columnar display of loss data. The data displayed may consist of losses incurred and reported, losses paid, the number of claims reported, the number of claims paid, or ratios of loss dollars to number of claims (average claim sizes). The triangle of known losses or claims is then used to project ultimate losses or claims from which IBNR reserves can be derived. When the dollar amount of losses is used in the triangle, it may include or exclude loss adjustment expenses.

Incurred and Reported Loss Development

Exhibit 9-1 shows a loss triangle based on incurred and reported losses. The figures shown in Exhibit 9-1 are hypothetical, but they were carefully selected to approximate data that might be produced by a rapidly growing book of medical malpractice insurance and to illustrate some of the problems likely to occur in the preparation and interpretation of a loss triangle. Because the figures are dollar amounts of losses and allocated loss adjustment expenses, the series of tables based on this data will project both losses and allocated loss adjustment

25

expenses, in total. Separate triangles could be used if separate projections for losses and ALAE were desired.

The first column of Exhibit 9-1 shows the accident years in which losses were incurred, ranging over the thirteen-year period 19X0 through 19Y2. Each line of the exhibit shows the losses incurred and reported (not including IBNR) for the given accident year, as estimated at the end of each calendar year, including the accident year and all subsequent calendar years. The second column of each line shows the estimated incurred and reported losses at twelve months of development; that is, on December 31 of the accident year. For example, the first data column on the line for 19X0 shows the estimated incurred and reported losses on December 31, 19X0 ($45,100). The second data column for 19X0 shows the losses incurred in 19X0 and reported in 19X0 and 19X1 as estimated on December 31, 19X1 ($240,400) and so forth.

For the purposes of this table, it is assumed that no further development is expected after 156 months. (An analyst desiring to project losses beyond this certified 156-month limitation could make estimates using a "tail factor," discussed later.) This assumption does not mean that all losses have been paid by that time, but only that all losses are known and their value can be accurately estimated by that time. The figure for 156 months of development would be, therefore, the ultimate losses for a given accident year. In the usual actuarial terminology, the losses have been developed to their ultimate level after 156 months. All of the data shown in Exhibit 9-1 are in dollars.

Loss Development Factors. Exhibit 9-2 was derived from Exhibit 9-1. It shows, in the triangular section at the top, the loss development factors for each accident year for each subsequent twelve-month period, that is, the development factor for the period from twelve months to twenty-four months, from twenty-four months to thirty-six months, and so forth. These factors are calculated by dividing the estimated amount of losses at the end of the period by the estimated amount of losses at the beginning of the period. For example, the loss development factor for the column headed 12-24 for accident year 19X0 in Exhibit 9-2 (5.33038) was calculated by dividing $240,400 (line 1, second column of the body of Exhibit 9-1) by $45,100 (line 1, first column of the body of Exhibit 9-1). Although loss data is shown for accident year 19Y2 in Exhibit 9-1, there are no loss development factors for that accident year in Exhibit 9-2. Two data points are required to calculate a loss development factor, and only one is shown for 19Y2 in Exhibit 9-1.

Data Inconsistencies. Exhibit 9-2 includes some anomalous data, as most loss development triangles do. For example, examine the

Exhibit 9-1
Loss Triangle Hypothetical Liability Loss and ALAE Data (Incurred and Reported)

Months of Development

Accident Year	12	24	36	48	60	72	84	96	108	120	132	144	156
19X0	$45,100	$240,400	$415,920	$485,520	$50?,337	$1,635,837	$1,767,037	$1,740,328	$1,918,578	$1,749,329	$1,891,829	$1,907,495	$1,862,485
19X1	928,350	1,587,650	1,884,850	2,043,888	7,149,908	6,482,428	6,373,195	6,387,455	6,975,955	7,201,372	7,733,206	8,353,737	
19X2	476,850	734,250	992,800	6,510,600	6,623,250	6,082,367	5,954,921	6,040,771	5,986,771	5,925,771	6,454,771		
19X3	698,400	1,008,600	5,943,350	6,550,650	8,03?,511	8,950,586	9,084,338	9,555,629	9,679,728	9,569,628			
19X4	108,750	2,930,235	6,422,295	7,944,635	9,963,864	10,543,051	10,797,616	11,611,739	11,033,139				
19X5	873,100	1,610,600	6,153,500	7,693,800	8,343,193	8,412,828	8,464,028	8,450,958					
19X6	510,000	3,384,027	6,910,833	9,727,058	12,282,933	11,264,311	10,584,787						
19X7	770,250	3,638,468	9,981,943	15,386,695	15,752,756	15,672,067							
19X8	85,098	4,989,543	16,177,091	18,332,248	18,292,711								
19X9	1,102,024	6,464,896	16,743,396	20,387,696									
19Y0	1,450,126	8,457,604	13,221,251										
19Y1	1,905,313	6,251,816											
19Y2	625,146												

Exhibit 9-2
Loss Development Factors from Hypothetical Data in Exhibit 9-1

Accident Year	Development During Period Shown in Months												
	12–24	24–36	36–48	48–60	60–72	72–84	84–96	96–108	108–120	120–132	132–144	144–156	156+
19X0	5.33038	1.73012	1.16734	1.03258	3.26295	1.08020	.98488	1.10242	.91179	1.08146	1.00828	.97640	1.00000
19X1	1.71018	1.18719	1.08478	3.49819	.90664	.98315	1.00224	1.09213	1.03231	1.07385	1.08024		
19X2	1.53979	1.35213	6.55782	1.01822	.91750	.97905	1.01442	.99106	.98981	1.08927			
19X3	1.44416	5.89267	1.10218	1.22713	1.11346	1.01498	1.05184	1.01299	.98863				
19X4	26.94469	2.19173	1.23704	1.25416	1.05813	1.05184	1.07540	.95017					
19X5	1.84469	3.92083	1.25031	1.08440	1.00835	1.07540	.99846						
19X6	6.63535	2.04219	1.40751	1.26276	.91707	.93967							
19X7	4.72375	2.74345	1.54145	1.02379	.99488								
19X8	58.63291	3.24220	1.13322	.99784									
19X9	5.86638	2.58989	1.25349										
19Y0	5.83232	1.56324											
19Y1	3.28125												
Average	10.31549	2.57777	1.77347	1.37768	1.27237	1.00390	1.02121	1.02976	.98063	1.08153	1.04426	.97640	1.00000
5-yr. avg.	15.66732	2.43619	1.31720	1.12459	1.01838	.99279	1.02847	1.02976	.98063	1.08153	1.04426	.97640	1.00000
3-yr. avg.	4.99332	2.46511	1.30939	1.09480	.97343	.98997	1.04190	.98474	1.00358	1.08153	1.04426	.97640	1.00000
Selected	10.31549	2.46511	1.30939	1.12459	1.01838	1.00390	1.00300	1.00350	1.00200	1.00150	1.00100	1.00500	1.00000
Cumulative	38.85904	3.76706	1.52815	1.16707	1.03777	1.01904	1.01509	1.01205	1.00953	1.00751	1.00600	1.00500	1.00000

series of loss development factors beginning in accident year 19X0 in the column headed 60-72 (3.26295) and proceeding diagonally leftward to accident year 19X4 and the column headed 12-24 (26.94469). Each of these five development factors is larger than the factors on either side of it. Such data should be questioned. For example, it may be that in calendar year 19X5, the claims manager of the company decided to increase case reserves on all accident years. A similar, but relatively smaller, tendency begins in accident year 19X0 in the column headed 120-132 (1.08146) and proceeds diagonally toward the lower left to 19X9, column 12-24 (5.86638).

Five possible interpretations of increases such as these are as follows:

1. The increases indicate a consistent practice of carrying inadequate reserves, so the current reserves are likely to be inadequate also.
2. The reserves were inadequate but are now adequate.
3. The reserves were inadequate but are now redundant.
4. The reserves were adequate and are now redundant.
5. The reserves were redundant and are now more redundant.

The first of those five scenarios is the one usually accepted, although the other four probably occur as frequently. There is no way to know from the loss triangle alone which interpretation is correct. That determination requires a careful analysis of claim files or more extensive claims data. Sufficient data for that purpose generally cannot be obtained without access to the internal, proprietary records of the insurer.

Another anomaly appears in the first data column of accident year 19X8 (58.63291) in Exhibit 9-2. The loss development factor there is much larger than those around it, although it does not appear to be related to a systematic reserve increase. Since Exhibit 9-1 (for 19X8, the column for twelve months of development) shows that the reported losses ($85,098) were unusually low at the end of accident year 19X8, this anomaly probably reflects a mere chance variation in claims reporting.

Ultimate Loss Projections. The goal of loss triangles is to project ultimate losses, the amount that will be paid out in losses (and, in this case, ALAE) when all losses for the accident year have been settled. The bottom five rows in Exhibit 9-2 represent the next step in that process.

Average Loss Development. The first of these rows, labeled "Average," shows the arithmetic mean of all of the numbers appearing in the column above it in the loss development triangle. In the second row, labeled "5-Year Average," the figure in each column is the average of the factors for the most recent five accident years in the loss development triangle above it. The five-year average and the average for all years are the same for the last six columns, in which only five or fewer accident years are represented.

In the third of these five rows, each figure is the average of the most recent three accident year figures above it. The three-year average, the five-year average, and the average for all years are all equal in the last three columns, in which three or fewer accident years are included.

Selection of Loss Development Factor. The fourth row, labeled "Selected," shows the loss development factor that the analyst elected to use for each of the twelve-month development periods. The method of selection used here, although not necessarily the only acceptable method, is one used by many actuaries:

1. If the three averages show a consistent downward trend in loss development factors, select the smallest of the three.
2. If the three averages show a consistent upward trend, select the largest of the three.
3. If the three averages do not show a trend, select the factor that is intermediate in value.
4. Adjust on a judgmental basis any factor that seems inconsistent with those adjacent to it.

The goal of this process is to derive loss development factors that can be used to forecast the future loss development expected in the next twelve months on each accident year that is not yet at its ultimate value. Often these factors decrease from a relatively high factor in the first period to a factor of one at the ultimate loss period, with no increases between, thus reflecting a normal decrease in new losses reported as more time elapses after the accident year ends. Some actuaries assure that this normal downward progression is reflected by fitting an appropriate curve to the data by mathematical means, but most practitioners make the necessary adjustments judgmentally.

Ultimate Losses. The final row in Exhibit 9-2, labeled "Cumulative," shows factors (multipliers) that can be used to project ultimate losses for any given accident year, given the reported losses for that accident year for any of the intermediate points in the table. Each of the development factors on the cumulative line was calculated by multiplying the factor at its immediate right, on the same line, by the factor immediately above it, on the "Selected" line. For example, the cumulative factor in the column headed 144-156, 1.00500, is the product of 1.00000 to the right with the 1.00500 above it. This number represents the cumulative factor from 144 to ultimate. Similarly, the cumulative factor in the column headed 132-144, 1.00600, is the product of the 1.00500 to the right with the 1.00100 above it. This number represents the cumulative factor from 132 to ultimate. The only exception is the last factor on the right, which is equal to the factor above it.

Exhibit 9-1 shows reported losses of $20,987,696 for accident year 19X9 developed to 48 months. Ultimate losses for that accident year can be projected by multiplying those reported losses by the cumulative loss development factor shown in the column headed 48-60 in Exhibit 9-2, 1.16707. These calculations for all of the accident years in Exhibit 9-1 are shown in Exhibit 9-3.

The ultimate losses for any given accident year may differ substantially from those projected by this technique (or any other technique). The goal for this process is to project reasonably accurately the total ultimate losses for all accident years combined, with the expectation that any errors in a given accident year will be offset by errors in the opposite direction in other accident years.

IBNR Development. The first column of Exhibit 9-3 shows the accident years. The second column shows the reported losses for each accident year as of December 31, 19Y2, the latest year available. Column 3 shows the appropriate loss development factor for each of the accident years, from the cumulative line in Exhibit 9-2. Column 4 shows the projected ultimate losses for each accident year, calculated by multiplying the reported losses in Column 2 by the loss development factor in Column 3. Column 4 is ultimate losses, including those already paid. The loss and ALAE reserve for December 31, 19Y2, could be found by deducting losses already paid for the accident years shown. Column 5 of Exhibit 9-3 shows the IBNR reserve for losses and ALAE. It is calculated by subtracting Column 2 from Column 4 for each accident year. The IBNR reserve shown in Exhibit 9-3 is an aggregate IBNR reserve, including both an element for losses not yet reported and an element for inadequate reserve on reported losses as developed from Exhibit 9-2.

Incurred Claim Count and Average Incurred Costs Loss Development

Exhibits 9-4, 9-5, and 9-6 demonstrate the use of loss triangles for the number of claims incurred. They are calculated in the same manner outlined for the dollar amount of losses and ALAE.

Method. Projected ultimate losses and ALAE can be calculated from Exhibit 9-6 by multiplying the projected ultimate number of

Exhibit 9-3

Developed Losses—Loss and ALAE Hypothetical Data
from Exhibit 9-1

(1) Accident Year	(2) Reported Losses	(3) Loss Development Factor	(4) Developed Losses	(5) IBNR Losses (Reserve)
19X0	$1,862,485	1.00000	$1,862,485	$ 0
19X1	8,353,737	1.00500	8,395,506	41,769
19X2	6,454,771	1.00600	6,493,500	38,729
19X3	9,569,628	1.00751	9,641,496	71,868
19X4	11,033,139	1.00953	11,138,285	105,146
19X5	8,450,958	1.01205	8,552,792	101,834
19X6	10,584,787	1.01509	10,744,511	159,724
19X7	15,672,067	1.01904	15,970,463	298,396
19X8	18,292,711	1.03777	18,983,627	690,916
19X9	20,987,696	1.16707	24,494,110	3,506,414
19Y0	13,221,251	1.52815	20,204,055	6,982,804
19Y1	6,251,816	3.76706	23,550.966	17,299,150
19Y2	625,146	38.85904	24,292,573	23,667,427
Totals	$131,360,192		$184,324,369	$52,964,177

claims in Column 4 by an appropriate average payment for losses, either including or excluding ALAE. A separate average could be used for each accident year or a single average for all accident years combined. The reserve for unpaid losses could then be calculated by deducting losses already paid from the projected ultimate losses.

The reserve for IBNR losses can be calculated by multiplying the number of IBNR losses from Column 5 of Exhibit 9-6 by an appropriate average dollar amount of loss. The calculation could be made separately for each accident year or in the aggregate for all accident years combined. The IBNR reserve calculated in this manner would be a pure IBNR reserve, including only claims not yet reported. An allowance for inadequate reserves would be provided by the projection of ultimate losses, outlined above, if an adequate average loss figure is used.

Adjustments. The average loss figures used in the foregoing calculations would be derived from the experience of the company

Exhibit 9-4

Loss Triangle—Hypothetical Data—Number of Claims Incurred

Accident Year	Months of Development												
	12	24	36	48	60	72	84	96	108	120	132	144	156
19X0	21	47	86	104	109	113	134	139	151	158	160	164	165
19X1	87	164	275	308	320	377	377	412	423	429	432	440	
19X2	97	203	257	294	337	362	368	382	390	394	396		
19X3	169	287	309	396	447	456	474	476	477	484			
19X4	77	175	357	425	429	439	456	467	472				
19X5	51	136	364	429	444	466	481	487					
19X6	32	161	347	434	451	462	474						
19X7	53	182	440	532	566	583							
19X8	65	292	658	789	828								
19X9	55	309	673	854									
19Y0	87	507	778										
19Y1	105	328											
19Y2	47												

Exhibit 9-5

Loss Development Factors from Hypothetical Data Shown in Exhibit 9-4—Number of Claims Incurred

Accident Year	Development During Period Shown in Months												
	12–24	24–36	36–48	48–60	60–72	72–84	84–96	96–108	108–120	120–132	132–144	144–156	156+
19X0	2.23810	1.82979	1.20930	1.04808	1.03670	1.18584	1.03731	1.08633	1.04636	1.01266	1.02500	1.00610	1.00000
19X1	1.88506	1.67683	1.12000	1.03896	1.17813	1.00000	1.09284	1.09670	1.01418	1.00699	1.01852		
19X2	2.09278	1.26601	1.14397	1.14626	1.07418	1.01657	1.03804	1.02094	1.01026	1.00508			
19X3	1.69822	1.07666	1.29155	1.12879	1.02013	1.03947	1.00422	1.00210	1.01468				
19X4	2.27273	2.04000	1.19048	1.00941	1.02331	1.03872	1.02412	1.01071					
19X5	2.66667	2.67647	1.17857	1.03497	1.04955	1.03219	1.01247						
19X6	5.03125	2.15528	1.25072	1.03917	1.02439	1.02597							
19X7	3.43396	2.41758	1.20909	1.06391	1.03004								
19X8	4.49231	2.25342	1.19909	1.04943									
19X9	5.61818	2.17799	1.26895										
19Y0	5.82759	1.53452											
19Y1	3.12381												
Average	3.36505	1.91860	1.20517	1.06211	1.05455	1.04840	1.03484	1.02936	1.02137	1.00824	1.02176	1.00610	1.00000
5-yr. avg.	4.49917	2.10776	1.22128	1.03938	1.02948	1.03059	1.03434	1.02936	1.02137	1.00824	1.02176	1.00610	1.00000
3-yr. avg.	4.85653	1.98864	1.22571	1.05084	1.03466	1.03230	1.01361	1.01125	1.01304	1.00824	1.02176	1.00610	1.00000
Selected	4.85653	1.98864	1.22571	1.05084	1.03466	1.03230	1.02759	1.02332	1.01859	1.00824	1.00700	1.00610	1.00000
Cumulative	14.53698	2.99329	1.50519	1.22802	1.16861	1.29946	1.09413	1.06475	1.04048	1.02149	1.01314	1.00610	1.00000

Exhibit 9-6
Developed Claims from Hypothetical Data in Exhibit 9-4—
Number of Claims Incurred

(1)	(2)	(3)	(4)	(5)
		Loss		
Accident	Reported	Development	Developed	IBNR
Year	Claims	Factor	Claims	Claims
19X0	165	1.00000	165	0
19X1	440	1.00610	443	3
19X2	396	1.01314	401	5
19X3	484	1.02149	494	10
19X4	472	1.04048	491	19
19X5	487	1.06475	519	32
19X6	474	1.09413	519	45
19X7	583	1.29946	658	75
19X8	828	1.16861	968	140
19X9	854	1.22802	1,049	195
19Y0	778	1.50519	1,171	393
19Y1	328	2.99329	982	654
19Y2	47	14.53698	683	636
Totals	6,336		8,543	2,207

appropriately adjusted for inflation and other factors that affect the average amount of loss. Also, open claims are likely to be larger, on average, than closed claims, because small claims usually are simpler and are closed more quickly. Some adjustment to the average paid claim may be necessary to reflect this relationship. Such an adjustment is especially necessary for IBNR losses. A substantial part of ultimate losses has already been paid, especially for the earlier accident years. The paid losses are now fixed and are not affected by future inflation or other future developments. However, IBNR losses, by definition, will be paid in the future, some of them far into the future. Consequently, some allowance for future inflation must be included in the average loss amount. In one case, an insurer projected the ultimate number of claims with reasonable accuracy, but its reserves were grossly inadequate because it used an inadequate average loss figure.

IBNR Development. Exhibit 9-7 shows projected ultimate losses and projected IBNR losses, based on the projected ultimate claim count and projected IBNR claim count in Exhibit 9-6. A different average loss amount (Column 5) has been used for each accident year in projecting ultimate losses, but the same average claim amount (Column 7) was used for all accident years in projecting ultimate IBNR losses.

Two other techniques that use triangles are the *paid loss technique* (as in Exhibits 9-1, 9-2, and 9-3, except that paid losses are used instead of incurred losses) and the *paid claim count and average paid costs loss development method* (as in Exhibits 9-4, 9-5, 9-6, and 9-7, except that paid claim counts and average paid costs are used).

Either the incurred loss technique, as illustrated by Exhibits 9-1, 9-2, and 9-3, or the incurred claim count and average cost method, as illustrated by Exhibits 9-4, 9-5, 9-6, and 9-7, or the two corresponding paid methods are satisfactory if correct statistics are used. Some actuaries use both techniques to be sure they produce similar answers.

COMPARISON OF RESERVING METHODS

None of the reserving methods described is satisfactory under all circumstances. The loss triangle techniques tend to be more satisfactory over a wider range of situations than do the techniques described in Chapter 8. However, they tend to be less reliable in the first year or two of development than they are in later stages, especially for very long-tail liability coverages. In addition, it may be necessary to adjust the data for anomalies. Because the loss triangle, loss ratio, tabular, and percentage methods each have particular strengths and weaknesses, combined methods have been developed that utilize the strengths of different methods.

Data Adjustments

Great care must be taken to be sure that the accumulated data have been correctly tabulated. Also, substantial judgment may be required to adjust for anomalous data. Such anomalies may result from (1) changes in case reserving or claims settlement practices, (2) chance variations in loss frequency or severity, or (3) for liability lines, changes in rules of law. For example, one state enacted legislation substantially shortening the statute of limitations for medical malpractice claims. An unusually large number of claims was filed in the last two months before the new law became effective. A person projecting losses for medical malpractice insurance in that state would need to make some adjustment to reflect (1) the sudden bulge in the frequency rate, and (2) a drop in frequency immediately after the law became effective because some of the claims that ordinarily would have been reported in that

Exhibit 9-7
Developed Losses and IBNR Losses—Hypothetical Data

(1) Accident Year	(2) Reported Claims	(3) Developed Claims	(4) IBNR Claims	(5) Average Loss Amount	(6) Ultimate Losses	(7) Average IBNR Loss	(8) Ultimate IBNR Losses
19X0	165	165	0	$18,500	$3,052,500	$25,000	$ 0
19X1	440	443	3	19,000	8,417,000	25,000	75,000
19X2	396	401	5	19,500	7,819,500	25,000	125,000
19X3	484	494	10	20,000	9,880,000	25,000	250,000
19X4	472	491	19	20,500	10,065,500	25,000	475,000
19X5	487	519	32	21,000	10,899,000	25,000	800,000
19X6	474	519	45	21,500	11,158,500	25,000	1,125,000
19X7	583	658	75	22,000	14,476,000	25,000	1,875,000
19X8	828	968	140	22,500	21,780,000	25,000	3,500,000
19X9	854	1,049	195	23,000	24,127,000	25,000	4,875,000
19Y0	778	1,171	393	23,500	27,518,500	25,000	9,825,000
19Y1	328	982	654	24,000	23,568,000	25,000	16,350,000
19Y2	47	683	636	24,500	16,733,500	25,000	15,900,000
Totals	6,336	8,543	2,207		$189,495,000		$55,175,000

Columns (2) and (3) are from Exhibit 9-6
Column (4) = Column (3) − Column (2)
Columns (5) and (7) are based on other data not shown
Column (6) = Column (3) x Column (5)
Column (8) = Column (4) x Column (7)

period had been reported early to avoid the effect of the new law. There is no statistical basis for such an adjustment, which would be entirely judgmental.

Advantages and Disadvantages of Individual Methods

Different loss reserving methods are better in different situations. Because no single method is always the best, it is important to recognize the strengths and weaknesses of each.

Loss Triangle Methods. Among the loss triangle methods illustrated, the incurred loss method (Exhibits 9-1, 9-2, and 9-3) and the paid loss method are perhaps the most useful, because the loss triangles used there can be constructed from the NAIC Annual Statement Schedule P, if statements for a sufficient number of years can be obtained. Schedule P, Part 1, shows, for each calendar year, the projected ultimate losses and IBNR reserves for a series of accident years. The reported losses, both paid and reserves, can be found by deducting the IBNR reserves from the projected ultimate losses. Loss triangles constructed in this manner, however, are no more accurate than the data in the Annual Statement.

Loss Ratio Method. The loss ratio method of establishing bulk reserves has little to recommend it, though it is very useful in the early stages of development of long-tail lines. The loss ratio method is required for the statutory minimum reserve for the auto liability, other liability, medical malpractice, and workers compensation lines of insurance (discussed in Chapter 8). The loss ratio method assumes that the ultimate losses will equal some pre-selected percentage of earned premiums. For the statutory minimum reserve, that percentage is prescribed by the NAIC Annual Statement blank. For other purposes, the expected or permissible loss ratio built into the rates, perhaps adjusting for the fact that rates may be less than fully adequate, usually is used.

The weakness of the loss ratio method as a long-term reserving technique is that the actual loss ratio seldom equals the expected loss ratio. The difference between them can be substantial. If the actual loss ratio is less than the expected loss ratio, the loss ratio method results in redundant reserves. If the actual loss ratio is greater than the expected loss ratio, inadequate reserves will result.

In spite of this weakness, the loss ratio method is used frequently in the early development stages for long-tail coverages. For those lines of insurance, the loss triangle methods are not completely reliable in the early stages of development—the first twelve, or perhaps twenty-four, months. After that period, they are likely to be more reliable than the loss ratio method.

Tabular Method. The tabular method (using mortality, morbidity, and remarriage tables) can be applied either on an individual claim or a bulk basis. The resulting reserve may be inaccurate for individual claims, but the method usually is accurate on a bulk basis.[1] The biggest weakness of this technique is its limited applicability. It is applicable primarily to income loss benefits under workers compensation, some structured settlements under liability insurance, and long-term disability health insurance. For those situations, it is clearly the method of choice.

Percentage Method. The final bulk reserving technique discussed here is the percentage method for establishing IBNR reserves. In this method, historical IBNR data are tabulated as a percentage of reported losses (or possibly earned premiums). IBNR losses, for Annual Statement purposes, would be those losses that happen during the statement year or an earlier year but were not reported until after December 31 of that year. If, historically, IBNR reserves after twelve months of development (on December 31 of the accident year) equaled 25 percent of reported losses, and IBNR losses after twenty-four months of development (December 31 of the year following the accident year) equaled 5 percent of the reported losses on that date, then these percentages would be applied to the reported losses to estimate IBNR loss reserves.

This method is acceptable for property insurance, for which losses (1) can be estimated with reasonable accuracy soon after reporting, and (2) are reported reasonably quickly. It is likely to be less accurate for liability lines, although the theory underlying it is not significantly different from the theory underlying the loss triangles used for liability lines.

Exhibit 9-8 shows an IBNR calculation as outlined above, based on the assumption that IBNR losses equal 20 percent of reported losses at twelve months of development, 10 percent at twenty-four months of development, and 5 percent at thirty-six months of development. Losses are presumed to have developed to the ultimate level at forty-eight months. The IBNR reserve for each accident year is calculated by multiplying the reported losses for that accident year by the IBNR factor. The total loss reserve, on the bottom line, is calculated by adding the total IBNR reserve to the total reported losses and deducting the total paid losses.

Exhibit 9-8

Calculation of IBNR Reserve for 19X4 by the Percentage Method from Hypothetical Data

(1) Accident Year	(2) Paid Losses	(3) Reported Losses	(4) IBNR Factor	(5) IBNR Reserve
19X1	$1,225,679	$4,725,679	0.00	$0
19X2	987,563	4,887,963	0.05	244,398
19X3	778,645	4,878,845	0.10	487,885
19X4	654,376	4,954,876	0.20	990,975
Totals	$3,646,263	$19,447,363		$1,723,258
Total Loss Reserve				$17,524,358

Combined Methods

The combined methods discussed here include the two-part combination method, the Bornhuetter-Ferguson method, and the three-part combination method.

Two-Part Combination. In order to realize the advantages of both the loss ratio method and the incurred loss triangle method, some actuaries have suggested that a weighted average of the two methods be used, with the weights varying with the length of development. Exhibit 9-9 shows a set of weights that might be used for a liability coverage.

At the end of the accident year (twelve months of development), the reserve would be based entirely on the loss ratio method because the reported loss data is too small to be a reliable indicator of the ultimate losses. Beginning at twenty-four months of development, the part of the reserve attributable to the incurred loss triangle method increases, and the part attributable to the loss ratio method decreases. At sixty months of development and thereafter, the reserve is based solely on the incurred loss triangle method.

The weights shown in Exhibit 9-9 do not have any theoretical basis. They are purely judgmental. Different weights might be selected for different lines of insurance.

Exhibit 9-9
Weights for Combining the Loss Ratio Method and
the Incurred Loss Triangle Method of Estimating Loss Reserves

Months of Development	Weights	
	Loss Ratio	Incurred Loss
12	100%	0%
24	50	50
36	25	75
48	10	90
60 or more	0	100

Bornhuetter-Ferguson. A variation of the two-part combination method that does not rely on judgmental weights is called the Bornhuetter-Ferguson method, named after two actuaries (each of whom subsequently became president of a reinsurance company). This method is used to set reserves in reinsurance. The method assumes that the losses reported to the reinsurer are not mature enough to be multiplied by a loss development factor for an ultimate loss calculation. This assumption reflects the reality that for some lines of insurance, particularly casualty excess treaties, losses reported to reinsurers lag behind reporting to primary companies. Exhibit 9-10 is an example of the Bornhuetter-Ferguson method applied hypothetically to reported losses under a casualty excess treaty.

Instead of multiplying reported losses by a loss development factor, the ultimate earned premium (Column 2) is multiplied by an initial expected loss ratio (Column 3) to yield initial expected losses (Column 4). Then, an expected percentage of unreported losses—an estimate of losses that have occurred that have not yet been reported to the reinsurer—derived from loss development factors is multiplied by the initial expected losses to yield expected unreported losses (Column 6). These expected unreported losses are the indicated IBNR for the reinsurer.[2]

For example, in Exhibit 9-10, in the year 19X5, the ultimate earned premium is estimated by triangulation methods to be $15,870,000. Due to inadequate pricing in 19X5, the initial expected loss ratio (Column 3) is 1.15. Multiplying the two figures yields initial expected losses (Column 4) of $18,251,000. The $18,251,000 is multiplied by 56.3 percent (Column 5), which is the projected percentage of losses that have been

Exhibit 9-10

Professional Underwriters of New Kalabaska Reinsurance Co.

Bornhuetter-Ferguson Technique—Casualty Excess from Hypothetical Data (000 omitted)*

(1)	(2)	(3)	(4)	(5)	(6)	(7)	(8)	(9)
Accident Year	Ultimate Earned Premium[1]	Initial Expected Loss Ratio[2]	Initial Expected Losses (2) × (3)	Expected Percent Unreported Losses[3]	Expected Unreported Losses (4) × (5)	Actual Incurred Losses	Ultimate Losses (6) + (7)	Ultimate Loss Ratio (8) ÷ (2)
19X0	$ 13,940	0.70	$ 9,758	14.5%	$ 1,415	$ 8,364	$ 9,779	0.702
19X1	13,940	0.75	10,455	17.8%	1,861	9,115	10,976	0.787
19X2	13,940	0.85	11,849	22.5%	2,666	9,610	12,276	0.881
19X3	19,110	0.95	18,155	30.8%	5,592	13,004	18,596	0.973
19X4	15,870	1.10	17,457	42.3%	7,384	10,283	17,667	1.113
19X5	15,870	1.15	18,251	56.3%	10,275	8,113	18,388	1.159
19X6	19,110	0.85	16,244	72.7%	11,809	4,641	16,450	0.861
19X7	31,310	0.80	25,048	82.5%	20,665	6,369	27,034	0.863
Totals	$143,090		$127,217		$61,667	$69,499	$131,166	0.917

1. Column (2) obtained by triangulating earned premium.
2. Column (3) obtained by estimating the premium adequacy level for each year relative to the current year.
3. Column (5) = 1 − (1 ÷ cumulative age-to-ultimate factors)

*Data provided by Jerome E. Tuttle, CPCU, ARM, FCAS, Vice President & Actuary, Mercantile and General Reinsurance Company of America incurred but not yet reported to the reinsurer under the treaty to yield the indicated IBNR for 19X5 under the treaty of $10,275,000 (Column 6). The balance of the information in Exhibit 9-10 is useful for purposes other than reserve development such as premium calculations for the treaty and so forth.

Three-Part Combination. A three-part combination system also has been suggested, combining the loss ratio method, the incurred loss triangle method, and case reserves established by the claims department. This combination would require three sets of weights, rather than the two sets specified in Exhibit 9-9. The weights would be set so they would give most or all of the emphasis to the loss ratio method in the first year. Thereafter, the loss ratio method would be phased out and the incurred loss triangle method phased in. Subsequently, the incurred loss triangle method would be gradually phased out, and more weight would be placed on case reserves. Finally, as losses approach ultimate, when all losses have been reported, and only a few remain open, the reserve would be based entirely on the case reserves of the claims department.

This final change in emphasis is based on a belief that in the final stages of development, when all claims have been reported, few are open, and much information has been gathered on the open claims, the case reserves established by the claims examiners are likely to be more accurate than statistically estimated reserves. Statistically estimated loss reserves are based on the application of the law of large numbers. In the final stages of development, the number of claims remaining open may not be sufficient for that law to operate successfully. Exhibit 9-11 shows a set of weights that might be used for such a combination. These weights are purely judgmental, and they are shown here for purposes of illustration only.

EXCESS OF LOSS REINSURANCE

Reinsurers use essentially the same loss reserving techniques as do primary insurers, and the reserving problems of pro-rata (proportional) reinsurance do not differ significantly from those of primary insurers. Excess of loss reinsurance is a different story. In that case, the problems in estimating loss reserves are much greater, and special considerations are involved. Data from the Reinsurance Association of America shows that excess of loss reinsurance typically experiences longer loss development patterns.

Exhibit 9-11
Examples of Weights for Three-Part Combination Method

Months of Development	Weights		
	Loss Ratio	Incurred Loss	Case Reserves
12	100%	0%	0%
24	50	50	0
36	25	75	0
48	0	100	0
60	0	100	0
72	0	100	0
84	0	100	0
96	0	100	0
108	0	90	10
120	0	75	25
132	0	50	50
144	0	25	75
156 or more	0	0	100

Problems in Estimating Loss Reserves

Excess of loss reinsurers have significantly greater problems in estimating loss reserves because of (1) the effects of social and financial inflation and (2) a much longer development period. In addition, the usual loss development techniques are more difficult for reinsurers to apply.

Inflation. Because the reinsurer, under an excess of loss treaty, covers the top of the loss, where the major effect of financial and social inflation is felt, its losses are affected by inflation to a greater extent than are the losses of the primary insurer. Also, some losses that were previously within the retention of the primary company are pushed over the retention by inflation, increasing the number of claims to which the reinsurer must contribute. These inflationary pressures are increased by the long development period (long time periods to trial or settlement) in excess of loss reinsurance.

Long Loss Development Period. The long development period in excess of loss reinsurance results from the nature of the contract. The reinsurer is not obligated to make any payment unless the amount of loss exceeds the retention of the primary company. Consequently, the primary company is required to report only those claims that it expects to exceed some agreed amount, ranging from 50 to 100 percent of its retention, depending on the terms of the contract. Some claims that eventually exceed the agreed amount may not be perceived initially as being that large. Consequently, the primary company may not initially report them to the reinsurer.

Problems with Usual Loss Development Techniques. Although reinsurers use the same loss reserving techniques as direct insurers, some of the techniques are more difficult to apply in practice for a reinsurer for reasons discussed. For example, the incurred loss technique for a reinsurer often shows a wide range of values for the development factors in each column, and it is a challenge to select a "reasonable" factor from the list. Further, reinsured losses arise from a large number of primary companies, there is little homogeneity among the losses, and there is a large variation in primary company case reserving and claim settlement practices (claim audits, discussed in the next chapter, help with this problem). The paid loss technique for a reinsurer suffers the same disadvantages, as well as the additional one that only a handful of claims may be paid through twelve or twenty-four months. Claim count and average claim methods also create problems for setting reinsurer reserves.

Special Excess of Loss Reserving Considerations

Setting reserves for excess of loss treaties requires consideration of the unusual nature of the business. These considerations include additional segmentation of loss data for greater homogeneity, greater use of expected loss ratio methods, segregation of certain treaties in special situations, reliance on external data, and retrocessional business.

Segmentation of Data for Greater Homogeneity. Data is more credible if it is based on similar exposures. This may mean that analysts responsible for generating loss reserves for reinsurers must segregate its data not only by line of business, but also into other categories whenever possible. Such additional categories may be by type of layer, such as working layers (where loss frequency is expected), intermediate layers, and clash layers. Such segmentation, however, means less information for each new category created and less statistical credibility for each such category.

Greater Use of Expected Loss Ratio Methods. Because few losses are reported early under an excess of loss treaty, expected loss ratio methods of setting reserves (such as the Bornhuetter-Ferguson method) should be considered. The use of loss ratio techniques is complicated by the fact that premium for excess of loss business is slow to develop. If losses are reserved based on a loss ratio and if premiums are underestimated, then the loss reserves of the reinsurer are also underestimated. Premiums must also be estimated (developed) to avoid inadvertent underreserving.

Segregation of Certain Treaties. Because each excess of loss treaty is individually negotiated with the reinsured, some treaties may have special terms and conditions, such as an aggregate limit so the losses of the reinsurer will not develop beyond the aggregate. Another treaty may have different loss development patterns than usual. While it would be useful for statistical credibility to combine results from treaties, it may be more useful to address the special features of an individual treaty separately from the larger book of business.

Reliance on External Data. Rarely does a reserve analyst believe that he or she has enough historical data to set the appropriate reserves. Therefore, the analyst must carefully consider how many years of "tail" to anticipate and to add to loss development factors. In some cases, analysts can use the data from the Reinsurance Association of America (RAA) and apply mathematical techniques to develop the additional loss development figures.

Retrocessions of Casualty Business. Reserve analysts for reinsurers active in writing assumed reinsurance casualty business, known as casualty retrocessions, are further disadvantaged in determining their ultimate liabilities. Each problem of reserve estimation discussed is exaggerated because of a further time delay in reporting the results to the reinsurer of the retrocession. To date, no published studies such as those of the RAA discussed below have been made for retrocession casualty business.

Reinsurance Association of America Data

The Reinsurance Association of America (RAA) has documented the longer development periods for excess of loss reinsurance in a series of monographs, published in odd-numbered years. Exhibits 9-12, 9-13, 9-14, 9-15, and 9-16 are from *Loss Development Study: 1987 Edition*. These exhibits compare the loss development patterns of

Exhibit 9-12
Comparison of Loss Development Patterns of Primary
Insurers and Reinsurers—Auto Liability Insurance*

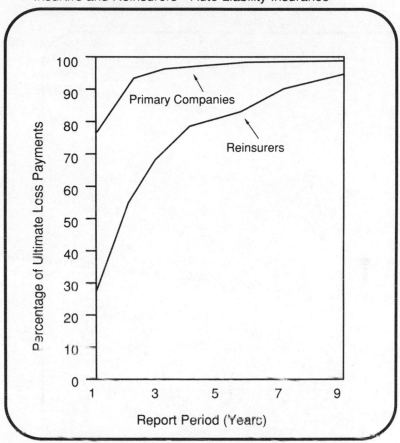

*Reprinted with permission from Reinsurance Association of
America, *Loss Development Study: 1987 Edition,* p. 15.

primary insurers and reinsurers for auto liability, general liability,
medical malpractice, and workers compensation insurance.

In preparing the graphs and table, the RAA included ALAE with
loss, and has included paid losses and case reserves, but not IBNR
reserves. Property damage losses have been included where applicable
and possible.

Auto Liability. Exhibit 9-12 shows graphically the difference
between the development periods for primary insurers and reinsurers
with regard to automobile liability insurance. There is a wide difference

Exhibit 9-13

Comparison of Loss Development Patterns of
Primary Insurers and Reinsurers—General Liability
Insurance Including Asbestos*

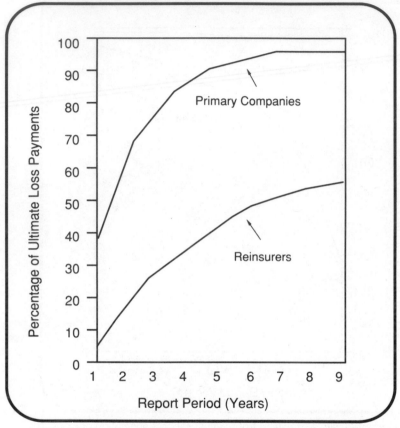

*Reprinted with permission from Reinsurance Association of
America, *Loss Development Study: 1987 Edition,* p. 16.

between the two lines at the end of the first year, indicating that the
reinsurer has received notice of only 25 percent of ultimate claims at
that point, although the primary insurer has received notice of 80
percent of ultimate claims. Even after nine years of development, the
reinsurer has notice of only 90 percent of ultimate losses, while the
primary insurer has notice of about 99 percent. The contrast between
loss development for reinsurers and that for primary insurers is even
greater for other third-party lines.

Exhibit 9-14
Comparison of Loss Development Patterns of
Primary Insurers and Reinsurers—Medical Malpractice
Liability Insurance*

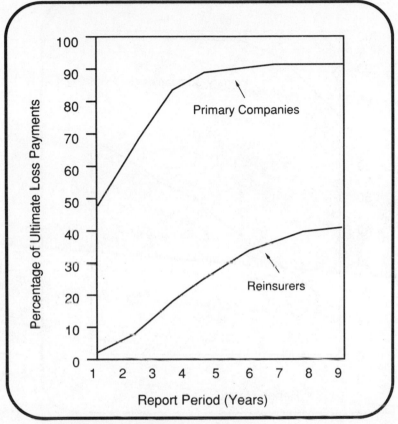

*Reprinted with permission from Reinsurance Association of
America, *Loss Development Study: 1987 Edition,* p. 17.

General Liability. Exhibit 9-13 shows a similar chart for
general liability, including asbestos claims. The spread between reinsurers and primary insurers is not as wide the first year for general
liability as for automobile liability insurance. However, the spread
becomes wider over the next few years, with a difference of about forty
percentage points remaining after nine years of development. The
inclusion of asbestos claims in the data accounts for some of this
spread. Some of the asbestos claims were not reported for forty years
or more after the alleged injury occurred. Also, the asbestos claims
probably constituted a larger percentage of total claims for reinsurers
than for primary insurers.

Exhibit 9-15
Comparison of Loss Development Patterns of
Primary Insurers and Reinsurers—Workers
Compensation Insurance*

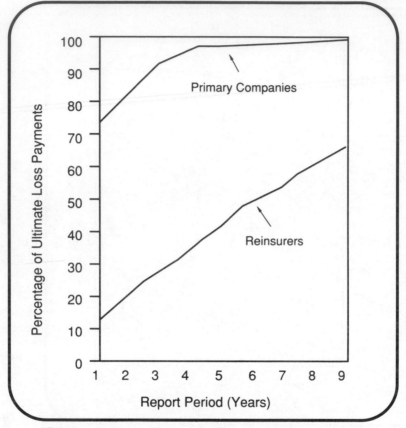

*Reprinted with permission from Reinsurance Association of
America, *Loss Development Study: 1987 Edition*, p. 18.

Medical Malpractice. Exhibit 9-14 shows medical malpractice
development patterns as reported by the RAA. The data used in
preparing this chart consisted of a mix of occurrence and claims-made
data, with the exact proportion of each unknown. The first year
development for primary insurers suggests a large proportion of
claims-made business, since development for primary insurers under
occurrence malpractice policies would be much nearer than that shown
for reinsurers in Exhibit 9-14. However, the distance between the two
curves in Exhibit 9-14 probably would be about the same if the data
were derived entirely from occurrence coverage or entirely from
claims-made coverage.

Exhibit 9-16
Comparison of Loss Development Patterns of Primary Insurers
and Reinsurers—Automobile Liability, General Liability, Medical
Malpractice Liability, and Workers Compensation Insurance*

	Percentage of Ultimate Loss Payments			
	First Year		Fourth Year	
	Reinsurer	Primary	Reinsurer	Primary
Automobile liability	25%	80%	75%	100%
Workers compensation	15%	75%	40%	95%
General liability (incl. asbestos)	3%	35%	25%	90%
Medical malpractice	1%	50%	20%	85%

*Reprinted with permission from Reinsurance Association of America, *Loss
Development Study: 1987 Edition*, p. 14.

Workers Compensation. Exhibit 9-15 shows development patterns for workers compensation insurance. The lag between development for primary insurers and reinsurers is even greater for workers compensation than for the other lines illustrated by the preceding exhibits in the first year of development, but narrows somewhat by the ninth year of development.

Lines Combined. The Exhibit 9-16 shows some of the same data in numerical form, contrasting the development of the various lines of the first and fourth years of development. The development factors for reinsurers vary somewhat according to their position in the reinsurance chain. Primary insurers sometimes buy their excess reinsurance in layers. In such situations, development is slower for the upper layers than for the lower layers. Also, development would probably be slower for retrocessionaires than for the reinsurer dealing directly with the primary insurer. As recently as 1987, losses from a hurricane that struck the U.S. Gulf Coast in 1983 were still being reported to retrocessionaires. All direct losses from the storm, excepting a few disputed claims, would have been paid several years earlier.

While the establishment of loss reserves is an art, it depends heavily on the science of mathematics. Considerable work has been done in the area that is beyond the scope of this text.[3] The challenge of establishing accurate reserves is considerable and will remain so into the future.

SUMMARY

Although much time and energy have been expended in an effort to improve loss reserving techniques, no completely satisfactory method, or combination of methods, has yet emerged. A large element of judgment still survives in even the most mathematical reserving methods.

There has been some experimentation with mathematical formulas and so-called expert systems. The results of the mathematical techniques, other than the tabular methods discussed, have been disappointing. The expert systems are too new to evaluate, but seem to offer some promise.

Estimating ultimate losses is less of a problem for property insurance than it is for liability lines, because property insurance losses are reported more quickly and can be evaluated more accurately. This is especially true for property lines that have frequent but relatively small losses, such as auto physical damage coverage. For such lines, even the most rudimentary techniques described in this chapter and in Chapter 8 are likely to prove adequate.

The real test of loss reserving methods comes from the long-tailed liability lines and from excess of loss reinsurance of such lines. Because losses for such lines are reported slowly, there is likely to be very little data to work with in the early years of development. Consequently, it may be necessary to resort to the loss ratio method of estimating reserves during early development periods. The loss ratio method is one of the least sophisticated reserving methods currently in use. However, greater sophistication is better only with adequate data.

Another problem with the long-tail lines is the uncertain value of such losses. Reasonably accurate evaluation of liability losses may be delayed for several years while medical treatment of the victims progresses and information is gathered through various legal proceedings. Precise valuation may not be possible until court decisions have been handed down, or even until all appeals have been exhausted.

The current asbestos claims illustrate the extreme problems possible with liability claims. Some people who worked in the shipyards during World War II are now suing, over forty years later, for injuries resulting from inhaling asbestos fibers at that time. It is doubtful that any reserving technique now known or to be developed in the foreseeable future can cope adequately with such extreme situations, but even the relatively normal liability claims, other than auto liability, pose serious reserving problems.

The only currently available techniques capable of coping adequately with liability loss reserving are the various loss development triangle techniques, possibly supplemented by the loss ratio method in the early years of development.

The reserving methods for reinsurance do not differ in principle from those used for primary insurance. However, the longer development period causes some difference in calculation and may place an even heavier burden on the judgment of the analyst.

Chapter Notes

1. In workers compensation the tabular method commonly reflects a factor discounting future payments to present value at some interest rate, often 3.5 percent. A $1 payment a year from now is reserved at $.965. If the $1 is indeed paid a year from now, then an arithmetical comparison of payments versus reserves shows that the $.965 reserve was deficient by $.035, representing the investment income earned on the reserves. There is disagreement within the insurance business as to whether loss reserves should be discounted.
2. R. Bornhuetter and R. Ferguson, "The Actuary and IBNR," *Proceedings of the Casualty Actuarial Society*, Vol. LIX, 1972, page 181.
3. There are a few publications that contain additional and more advanced concepts in loss reserving including:

   American Academy of Actuaries, *Casualty Loss Reserve Seminar Transcript* (annual), Washington, DC.
   Casualty Actuarial Society, *Statement of Principles Regarding Property and Casualty Loss and Loss Adjustment Expense Reserves*, New York, NY, 1988.
   T.M. Peterson, *Loss Reserving Property/Casualty Insurance*. Ernst & Whinney, Cleveland, OH, 1981.
   R.E. Salzmann, *Estimated Liabilities for Losses and Loss Adjustment Expenses*, Prentice Hall, Inc., Englewood Cliffs, NJ, 1984.

CHAPTER 10

Reinsurance Audits

An audit is a formal, systematic examination of accounts or financial records conducted by an independent party to verify their correctness. Reinsurance "audits" tend to be less structured than accounting audits and are done for several purposes, only one of which involves verifying the accuracy of financial records.

Historically, reinsurers have relied upon the principle of *uberrimae fidei* (utmost good faith) between the parties to the reinsurance contract. In fact, a reinsurance treaty (a contract) is generally such that a reinsurer depends upon full and voluntary disclosure to reinsurers by reinsureds of any policies issued, premiums written or earned, and losses after the contract is executed. Breach of utmost good faith is legally accepted as grounds for any necessary contract remedy, including reformation and rescission of the treaty.

In the early 1980s, primary and reinsurance loss experience deteriorated, driven in part by rate competition, increasing verdicts for torts involving toxic substances and pollution, and liberal interpretations of policy provisions. Reinsureds found many of their reinsurers in financial trouble, and both insurers and reinsurers failed at an accelerating rate. The increasing number of impaired insurers and reinsurers caused an increase in the number of all types of audits. The audits themselves increased in scope and uncovered many practices perceived as breaches of utmost good faith.

This chapter examines the procedures involved in reinsurance audits. It also examines in detail three types of reinsurance audits—underwriting, transactional, and claims—and considers the special problems of auditing managing general agents. It is in the best interests of the reinsurer to understand practices of the reinsured, to establish those practices that will facilitate a successful reinsurance

55

Exhibit 10-1
Sample Access to Records Clause

ARTICLE ___ – ACCESS TO RECORDS
The Reinsurer or its duly authorized representatives shall have the right to examine, at all offices of the company at all reasonable times, all books and records of the company relating to any business which is the subject of this Agreement. This right shall survive termination of the Agreement and shall continue so long as either party has any rights or obligations under this Agreement. Upon request, the Company shall supply the Reinsurer, at the Reinsurer's expense, with copies of any such books or records.

program, and to provide for audits as one form of early warning of trouble to the reinsurer.

AUDIT PROCEDURES

Reinsurers have the right to conduct audits because of the "Access to Records" article contained in virtually all contracts of reinsurance. A sample showing typical wording of this article is shown in Exhibit 10-1. Even in the absence of this or similar wording, the reinsurer may assert a right to audit under common law. In many respects, a reinsurance agreement creates a fiduciary relationship. It is well established that a fiduciary must be permitted to perform the actions necessary for fulfilling the fiduciary responsibilities.

Further empowerment for the performing of audits may arise from business practices outside the individual contract. For example, the American Institute of Certified Public Accountants requires that a reinsurer establish internal controls ". . . for assessing the accuracy and reliability of data received from the ceding company. . . . Principal control procedures of the assuming company may include. . .visiting the ceding company and reviewing and evaluating its underwriting, claims processing, loss reserving and loss reserve development monitoring techniques."[1]

While reinsurance intermediaries are important to many reinsurance relationships, they are not usually subject to underwriting, transactional, and claims reinsurance audits. The broker is not a party to the reinsurance contract. A reinsurance intermediary that is the underwriting manager for the assuming reinsurer, however, is subject to audits either as a signatory to the reinsurance document or under the agency contract with the reinsurer principal.

Purpose

Reinsurers normally conduct audits to obtain information necessary to evaluate the reinsurance agreement. The information may be specific—for example, claims data on specific claims—or general—for example, to establish a comfort level concerning loss reserving practices.

A second purpose for conducting audits is to provide a service to the client, the reinsured company. For example, the reinsured might ask for advice concerning a computer system with which to record cessions to a surplus share treaty. The service aspect, however, is usually not freestanding but arises as a side benefit from an information-seeking audit.

Timing of Audits

Audits may be done before an agreement is signed (pre-quote audits) or after the agreement is executed (at-risk audits).

Pre-Quote Audits. Audits made by a reinsurer prior to making a commitment to a new relationship are called "pre-quote audits." Normally these are underwriting audits, claims audits, or both and are used for the purpose of gathering information. For example, to rate a given contract, the underwriter might desire to know the number of policies and the premium dollars associated with specific ranges of limits of liability. For a similar purpose, a claims auditor might review past claims patterns to evaluate and project incurred but not reported (IBNR) losses.

At-Risk Audits. Audits made after the reinsurer has made a commitment are known as "at-risk audits" and involve all three types of audits discussed in this chapter. An underwriter might wish to update a limits profile to make sure the exposure is not increasing faster than the premium of the treaty. A claims person might wish to verify that there has not been an inappropriate change in the loss reserving practices of the reinsured. A financial auditor (in this chapter referred to as a "transactional" auditor, distinct from a public accountant) might wish to make sure that the premiums ceded to a surplus share treaty are in accord with the liabilities the reinsurer is assuming. In all of these examples, the purpose of reinsurance audits is to gather information, but any or all of them could produce suggestions for changing systems or methodologies that would be offered to the reinsured as a service.

Preparation

Whatever the type of audit, the auditor should perform certain tasks in advance. There is always more auditing to be done than can be accomplished, so the desired audits must be prioritized. Each audit must be defined in terms of the objective, including expected outputs. The outputs may suggest the timing of the audit. For example, if a primary insurance company is entering a new line of business and a limits profile is the desired output, it would be useless to schedule the audit before sufficient time has passed for a representative portfolio to be written.

A decision concerning the audit approach must also be made. It could be very organized or flexible. The desired outputs influence this decision, but knowledge of the reinsured may also be a factor. For example, most audits occur in a friendly rather than adversarial atmosphere and are conducted to foster the long-term relationship between the parties. Some primary companies, particularly smaller ones, view an "audit" as an activity similar to an IRS audit, but have no difficulty with the idea of an "underwriting review." This softening of terms may suggest a more flexible auditing approach.

Whatever the approach, the auditor should analyze the sources for the desired information and possibly design forms to facilitate its collection. The auditor should also employ a sampling technique to assure that a representative portfolio is reviewed. This sampling may require some knowledge of the filing system of the reinsured. Whenever possible, the auditor should communicate his or her needs to the reinsured so that the necessary files may be pulled prior to the auditor's arrival.

UNDERWRITING AUDITS

The purpose of an underwriting audit is three-fold. First, it is an avenue for the reinsurer to gain first-hand knowledge of a primary company, its management, its underwriters, and its book of business. Second, it serves to verify the correct usage of the reinsurance treaty. Third, the underwriting review provides a service to the reinsured in the form of audit findings and recommendations.

Preparation

The quality of the underwriting audit depends largely on the auditor's ability to speak to the reinsured's key people and to have available the desired files for review. If possible, key people should include senior management, underwriting management, and line underwriters. The file sample requested should include not only active files that are a fair representation of those risks exposing the treaty but also nonrenewed and declined accounts. Reviewing these latter groups often provides insight into current underwriting policy.

Prior to conducting the audit, as much information as possible should be gathered about the treaty and the reinsured. Information about the treaty should include a review of the underwriting file, the contract wording, and experience reports. Coordination with the reinsurer's claims department and accounting department may help to identify any problems pertaining to these areas that need to be discussed during the audit. Publications such as *Best's Reports* also provide information about the reinsured. Reports on any previous audits should be reviewed prior to visiting the reinsured.

Preparation of an audit worksheet is useful to assure consistent gathering of data as files are reviewed. The worksheet should provide for the collection of data such as the name of the insured, nature of the operations of the reinsured, policy limit, and premium. In addition, the worksheet should be tailored to facilitate the gathering of information relevant to specific concerns that the reinsurer may have regarding the particular treaty.

Senior Management Interview

Senior management should be interviewed to determine the philosophy, controls, company structure, future directions, and competition of the reinsured.

Philosophy. Interviews with management of the reinsured are valuable in collecting first-hand knowledge about the company. It is at the senior management level that company policy and underwriting philosophy are established. Through these interviews the reinsurer can determine whether the philosophy of the reinsured is compatible with its own and whether the position of the reinsured on current issues fits with the position of the reinsurer.

Controls. The presence of appropriate management controls is essential to the effective management of a company. Therefore, the reinsurer wants to know not only about the philosophy of management but also about the mechanisms that convey these philosophies to the front line underwriters. Once the philosophy is communicated, auditors should verify that (1) controls are in place to verify front line adherence to policies; (2) management reports capture the information needed to judge compliance with company policy; and (3) open lines of communication are in place.

Company Structure. Management can also provide information to the reinsurer regarding the structure of the company. The reinsurer should determine the number and location of branches and divisions. This information helps the reinsurer to understand the possible territorial differences in the business covered. The reinsurer should also determine the sources of the primary company's production: large brokerage houses, independent agents, managing general agents, or company employees. In addition, the reinsurer should evaluate how the company monitors and controls these production sources, such as through the identification of poor sources of business and by putting programs in place to deal with such sources. The commission levels paid to producing sources is important to determine, especially when the reinsurer is providing a pro-rata treaty with a ceding commission. Auditors can verify that commissions are stable and that the commission structure offers incentives for the placement of profitable business.

Future Directions. Interviews with management are the best means of determining the plans of the reinsured that might affect the business subject to the reinsurance agreement. Changes in direction might include changes in the lines of business written, production sources used, new ventures or acquisitions, or a change in the geographic spread of business. Projections of future premium levels help the reinsurer to assess whether there will be an adequate level of premium to fund the reinsurance limits provided.

Competition. An interview with senior management serves as a forum to discuss the major competitors of the reinsured. Understanding these competitors leads to a better appreciation of the market environment and factors affecting the reinsured.

Staff Interview

In addition to senior management, reinsurance auditors should become familiar with members of the underwriting staff to evaluate their strengths and weaknesses. The size of the staff and the relative workload are important. Underwriters' authority levels for binding business should be assessed to determine whether they are commensurate with experience. The reinsurer should become familiar with the controls that assure appropriate use of authority levels and adherence to other company policies. Questions for underwriting staff include the following:

- Are training programs in place?
- Are internal audits conducted?
- Are files reviewed by superiors?

File Review

Files are reviewed to determine pricing, limits profile, and risk selection techniques.

Pricing. A determination of pricing adequacy and trends is an important output of the review process. If pricing follows ISO manuals, the reinsurer may wish to sample the debits and credits used against manual rates. Trends in these factors from year to year help the reinsurer to judge the ultimate loss ratio on the book of business, as well as the commitment of the primary company to pricing integrity over the long term. While this information is particularly useful for a pro-rata treaty, it is also necessary if the reinsurer is pricing an excess of loss treaty on an exposure rating basis. Rate deviations should be warranted and properly supported with the appropriate documentation. The reinsurer should review the methods of monitoring these rate deviations.

Pricing may also be done using a primary company-developed rating approach. The reinsurer should review the approach of the reinsured as it is applied to the sample files. Questions include:

● Is the approach used consistently?
● Are the rating procedure and deviations documented?
● Does the rating approach adequately address all exposures being submitted to the underwriters?

Comparison of company rates from year to year is instructive for judging market fluctuations and adequacy of primary rates. Questions include:

● Does the company monitor these rate changes?
● Are the rates from prior years readily available to the underwriter when evaluating an account?
● Does the company have a regulation regarding the maximum decreases allowable?

By requesting pricing information from prior years, the reinsurer can judge the direction and extent of pricing fluctuations from year to year.

Limits Profile. A sample of policies may be reviewed to construct a limits profile. A limits profile helps the reinsurer to understand the number of times and the amounts for which the treaty is exposed to loss from (or by) the policies issued by the reinsured relative to the entire portfolio of the reinsured. Notes should be taken during the analysis to help the reinsurer decide when to reinsure at higher limits and when to restrict coverage to a lower limit. The analysis also helps determine whether the reinsured is using higher policy limits for only the larger and more hazardous risks, resulting in adverse selection to the reinsurer.

Risk Selection Techniques. The business of the reinsured can be only as good as its underwriters' ability to evaluate and select risks with qualities commensurate with the pricing and coverages provided in the policy forms used. The reinsurer should analyze a sample of files to review the quality of the primary insurer's risk selection. Review of active, canceled, and declined files reveals the underwriters' selection process. This review should include the primary company underwriters' analysis of the exposures presented by particular risks. Documentation of analysis is important so that, from year to year, the underwriters can monitor differences in the treatment of exposures. If the underwriter identifies exposures not contemplated in the policy form or in the pricing, the reinsurer should feel confident that these exposures have been addressed. Questions include:

- Have these exposures been excluded?
- Has the underwriter offered inspection or engineering recommendations to deal with the hazard?
- Does the pricing reflect to exposures accepted?

The reinsurer should verify that the underwriters of the reinsured are selecting risks in accordance with the underwriting guide. The underwriting guide provides the underwriter with assistance to determine when inspections are needed, when motor vehicle registration checks should be made, when financial information of the risk should be analyzed, and so forth. During the audit, the reinsurer should verify that each file in the sample complies with the primary company's underwriting guide.

Use of Reinsurance Agreement

When entering into or considering a reinsurance agreement, the reinsurer has certain expectations. These include not only an estimate of the amount of subject premium but also an understanding of the types and quality of risks that will be subject to the agreement. Verification that the correct amount of subject premium is reported to the reinsurer is usually the function of a transactional audit, discussed later. However, the underwriting review is the appropriate time to verify that the quality of risks transferred is in line with the assumptions of the reinsurer regarding the agreement.

If the reinsurer understands the agreement to be a mechanism for the reinsured to increase its premium-writing capacity, the reinsurer should verify that additional capacity is being used on the better risks for which the reinsured should want to allow additional capacity. A review of a random sample of the policies subject to the agreement should verify that there is a strict selection process as to which risks are written with the additional capacity. The review should also verify that the agreement is not being used to allow additional capacity on all risks and certainly not on the less attractive risks.

Finally a review of the random sample should verify that the agreement is not used for risks that are specifically excluded. If it is, this fact may indicate that the primary company and the reinsurer do not have a mutual understanding of the exclusion wording of the agreement.

The documentation of the cessions to any treaty should be verified. The correctness of the cession information and the timeliness with which the information is conveyed should also be noted. Incomplete or late documentation regarding the fact that a particular risk is subject to a treaty can eventually lead to delayed or confused reporting of claims to the reinsurer.

Audit Results

At the completion of the underwriting audit, the reinsurance underwriters should have gained an appreciation for both the strengths and weaknesses of the reinsured and its underwriting approach. While it is important to convey to the reinsured favorable findings of a review, it is essential to communicate any concerns of the reinsurer about the less favorable findings as well. The reinsurer should provide constructive criticism and well-thought-out recommendations for improvement. Such comments can be instructive for the reinsured and, as such, should be viewed as a value-added service provided by the reinsurer. This communication could take place in a wrap-up session at the conclusion of the audit, or the findings may be conveyed via a written letter or report after the conclusion of the audit. If a long-term relationship is to be established between the reinsurer and the reinsured, good communication and a willingness on both parts to work toward common goals are a necessity. Each party must agree to the functions and uses of the treaty, and each must feel comfortable that the contract is being used in the agreed-upon manner.

Upon completion of the audit, the reinsurance underwriters should document all findings for their files. This documentation not only serves to inform senior management and other members of the department about the findings, but it also serves as a document to be reviewed prior to any future audits. In this way, future auditors will note the recommendations that were made and will be able to follow up on progress that was or was not made in conforming to these recommendations.

TRANSACTIONAL AUDITS

The purpose of transactional reinsurance audits is to verify the accuracy of premium and loss data reported by the reinsured to the reinsurer and to determine whether the reinsured is complying with reinsurance contract terms. In addition, the transactional audit team evaluates the control structure of the reinsured over reinsurance reporting. Unlike underwriting audits, a transactional audit does not assess the quality of the risks subject to the reinsurance agreement or the rating philosophy employed by the reinsured in pricing the risks. Similarly, a transactional audit does not test the adequacy of loss reserves posted by the reinsured, as is the case during a claims audit.

Transactional audits provide at least five advantages to reinsurers and reinsureds:

- They provide the underwriter of the reinsurer with an evaluation of whether the financial data reported to the reinsurer by the reinsured are accurate and in compliance with reinsurance agreement.
- They furnish an opportunity for the reinsurer to provide a unique service to the reinsured in the form of an independent evaluation of the reinsurance reporting system of the reinsured. Because of this service element, many reinsurance underwriters view transactional audits as a valuable marketing tool.
- They determine whether additional funds are due the reinsured or the reinsurer.
- They represent opportunities for the reinsured to examine alternative approaches to achieving a more efficient and cost-effective reinsurance processing system. The auditors' efficiency recommendations may include changes in the workflow through various processing units, increased automation, and systems edits.
- They provide the underwriter of the reinsurer with assurances that premiums and losses are accurately processed internally and properly reflected on the books of the reinsurer.

In determining which reinsurance programs are most appropriate for transactional audits, many reinsurers focus attention on treaty rather than on facultative business. Since a treaty covers an entire book of business, it is difficult for the reinsurer to determine readily whether the financial information reported by the reinsured is reasonable and accurate. As a result, the reporting of financial data pertaining to a treaty presents a greater risk to the reinsurer than the reporting of data relating to a facultative certificate, which insures only a single risk. The assumption here is that the transactional audit program focuses on treaty business.

Many reinsurers have developed pro forma transactional audit manuals that serve as a set of guidelines for conducting transactional reviews. The audit manual is not intended to be a list of instructions for completing all phases of the audit, but rather, serves the audit team in three ways:

1. It identifies the typical transactions that take place during the course of a reinsurance treaty: premium cessions, loss recoveries, ceding commissions, brokerage fees (if applicable), contingent profit-based commissions, portfolio transfers, loss reserves, salvage, and subrogation.
2. It suggests methods for verifying the accurate processing of these transactions by the reinsured and the reinsurer.
3. It provides a systematic approach for evaluating the control structure of the reinsured over reinsurance processing.

Establishing Audit Contacts

Prior to on-site testing, the appropriate audit contacts at the reinsured are determined by consulting the reinsurer's underwriter, who has account responsibility, and the broker, if applicable. The audit contacts assist in scheduling the review and represent key departments of the reinsured, including underwriting, claims, and accounting. During the entrance conference, the audit contacts can trace the flow of insurance and reinsurance information through the primary insurer's processing units. This workflow description enables the auditors to identify any control concerns applicable to the operation that require further evaluation.

Premium Accounting

The methods the audit team employs to verify the accuracy of premium data reported to the reinsurer depend on the type of reinsurance treaty reviewed. Premium audit testing for pro-rata and cessions-basis excess of loss treaties is discussed in the next section, followed by a discussion of premium testing for rated excess of loss treaties. Cessions-basis excess of loss treaties are agreements under

Exhibit 10-2
Sample Reinsurance Account for Quota Share Treaty

XYZ Insurance Company
Property Quota Share Treaty
in Account with:
ABC Reinsurance Company
for Quarter Ending: March 19X6

Written Premiums	$3,274,195.00	
LESS: Cancellations	0	
Net Written Premiums		$3,274,195.00
Ceding Commissions at 25%	818,548.75	
Paid Losses	364,264.78	
Paid Loss Adjustment Expenses	28,765.93	
Brokerage @ 1% of Written Premiums	32,741.95	
LESS: Total Reinsurance Deductions		1,244,321.41
Net Due Reinsurers		$2,029,873.59
Net Due ABC Reinsurer @ 30% Share		$ 608,962.08

which the primary company cedes premiums by policy according to a schedule of rates that vary according to the limits of liability of the policies.

Pro-rata and Cessions-Basis Excess of Loss Treaties. Prior to visiting the reinsured, the auditors reconstruct the premium data reported to the reinsurer from the summary accounts sent by the reinsured or the broker. Exhibit 10-2 shows a sample reinsurance account for a quota share treaty. The auditors extract the following information from the reinsurance accounts: gross written premiums, ceding commissions deducted by the reinsured and, if applicable, brokerage fee. The use of a personal computer-generated spreadsheet often eases the compilation of such data in the form of an account reconstruction.

While on-site, the audit team requests the premium bordereaux

Exhibit 10-3
Sample Premium Bordereau for Quota Share Treaty

XYZ Insurance Company
Quarterly Premium Bordereau
Property Quota Share Treaty
January–March, 19X6

Insured	Policy Eff. Dates	Policy No.	Gross Premium
Bronte, Charlotte	3/25/X6 – 3/25/X7	89-6987	$69,824
Bronte, Emily	1/26/X6 – 1/26/X7	89-1295	978,137
Carton, Sidney	2/2/X6 – 2/2/X7	89-2469	657,942
Copperfield, David	1/30/X6 – 1/30/X7	89-6547	62,172
Dickens, Charles	2/14/X6 – 2/14/X7	89-6952	654,896
Dickinson, Emily	1/10/X6 – 1/10/X7	89-2694	66,713
Faulkner, William	3/15/X6 – 3/15/X7	89-6973	568,413
Jennings, Peter	2/18/X6 – 2/18/X7	89-4369	10,025
Koppel, Ted	2/4/X6 – 2/4/X7	89-9547	97,423
Manet, Lucy	1/6/X6 – 1/6/X7	89-2375	19,235
Walters, Barbara	1/9 X6 – 1/9/X7	89-3574	89,415
Quarter Totals			$3,274,195

Total premium per the premium bordereaux of $3,274,195 appears on
the reinsurer's quarterly account in Exhibit 10-2.

that support the summary accounts. They compare the written
premium totals documented on the bordereaux to the written premium
totals shown on the account reconstruction. Exhibit 10-3 shows a
sample page from a premium bordereau for a quota share treaty. For
those accounts that cannot be reconciled to the supporting premium
bordereaux, the auditors follow up with appropriate broker or reinsured personnel or both to determine the cause of the discrepancy.
Upon confirming the existence of a difference, the team calculates the
additional sums due either the reinsurer or the reinsured.

After verifying the accuracy of the premium data reported on the
reinsurance accounts, the auditors conduct a review of a judgmental
sample of policies ceded to the treaty. (The manner of selecting this
sample is discussed in the "Loss Accounting" section for pro-rata and
cessions-basis excess of loss treaties.) During the policy file review, the
following factors are tested:

● Is the policy effective date within the effective dates of the
  reinsurance treaty?

- Are the lines of business covered by the policy in compliance with the terms of the reinsurance treaty?
- Is the policy limit of liability within the limits of liability of the reinsurer for this treaty?
- Was the treaty share of the policy premium traced to the premium bordereaux?
- Is premium ceded to the reinsurers in a timely manner?
- Was the premium applied to the correct underwriting period?

Rated Excess of Loss Treaties. Prior to the on-site review, the audit team reviews the deposit premiums rendered to the reinsurer and verifies that these amounts are in accordance with the reinsurance treaty terms. In addition, the audit team reviews each annual premium adjustment account for accuracy and tests the premium rate applied to the subject premium base for compliance with treaty terms. A sample annual premium adjustment account appears in Exhibit 10-4.

While on site, the auditors request documentation for the subject premium base. Such support may consist of Part 2 (Premiums Earned) or Part 2B (Premiums Written) of the Underwriting and Investment Exhibit of the reinsured's Annual Statement or premium worksheets compiled that document the calculation of the subject premium base. These worksheets may include various manual adjustments in calculating the premium base, such as the deduction of facultative reinsurance premiums. In reviewing the Annual Statement or premium base worksheets, the audit team should verify that only lines of business specified by the treaty terms are included in the premium base calculation.

After verifying the accuracy of the subject premium base reported to the reinsurer, the auditors select a sample of policy files for review. (The manner in which the policies are selected is discussed in the "Loss Accounting" section for rated excess of loss treaties.) During the policy file review, the audit team verifies that the policy effective dates are within the effective dates of the reinsurance treaty. In addition, the team verifies that the lines of business covered by the policy are not excluded by the terms of the reinsurance treaty.

Loss Accounting

Similar to the verification of reported premiums, the methods employed by the auditors to verify the accuracy of loss data reported to the reinsurer depend on the type of reinsurance treaty reviewed. A discussion of loss audit testing for pro-rata and cessions-basis excess of loss treaties is provided below, followed by an explanation of loss testing for rated excess of loss treaties.

Exhibit 10-4

Sample Reinsurance Account for Rated Excess of Loss Treaty

XYZ Insurance Company
Property Excess of Loss Treaty
in Account with:
ABC Reinsurance Company
Premium Adjustment Account for
Year Ending 19X7

Fire	$31,265,478
Allied Lines	4,655,332
Extended Coverage	123,987
Homeowners Multi Peril	3,365,498
Commercial Multi Peril	4,569,835
Motor Truck Cargo	2,365
Burglary	2,641
Fidelity	13,654
Earthquake	0
Auto Physical Damage	665,498
Total Subject Earned Premium	$44,664,288
Rated @ 2.75%	$1,228,267.92
LESS: Annual Deposit Premium	1,000,000.00
Difference	$228,267.92
Additional Premium Due ABC Reinsurer @ 10% Share	22,826.79
LESS: 10% Brokerage	2,282.68
Net Adjustment Due ABC Reinsurer	$20,544.11

Pro-rata and Cessions-Basis Excess of Loss Treaties.
Prior to visiting the reinsured, the audit team reconstructs the paid loss
and loss adjustment expense data reported to the reinsurer. The loss
reconstruction is frequently completed in conjunction with the premium
reconstruction. The audit team extracts the following information from
the summary accounts sent to the reinsurer by the reinsured or broker:
gross paid losses and loss adjustment expenses, salvage and subroga-

tion, and current outstanding loss and loss adjustment expense reserves.

While on-site, the auditors request the supporting paid loss and outstanding loss reserve bordereaux. They compare the paid loss and paid expense totals documented on the bordereaux to the paid loss and paid expense totals shown on the account reconstruction. Similarly, they compare the total outstanding loss reserves as of the current period as shown on the bordereaux to the outstanding loss reserves documented on the account reconstruction. Exhibit 10-5 illustrates a sample page from a paid loss and outstanding loss reserve bordereau. For those accounts that cannot be reconciled to the supporting loss and expense bordereaux, the audit team follows up with the appropriate broker or reinsured personnel to determine the cause of the discrepancy. Upon confirming the existence of a difference, the team calculates the additional sums due either the reinsurer or the reinsured.

From the paid loss bordereaux, the auditors select a sample of claim files, skewing or adjusting the sample to include higher dollar paid loss amounts. For each claim selected, the audit team also requests the corresponding policy files (see the section on "Premium Accounting" for pro-rata treaties). In conducting the claim file review, the following factors are tested:

- Did the date of loss occur within the policy period?
- Is the cause of the loss or accident covered by the policy terms and reinsurance treaty terms?
- Was the paid loss properly calculated (were the policy deductible and retention of the reinsured properly applied)?
- Are all paid losses and loss adjustment expenses adequately supported by the contents of the claim file?
- Were salvage and subrogation recoveries pursued and credited to the reinsurers?
- Were all paid losses, loss adjustment expenses, and current outstanding loss reserves traced to the reinsurance loss bordereaux?
- Were paid losses, loss adjustment expenses, and current outstanding loss reserves entered into the reinsurance reporting system of the reinsured in a timely manner?
- For surplus share treaties, was the loss recovery percentage consistent with the premium cession rate?
- Were the losses, expenses, and reserves applied to the correct underwriting period?

Rated Excess of Loss Treaties. Prior to the on-site review, the auditors select a sample of individual losses reported to the reinsurer based on higher dollar paid loss amounts. While reviewing the

Exhibit 10-5
Sample Loss Bordereau for Quota Share Treaty

XYZ Insurance Company
Quarterly Loss Bordereau
Property Quota Share Treaty
January – March 19X6

Insured	Policy Eff. Dates	Date of Loss	Claim No.	Policy No.	Paid Losses	Paid Expenses	Outstanding Loss Reserves
Bronte, Charlotte	3/25/X6–3/25/X7	3/30/X6	4695	83-5987	$152,611.68	$165.60	$362,569
Copperfield, David	1/30/X6–1/30/X7	2/25/X6	5492	89-6547	23,693.62	13,289.00	5,642
Dickens, Charles	2/14/X6–2/14/X7	3/1/X6	3621	89-6952	52,685.73	596.33	101,269
Jennings, Peter	2/18/X6–2/18/X7	3/1/X6	2643	89-4369	72,244.97	7,289.00	83,695
Manet, Lucy	1/6/X6– 1/6/X7	1/15/X5	9853	89-2375	63,028.78	7,426.00	10,094
Quarter Totals					$364,264.78	$28,765.93	$563,269

Paid loss, paid expense, and outstanding loss reserve amounts shown on loss bordereau
match amounts shown on first quarter 19X6 account per Exhibit 10-2.

reinsurer's claim files pertaining to the treaty, the audit team documents the following data for each claim: the policy and claim file numbers of the reinsured, paid losses, paid expenses, salvage, subrogation, and current outstanding loss reserves.

During the on-site review, the auditors review the claim files of the reinsured for the sample selected, as well as the corresponding policy files of the reinsured (see the section on "Premium Accounting" for rated excess of loss treaties). For each claim, the audit team compares the loss data documented in the file to the loss data reported to the reinsurer as shown on its claim reconstruction. Specifically, the auditors verify the accuracy of the paid loss and paid expense amounts reported to the reinsurer, review the timeliness of claim reports including changes in outstanding loss reserves, and verify cessions of salvage and subrogation.

Evaluating the Control Structure over Reinsurance Reporting

To facilitate evaluating the controls of the reinsured over the accuracy of reinsurance reporting, the auditors prepare control questionnaires pertaining to each of the key functions of the reinsured. These functions include underwriting, accounting, claims, and auditing. The auditors may distribute the questionnaires prior to or during on-site testing or use them as an agenda for the entrance conference and for interim meetings during the on-site review.

The audit team must be flexible in developing the questionnaires and tailor them according to the insurance operation under review. For example, the control questionnaires developed for a captive insurance company or a small managing general agent writing a single specialized line of business would differ significantly from the questionnaires for a large multi-line property-liability insurer with branches worldwide.

The control questionnaires help in gaining an understanding of the reinsured's premium and loss processing functions and the associate controls over those functions. The underwriting and accounting questionnaires determine how the business is marketed, how premiums are recorded on the books of the reinsured and collected, and how premiums are reported and remitted to the reinsurers. The auditors often request information concerning the following:

- Marketing strategy employed
- Diary system for collecting premium balances from agents
- Edit checks in the premium processing system of the reinsured

- Internal controls that help to ensure that all business that should be ceded to the treaty is actually ceded
- Management review of reinsurance accounts prior to release

Similarly, the claim questionnaire determines how coverage is verified and how losses are recorded on the books of the reinsured and charged to the reinsurers. Typical points covered on the claim questionnaire are as follows:

- Reporting of losses to the insurer by the insured
- Coverage verification
- Initial reserve posting and reporting to reinsurers
- Timeliness of reporting reserve changes to reinsurers
- Compliance with paid loss and reserve authorization levels
- Use of outside loss adjusting firms
- Use of defense counsel and monitoring defense costs
- Internal diary system for monitoring file status
- Accuracy of reinsurance loss cessions, including proper application of the policy deductible, the retention of the reinsured, and the participation share of the reinsurer

Finally, the auditing questionnaire determines whether the reinsured has a formal internal audit unit responsible for periodically reviewing the control structure over its key functions. In addition, the questionnaire determines whether other reviews have been conducted by state examiners, the public accounting firm of the reinsured, and other reinsurers. Also, the questionnaire is designed to identify any internal quality review programs that regularly monitor the accuracy of transactions processed. The completion of the auditing questionnaire assists the team in gathering information regarding the primary company's controls over its reinsurance processing system.

Implementing Audit Recommendations

One of the primary reasons for conducting a transactional review is to improve procedures where appropriate. Therefore, it is necessary to discuss and confirm all discrepancies, especially those resulting in a financial impact to the reinsured or reinsurer, with the audit contacts during all phases of the review. At the conclusion of the review, the audit team holds an exit conference with the appropriate personnel to summarize all discrepancies and control concerns.

To facilitate the timely resolution of audit findings, the auditors prepare point sheets to distribute to the primary insurer's personnel. These point sheets document the following information for each concern: the applicable standard procedure, the deviation from that standard, the cause of the deviation, and the effect of the deviation. Also, the team provides to the reinsured other useful data where appropriate, such as the reinsured's policy and claim file numbers and the corresponding insured's name. The point sheets serve as an agenda for the exit conference as well as a summary of audit findings. Upon reviewing the point sheets, the auditors work with the primary company to obtain agreement regarding appropriate corrective action and benchmark dates for the disposition of all discrepancies.

In addition to discussing specific discrepancies, the exit conference is an opportunity to offer the reinsured efficiency recommendations to improve its control structure, reduce its costs, and enhance its operations. Upon completing on-site testing, the team communicates the results of the review to the underwriter of the reinsurer and to the broker, if applicable. Finally, the audit team establishes a diary system for monitoring the status of open audit points until all outstanding issues are adequately resolved.

Challenges

The scope of the transactional audit program of the reinsurer depends upon the targeted markets established by executive management in its long-term strategy. For example, if the reinsurer establishes an objective to increase its automatic facultative or treaty premium volume, the company must adjust the focus of its audit programs to address the concerns associated with those types of coverages.

One factor that has caused many reinsurers to adjust audit scope has been the recent wave of insurance company insolvencies. Specifically, some reinsurers are currently expanding audit coverage to include the review of the financial statements of the reinsured and an evaluation of the solvency position of the reinsured.

Another factor influencing the focus of the transactional audit program is the revision of insurance and reinsurance contract provisions. For example, the reinsurer needs to assess the impact of increased use of certain reinsurance contract provisions, such as the claims-made form, the extra-contractual obligations (ECO) clause, and any hold-harmless provision, and reflect its assessment accordingly in its audit program.

Finally, the transactional audit program must respond to technological advances. Specifically, the reinsurer needs to consider the level of automation of the reinsurance reporting system of the reinsured, including edit checks, interfacing of premium and loss computer subsystems, and the use of personal computer applications in generating reinsurance reports.

The transactional auditor needs to address the challenges discussed by consistently assessing changes in the insurance and reinsurance markets. This evaluation is facilitated by continuing insurance education and membership in various insurance associations. An understanding of the nature of the coverages provided by the reinsured with whom the reinsurer contracts and the market conditions that affect those coverages is of primary importance in the effective execution of a transactional audit program.

CLAIMS AUDITS

Whenever practical, given time and expense considerations, the reinsurer should regularly exercise its right to inspect the claims records of the reinsured, particularly in light of the increasing volume of torts involving toxic substances, including pollution claims, and the trend toward liberal court judgments and verdicts.

Different types of claims audits apply to different situations. The pre-quote or pre-binding audit assesses the quality of the claim operation of the reinsured. The at-risk claims audit is the periodic (generally annual or biannual) review of specific reinsurance claims fitting defined criteria, as well as a random sample of claims in the office of the reinsured that have not been reported to reinsurers. The primary reasons for conducting routine, periodic claims audits include evaluating the claims management staff of the reinsured, as well as its systems, procedures, controls, reserves, and reinsurance claims reporting practices. At-risk audits also provide the opportunity to establish a supportive team relationship between the reinsured and reinsurer. The success and profitability of the reinsurance relationship depends upon the technical skills of both the reinsured and the reinsurer.

A third type of audit arises when the reinsured or a reinsurer requests a meeting to discuss a specific claim. At one time such audits were rare. However, with the ever increasing numbers of complex asbestos cases and torts involving toxic substances, the frequency of this type of review is increasing. Generally, during the meeting the reinsured explains to all reinsurers the coverages included in the insured's policy, the circumstances of the claim, its evaluation, and the proposed course of action. The primary reasons for meeting with reinsurers are to ensure that all questions are addressed up front, to obtain objective evaluations of the proposed course of action, and possibly, to solicit additional recommendations from reinsurers on other available options. The reinsured generally attempts to obtain the agreement of the reinsurer prior to committing to a course of action. Willingness of reinsurers to participate in these special reviews varies. On occasion, reinsurers decline to give any "counsel and concurrence" for fear the courts may bring them into the case. These individual claim reviews may require unique planning on the part of the reinsurer. Each situation should be carefully assessed, specific objectives established, and information gathered as deemed appropriate. Due to the many variations associated with individual claim reviews, the following discussion focuses on pre-quote and at-risk audits only.

Preparation

Prior to scheduling a claims audit, the reinsurer should obtain and review:

- Copies of pertinent reinsurance agreements, underwriting information, and sample policies, with particular attention to information on additional reinsurance protection the reinsured may have purchased that inure to the benefit of the agreement(s) in question, as well as the intermediary and sunset clauses
- Reinsured company profile
- Review of applicable insurance reports (for example, A.M. Best's Insurance Reports)
- Individual reinsurance loss experience detail (reinsurer should compare its records with that of the reinsured and the intermediary, or both)
- List of open receivables and payables between reinsured and reinsurer to determine whether there is a lag in reporting losses
- Loss ratio and loss development reports
- Prior year audit and actuarial reports
- Specific claim files of the reinsured to be targeted for review
- Recent awards in the jurisdiction(s) where the reinsured does business
- Copies of the internal procedure manuals, forms, and instructions of the reinsured (for example, claims coding forms, clerical instruction form, large loss form). These could be reviewed on-site once the audit has begun.
- List of outside attorneys and adjusters used by the primary company

The reinsurer should formally define the objectives of the audit, including its purpose, scope, and testing methodology. The reinsurer should determine whether the reinsured prefers a specific time of the year for reinsurer audits. Many companies routinely reserve a specific time, making space and files available to all reinsurers. This practice reduces the disruption to the claims operation of the reinsured.

However, individual reinsurers must first determine that this practice is acceptable.

Objectives for Claims Audits. The objectives of claims audits are determined by the purpose of the audit. Claims audits may have any one of three purposes: (1) to determine whether the reinsurer should participate in a reinsurance agreement, (2) to perform a routine periodic review of existing claims, or (3) to review the details of a specific claim.

To Determine Whether the Reinsurer Should Begin or Continue To Participate in a Reinsurance Agreement. In this case, the auditors need to assess the claims handling expertise, systems, and controls in the office of the reinsured. They also need to assess the adequacy of reserves and reinsurance claim reporting to evaluate the loss experience data provided. This type of review could include an examination of the financial statements of the reinsured company. It should include a review of a sample of policies written under prior reinsurance agreements to ensure conformity to the reinsurance agreement. Once this information is gathered and studied, the reinsurer can determine whether it wants to participate in the reinsurance agreement and, if so, how large a line to accept.

To Perform a Routine Annual Audit of Claims on Existing Agreements. If the audit is routine, the reinsurer reviews the personnel, systems, controls, reserves, and reinsurance claim reporting of the reinsured. Specific claims with serious injuries on large reserves may be targeted for in-depth review. Auditors should also review a sample of claims not reported to reinsurers. This sample can reveal whether the claims are reported in accordance with the terms of the agreement and indicate the adequacy of the primary insurer's reserves.

To Review a Particular Claim or Series of Claims. In this instance, the objectives of the reinsurer are to determine whether the claim is (1) covered in the original policy, (2) handled properly, and (3) adequately reserved. This type of review generally occurs with complex files involving asbestos, toxic dump sites, and other toxic substances. After reviewing the policy, claim, reserves, and reinsurance agreement, the reinsurer can offer suggestions, agree with handling and coverage, or issue a reservation of rights letter.

Questions for a Claims Audit. The questions cover general questions, specific concerns, the timing of the audit, nature of the audit report, and the quality of claims personnel at the primary company.

General Questions. The following general questions should be addressed:

- What are the experience and authority levels of the staff?

- What procedures, systems, and controls are in place to ensure proactive claims settlement practices, consistent monitoring of reserves, and handling of routine, as well as critical, large losses?
- How much supervisory and management involvement are present in the files?
- Does the reinsured regularly collectively review files? Specifically, is there a mechanism whereby senior claims personnel, in conjunction with underwriting and management staff, review and evaluate the handling and reserving of large or complex cases?
- Does the reinsured wisely use legal counsel, providing direction rather than merely assigning the file?
- How is the reinsured structured (one office or home office with multiple branches and many locations)?
- If the reinsured has multiple branches, are regular audits performed by the home office or regional office?
- Is the reinsured properly reporting claims with potential reinsurance exposure in a timely manner?
- How does the reinsured bill and monitor reinsurance loss recoverables and payments?
- If the reinsured has multiple branches, who coordinates reinsurance reporting?

Specific Concerns. The audit should address the reinsurer's specific concerns through the following types of questions:

- Has there been a pattern of late reinsurance loss reporting?
- Has there been a pattern of unexpected verdicts drastically above case reserves?
- Is there evidence of recoveries that have not been promptly refunded to reinsurers?
- Is the reinsured providing sufficient loss detail and responding promptly to questions of the reinsurer?
- Has there been increased turnover in the claims department or in the company overall?
- If the reinsured has multiple branches, has the reinsurer identified a difference in reporting and responsiveness among the branches?
- Has there been a pattern of "bad faith" lawsuits against the reinsured for improper claims handling?

Timing of the Audit. The length of time available for the audit imposes limits on what can be accomplished. The audit team must determine the number of files and any specific loss files that need to be examined. The audit team may request the reinsured to provide a comprehensive loss list prior to the audit to sample unreported claims. The audit team should estimate the time required to interview the appropriate staff of the reinsured and estimate the total time required for the audit—including the wrap-up meeting. The timing of the audit may require the reinsurer to decide which personnel to make available for the audit. It may be necessary to schedule visits not only at the primary company's home office but also at its branches. The audit team should contact the reinsured or its intermediary to schedule the audit and to notify the reinsured of the information it wishes to review.

Once all of this is accomplished, the reinsured or its intermediary schedules and confirms the audit. If an intermediary is involved in the agreement, it often chooses to attend the reinsurance claim audit and participate in the "wrap-up" meeting.

Nature of the Audit Report.   The type of report to be compiled after the review should be determined in advance so that the auditors may do the following:

- Establish the format necessary to record the results
- Determine whether this will be confidential or shared with the reinsured, the intermediary, or both
- Determine whether a "wrap-up" meeting will be held with the reinsured to discuss the results of the review and who should attend

Assessing the Claim Personnel of the Primary Company. One of the most critical aspects of assessing the primary insurer's claims handling ability is the quality of the personnel in its claims department. Therefore, the reinsurer generally requires certain information concerning the background and experience of claims personnel. The background information may be requested prior to or during the audit. Generally, the reinsurer also conducts several staff interviews during the audit. As a minimum, most reinsurers request information concerning:

- Department heads (vice president, manager, supervisor)
    - Biographical sketches (education, previous experience, years with the reinsured, and in what capacities)
    - Authority levels for each individual
    - What is each individual's involvement in setting reserves and negotiating settlements?
    - What is the individual's involvement in executing a routine claim audit program?
    - When are claims referred to management, and how does the reinsured ensure that this will happen?

- Does the individual have input into the underwriting philosophy and guidelines of the company?
- What is the general claim philosophy of the reinsured (aggressive or passive)?
- What type of management diary system exists, what are the time parameters, and who monitors the diary?
- General claims staff/adjusters
  - What is the hiring/promotional philosophy of the company?
  - Who has hiring authority?
  - What is the type and length of training provided to new hires?
  - What is the average experience level of the staff?
  - What is the average workload of the staff and how is it determined?
  - Does the claims staff specialize (workers compensation adjusters, medical malpractice adjusters, property adjusters, and casualty adjusters), and how are specific claims assigned?
  - What standards of performance exist; who sets the standards; and how does the reinsured monitor performance to standard?

Auditing Reinsurance Claim Reporting

Another priority for a reinsurer performing a pre-quote or an at-risk claims audit is evaluation of loss reporting to reinsurers based upon the criteria established in the reinsurance agreements (both excess of loss and pro rata).

General Process. A reinsurer also wants to determine whether the primary insurer's reported reserves are adequate or whether the reinsurer should establish an additional case reserve (ACR). An ACR is an internal mechanism that allows the reinsurer, in bulk or per file, to establish an additional reinsurance incurred reserve above that established by the primary company.

Prior to conducting an on-site audit, the auditors often prepare a matrix of reinsurance coverage purchased by the reinsured to show graphically how the individual reinsurance agreements interrelate. The reinsurer then reviews targeted claims (reinsurance reported as well as a sample of unreported) to verify proper and accurate reporting. The reinsurer should pay particular attention to management controls, internal audits, and reinsurance reporting guidelines. The reinsurer should review how the primary company monitors reinsurance coverage, by the reinsured, how claims are identified for reporting, who handles the reporting, and the frequency and content of the information provided to the reinsurers.

In addition, the reinsurer should review documented procedures and verify the understanding and implementation of these procedures by claims personnel. Any gaps between the directives and the execution of those instructions should be discussed with the reinsured during the audit wrap-up.

The reinsurer should evaluate reinsurance reporting (format, information, and timeliness) and validate its own reinsurance reserves. Often, as a reinsurer reviews individual claim files, it identifies files needing increased reserves. The reinsurer has the opportunity to offer suggestions and guidance, overall or on individual files, during the audit wrap-up. The primary company may accept or disregard the advice given. Should the primary company not choose to increase the reserves, the reinsurer may then choose to establish an internal additional case reserve for specific claims.

While reviewing the sample of unreported claims, the reinsurer may identify claims which could or should be reported to reinsurers. These files should also be discussed and a request made for a report at the wrap-up. If the number of unreported claims is high or the overall reserves appear low, the reinsurer may ask to review a larger sample immediately, schedule a second audit within the next few weeks, or step up the frequency of reinsurance claim audits with that reinsured. The reinsurer may also advise its underwriters to decline to renew the agreement.

Reserving Practices. The financial results of a company reflect the timing and accuracy of the claim department's reserve estimates. Those estimates involve many considerations, including the following:

- Does the policy cover the allegations against the insured?
- Do the facts as originally presented favor the party bringing the claim?
- Are there additional circumstances that would make the claim difficult to defend?
- Is the alleged injury or damage serious?
- Is the jurisdiction in which the claim is brought conservative or liberal?
- If in suit, what is the technical competence of opposing counsel?

An insurer must develop the facts of a claim quickly to ensure that the claim reserve properly reflects the exposure to both the insured and the company.

If an insurer consistently avoids aggressively pursuing timely investigations of reported losses, there is a need for change in reserving or investigative philosophies. A reinsurance claim audit can be used to determine the primary insurer's overall approach to claim reserving and handling. The reinsurer is in a position to become actively involved by identifying deficiencies and suggesting improvements. In some cases, a reinsurer might decide to terminate a relationship with a reinsured if reserving philosophies are not commensurate with those of the reinsurer. In other cases, a stronger relationship can be established as the parties work together to improve any deficiencies.

Reserve Changes. All reserve changes should be documented in the claim file, including the amount and date of the change and the reason for the change. Reserve entries should be dated and signed, or initialed, by appropriate claim personnel. Procedures should be in place for management review of significant reserve changes, and reinsurance guidelines should be clearly communicated to staff so that reinsurance recoverables are reported as appropriate.

"Reserve Creep." Claim files should be reviewed to determine whether significant or last minute changes in reserves occur often. Significant differences between an initial reserve and the ultimate value established either through settlement or judgment may be indicative of reserving problems. This "stair-step" or "stepladder" (each addition to reserves is a stair step) reserve development may reflect a claim that has not been aggressively investigated to determine liability and damages. On occasion, this reserve development might not be under the control of the claim department (because, for example, high-dollar jury verdicts have become common), and a claim audit can determine whether this is a trend. Slow development of claim files with large, unexpected increases can adversely affect the financial results of an insurer and its reinsurers.

Precautionary Reserve Practices. At times insurers reserve for nominal amounts if the exposure to the insured is deemed to be limited. There are three reasons an insurer might establish a precautionary reserve.

1. An umbrella file might be established with a minimal reserve if the insurer writes both the underlying and excess coverage. The file acknowledges the excess coverage and its potential exposure.
2. An insured, or a number of insureds, might be the subject of certain types of claims, such as asbestos, in which the insurer participates in an upper layer of coverage that is not expected to have to respond in light of the circumstances of the losses.

3. Coverage might attach at a level above for a specific insured's retention.

In all such cases, the audit team should obtain loss lists and review claims to determine the validity of this particular reserving philosophy. Some insurers have procedures for specific insureds to file incident reports. These incidents may or may not pose an exposure to the insured. A random sample, including a review of claims already established, can provide an insight into proper claim procedures.

Prompt and Complete Investigation. The early and accurate determination of liability and damages is essential to enable a book of business to produce a profit. Although accuracy is important in documenting liability on behalf of an insured, a claim adjuster must be aware of all intervening factors influencing a given claim. Opportunities to settle throughout the course of an investigation should not be lost because of that "last detail" that needs to be uncovered. An experienced claim professional weighs the facts along with the economics of an early resolution of a claim against an insured. The reinsurance claim auditor should look for procedures that encourage an early, accurate liability and damage investigation, plus a philosophy of sound claim negotiation priorities. A thorough and complete investigation should be balanced by an understanding of claim costs associated with claim files that remain open for an extended period. A well run claims department completes its investigations in a timely fashion to allow early resolution of disputed losses.

Early Evaluation. An insurer must have claim personnel capable of promptly recognizing and evaluating exposure under its policies. Generally, the longer a claim stays open, the more expensive it becomes to settle. There should be procedures in place to ensure that claims are initially reviewed by highly trained technical personnel and that these reviews continue at regular intervals. Reviews should reflect progress toward an early determination of value and settlement.

Early Settlement Authority. Once it has been determined that there is coverage for a specific loss, and liability has been established, early settlement negotiations should be initiated. Procedures should be in place to enable a claim handler to obtain settlement authority up to the value of the claim and to control overall claim payments made. The absence of consistent investigation, evaluation, and settlement efforts may suggest that the department is in need of additional controls.

Use of Counsel. Often, the insurer finds it necessary to be represented by an attorney during the claim process. One area the reinsurer should assess during the audit is how much direction claims personnel provide to the attorney. In most cases, it is inappropriate merely to turn the file over to attorneys because this generally results in increased loss adjustment expenses. Specific, ongoing instruction should be provided to the attorney to minimize costs.

"Wrap-Up"

At the conclusion of the audit, the reinsurer holds a wrap-up meeting with claims management personnel (and perhaps a representative from the intermediary). The reinsurer presents a summary of its findings, acknowledges the primary company's strengths, and highlights those areas where deficiencies were identified. The reinsurer may suggest increasing reserves on particular files, handling files more aggressively in general, hiring more skilled claims technicians, and so forth. The reinsurer may also request that particular unreported claim files be reported to reinsurers. Both the reinsured and intermediary should take careful note of the audit conclusions.

AUDITING MANAGING GENERAL AGENTS

A managing general agent (MGA) has authority to act on behalf of an insurance company. The MGA may have complete underwriting and claims authority, depending on its agency agreement. Any of the three types of audits discussed can apply to an MGA. When auditing an MGA, the auditor should seek some additional facts beyond the normal audit inquiry. The auditor should take special care to understand the nature and scope of the agency relationship. Moreover, the auditor should evaluate the quality of that relationship. (For example, is there adequate communication between the MGA and the issuing company concerning underwriting and claims administration?) Finally, the auditor should be satisfied that the MGA has the financial strength and technical expertise to protect the interests of the issuing company and reinsurer.

Nature and Scope of the MGA Authority

Most MGA relationships are governed by written contracts that should be made available to auditors. The agreement sets forth the specific authorities delegated to the MGA, such as underwriting authority for specific lines of business, claims administration and settlement authority up to a fixed dollar limit, and the right to place reinsurance coverage for the benefit of issuing companies. In addition, the agreement usually sets forth the reporting obligations of the MGA and specifies the compensation to be provided to the MGA.

Auditors should review the underwriting authority of the MGA and specifically note any restrictions, either in limits, lines, or geographic exposure. Any limitations on premium volume should be noted. The auditor should take note of any provision within the MGA agreement that limits the authority of the MGA. The auditor should then compare these provisions with the business ceded to the reinsurer. Inconsistencies should be brought to the attention of the MGA immediately with a request that the issuing company by notified of these discrepancies. Any record-keeping requirements within the MGA agreement should also be audited for compliance. An MGA not in compliance with reporting or record-keeping requirements may find itself in a dispute with its principal before long.

Understanding the nature and scope of the MGA relationship enables the auditor to determine whether business is being properly underwritten and ceded under the reinsurance agreement. The key goals in this investigation is to eliminate, or at the very least minimize the possibility of disputes between the MGA and issuing company with potential adverse impact on reinsurers.

Relationship Between the MGA and the Issuing Company

Auditors should also make a qualitative evaluation of the relationship between the MGA and the issuing company. If the issuing company takes a hands-off approach with the MGA, the auditor may have to take additional steps to verify that the MGA is fully meeting its obligations under the MGA agreement. If the issuing company conducts regular audits of the MGA to verify compliance with the MGA agreements, the auditor may simply want to review reports of these audits. The greater the communication between the MGA and the issuing company, the less concern on the part of the auditor to confirm that the issuing company is aware of and has approved or ratified the actions of its agent. To the extent that the MGA and issuing company are not communicating critical underwriting, premium, claims, and accounting information regularly, the possibility of disputes is enhanced, thereby increasing the likelihood of a negative impact on reinsurance results.

Stability of the MGA

In addition to confirming that the MGA is acting within the scope of its authority, and assuring that the MGA and the issuing company have adequate lines of communication, the auditor should also assess the strength of the MGA operation itself. Although the issuing company is ultimately responsible for the actions of the MGA, any shortcomings in the operations of the MGA can easily result in increased exposure to the reinsurer through poor claim administration and lax underwriting.

MGA operations that run "lean" backrooms should be examined for technical expertise and support. Moreover, an MGA that does not have a financial stake in the quality of business written, but instead has incentive only to produce business, should be carefully examined in the underwriting area. Without the financial incentive to produce profitable business, the reinsurer may be exposed to poorly priced, highly volatile business.

Finally, the commitment of the MGA to the insurance business should be evaluated. Operations that are relatively young and have not yet established a proven track record should be scrutinized for evidence of long-term commitment to the issuing company, particularly when it writes long-tail casualty business.

Reinsurance auditors faced with business produced and ceded by an MGA should verify that the MGA is acting within the scope of its authority, that the issuing company is aware of and receives timely information on the activities of the MGA, and that the MGA has the financial and technical resources to fulfill all management responsibilities through the run-off of the business written.

SUMMARY

Both parties, the reinsured and the reinsurer, have much to gain through the audit process. Not only can knowledge and comfort levels be increased, but enduring professional relationships can be fostered that help to assure a smooth flow of information and early identification and resolution of potential issues related to the administration of the reinsurance agreement.

Reinsurance audits generally examine underwriting, transactions, or claims. Reinsurance audits typically arise from the access to records clause and are required by the AICPA although they also may be allowed by common law. Pre-quote reinsurance audits determine whether the reinsurer will accept the insurance company's business while at-risk audits are conducted after an agreement is signed.

Preparation is important regardless of the timing and type of audit. Background information on the reinsured is gathered and specific objectives for the audit are established prior to the audit.

The audit usually begins with interviews with senior staff of the reinsured. These are followed by interviews with the staff of the department involved (line underwriters, claims supervisors, and so forth).

An underwriting audit seeks information on the marketing philosophy of the reinsured and examines the structure of the company, future direction of the company, its competition, and the controls in place to implement its philosophy. The audit team reviews files to determine (1) how the reinsured prices its products, (2) its typical limits profile, and (3) how individual risks are selected.

Transactional audits examine controls over the recording of premiums and losses subject to the reinsurance agreement. Both premium and loss accounting audits are conducted using different approaches, depending on the nature of the reinsurance agreement (pro-rata versus excess of loss). While controls are important to any reinsurance audit, they are the primary focus of a transactional audit.

Claims audits examine general information about the primary company and also focus on such specific claims issues as initial reserving, reserve changes, patterns of "reserve creep," precautionary reserves, loss evaluation, settlement authority, investigation practices, and use of counsel. Longer term claims patterns are audited by examination of the annual financial statements of the reinsured and certain underwriting practices.

Any type of audit is concluded by issuing an audit report. The contents of the report should be discussed with the reinsured and be made available for future audits. The report summarizes the findings of the auditors and includes both the positive and negative audit results. Conducted professionally and in good faith, any reinsurance audit provides the opportunity to improve the business relationship among the reinsurer, reinsured, and intermediary (if any) and to verify that the reinsurance agreement is being carried out in accordance with its terms.

Some reinsurance audits focus on managing general agents. If the audit involves a managing general agent, the nature and scope of the MGA authority, the relationship of the MGA and its principal (the issuing company), and the stability of the MGA are the principal concerns.

Chapter Note

1. American Institute of Certified Public Accountants, "Auditing Property and Liability Reinsurance," *Audits of Fire and Casualty Insurance Companies,* 4th ed. (New York: American Institute of Certified Public Accountants, 1982), pp. 95-96.

CHAPTER 11

The Annual Statement

All property-liability insurance companies, including reinsurance companies, are required to file an annual financial statement with the regulatory authorities in each state (including Puerto Rico and the District of Columbia) in which it is licensed or authorized. The Annual Statement is prepared on a form acceptable to all states, though nearly all states require supplementary data.

The uniform Annual Statement blank is promulgated by the National Association of Insurance Commissioners (NAIC) and is sometimes referred to as the NAIC statement blank. It also is known as the "convention blank," after the National Convention of Insurance Commissioners, a predecessor of the NAIC, that developed the first uniform Annual Statement blank. The NAIC Annual Statement blank in 1989 was eighty-eight pages in length, but a completed Annual Statement for a large insurer may have many more pages because of the lengthy schedules of investment securities and investment transactions. Each schedule in the Annual Statement appears on a specific page. If additional pages are required to complete the detail of a schedule, the additional pages carry the same number with a decimal point designation. For example, if a schedule begins on page 44 and it has two additional pages, the page numbers for that schedule are numbered 44, 44.1, and 44.2.

The NAIC revises the statement blank annually as changes in the insurance business require new information for effective regulation. For example, financial guaranty insurance was added recently to the lines of insurance for which statistics are shown separately in the Annual Statement. Also, as reinsurance became a major regulatory concern, Schedule F was expanded to provide additional information concerning the reinsurance activities of the company, especially ceded reinsurance.

The Insurance Expense Exhibit (IEE) is a separate document filed along with the NAIC Annual Statement. The primary purpose of the IEE is to provide a detailed breakdown of expenses for each line of insurance, although some additional schedules also are included. The remainder of this chapter provides more detailed information concerning the NAIC Annual Statement blank as promulgated in 1989 and the Insurance Expense Exhibit. This text includes the 1989 blank as an appendix.

The NAIC Annual Statement blank consists of the following items:

- Statement of Assets, Liabilities, Surplus and Other Funds (balance sheet) with supporting exhibits and schedules
- Underwriting and Investment Exhibit (income statement) with supporting schedules
- Statement of Cash Flow
- General interrogatories

Each of these items is discussed below.

Accountants who keep the books of an insurer usually record entries on a cash rather than on an accrual basis. These entries are the source for all ledger assets and for the reconciliation of ledger assets. Once these figures are compiled, the "quantifying" of nonledger and nonadmitted assets is completed along with the liabilities of the insurer. Once these accounting and actuarial activities are completed, the statutory balance sheet, income statement, and statement of cash flow are completed.

BALANCE SHEET WITH SUPPORTING EXHIBITS AND SCHEDULES

The balance sheet is found on pages 2 and 3 of the Annual Statement. It includes the items usually found on balance sheets of any business, such as cash and real estate, but it also includes many items unique to insurance operations, such as reinsurance recoverable and the unearned premium reserve.

Assets

Page 2 of the NAIC Annual Statement summarizes the insurer's assets. Supporting schedules provide more detail regarding particular categories of assets. For most property-liability insurers, investment securities constitute the largest asset. Consequently, the first eight lines (some of them with subparts) are reserved for investment (or invested) assets. For this purpose, cash (on hand and on deposit) is considered to be an invested asset. Line 8A is the subtotal of cash and other invested assets.

Bonds. Bonds are the largest category of investments for most property-liability insurance companies. The value of bonds appears on the first line of the asset page. The value shown generally is the amortized value, less any liability to transfer bonds to others under put options.[1]

The amortized value of the bonds, as shown in the balance sheet, is taken from Schedule D, line 30, column 6. The supporting details are shown in Schedule D, Part 1, discussed in detail below.

Stocks. After bonds, the next largest asset category of most property-liability insurers is stock. Both common stocks and preferred stocks may be held, but the amount invested in preferred stocks is likely to be smaller than that in common stocks.

Preferred stocks and common stocks are shown separately in the Annual Statement, with preferred stocks on line 2.1 and common stocks on line 2.2. Valuation of stocks is established by the NAIC Security Valuation Office (SVO) and is shown in the Annual Statement. That value per share usually is the market price on the last business day of the year, but some value other than the market price may be selected by the SVO under unusual circumstances. Stocks for which no market exists (such as stocks of wholly owned subsidiaries) are shown at their net asset value (the net worth of the issuing company divided by the number of shares outstanding).[2] Preferred stocks may be shown at market price, if they are in good standing, or at cost if callable and backed by a full sinking fund.

The value shown on the balance sheet for preferred and common stock is taken from Schedule D, column 3, lines 48 and 66 respectively. Details of these amounts are shown in Schedule D, Part 2, Sections 1 and 2.

Mortgage Loans on Real Estate. Most property-liability insurers do not invest in mortgage loans. However, a line is provided on the balance sheet for those companies that hold such investments. Mortgages usually are valued at their unpaid balance less any unamortized discounts. Discounts arise when a mortgage is purchased at a price less than its outstanding balance at the time of purchase. This situation usually occurs when market interest rates have increased since the mortgage was originally entered into. The value of mortgages held is shown in Schedule B of the Annual Statement.

Insurance companies are prohibited from making other than first lien mortgage loans or mortgage loans in an amount greater than the market value of the mortgaged property. If such loans are made, the amount of the mortgage in excess of the property value or second mortgages are nonadmitted assets. Nonadmitted assets are not shown on the balance sheet, but are shown in Exhibit 2—Analysis of Nonadmitted Assets, on page 12 of the Annual Statement.

Real Estate. Real estate is not a major investment item for property-liability insurance companies. In most cases, they own only the real estate necessary for their own operations. Real estate usually is shown on the Annual Statement at its depreciated cost, calculated as the sum of the original cost, plus any additions or improvements, less depreciation of any buildings or improvements, less any outstanding mortgages. Land does not depreciate, so depreciation applies only to buildings and other improvements to land.

Real estate is shown on the balance sheet in two lines: line 4.1 for property occupied by the company and line 4.2 for other property. Mortgages are deducted in each case.

Collateral Loans. The balance sheet includes a line for collateral loans, but very few property-liability insurers hold such investments. Collateral loans are similar to mortgages except that the security is personal property, not real estate. Collateral loans are considered to be admitted assets, and are valued at the unpaid balance, provided (1) the amount of the loan does not exceed the value of the collateral, and (2) the collateral qualifies as an admitted asset.

Cash on Hand and on Deposit. Cash and deposits in solvent U.S. banks are shown at this face amount. Foreign coin and currency and deposits in solvent foreign banks are shown on the balance sheet at their value in U.S. currency.

Deposits in insolvent depositories are divided between admitted and nonadmitted assets. The estimated amount to be recovered from the insolvent bank is shown as an admitted asset. The remainder of the account is a nonadmitted asset.

Short-term Investments. Short-term investments include commercial paper, certificates of deposit, bonds, notes, and similar securities with a maturity period of one year or less at the time of purchase. Such securities are shown at the value assigned to them in the *NAIC Valuation of Securities Manual*, which usually is their market value. Short-term investments are listed in Schedule DA of the Annual Statement.

Other Invested Assets. An insurer may own other property not included within the categories described above. These items can be shown on line 7 of the asset page as "Other invested assets," or on line 8, as "Aggregate write-ins for invested assets." Examples of "other invested assets" are transportation equipment, timber deeds, mineral rights carried as admitted assets, and, more commonly, cash surrender values of life insurance policies held on insurance company executives. Space is provided at the bottom of the asset page for a detailed listing of items included in line 8. Items are not included on either of these lines unless they qualify as admitted assets.

Line 8A of the asset page (page 2) is a subtotal of all invested assets, including cash and bank deposits. Assets listed below that line (lines 9 through 21) also are admitted assets but are not invested assets.

Agents' Balances or Uncollected Premiums. Many companies that operate through the American agency system permit their agents to bill and collect premiums for policies. The agencies deduct their commissions from the premiums and remit the balance to the company. The agency contract usually specifies how long after issuance of a policy the agent is required to remit to the company (usually thirty to forty-five days). These amounts are shown on line 9.1 of the asset page (less any amounts more than ninety days past due).

Most direct writers and some agency companies bill the insured directly for premiums, without the assistance of an agent. These insurers show the premiums billed but not yet collected on line 9.1 of the asset page, provided such premiums are not over ninety days past due. Premiums over ninety days past due, whether from agents or directly from insureds, are nonadmitted assets. They do not appear on the balance sheet, but are shown in Exhibit 2 on page 12 of the Annual Statement.

Line 9.2 of the asset page is for agents' balances or installment premiums that have been recorded on the books of the insurer but are not yet due. Such premiums may not be due either because the effective date of the policy has not yet been reached or because the due date for an installment payment has not been reached.

If the company accepts bills or notes for future premium payments, it shows the amount of such bills or notes (if not past due) on line 11 rather than on line 9. Past due notes and bills are nonadmitted assets.

Funds Held by or Deposited with Reinsured Companies. A company that assumes reinsurance may permit a reinsured company to hold assets as security for amounts that the reinsurer may owe the reinsured under the reinsurance agreement (usually this is the amount of the unearned premium reserves and loss reserves ceded to the reinsurer). In other cases, regulatory authorities may require such security as a condition for permitting the reinsured company to take credit for the reinsurance in its Annual Statement. These amounts are shown on line 10.

These deposits were common in the past. In most cases, they are now replaced by letters of credit or trust agreements.

Reinsurance Recoverable on Loss Payments. Line 12 of the asset page is for reinsurance recoverable on paid losses. Reinsurance recoverable on losses that have not been paid is not shown as an asset, but as a reduction of loss reserves on the liability page of the Annual Statement.

Reinsurance recoverable on losses, both paid and outstanding, is shown in detail in Schedule F, Part 1A, of the Annual Statement. The total of column (1) of that schedule should agree with line 12 of the asset page.

Federal Income Tax Recoverable. An insurer that has an operating loss in a given year may be able to recover some of the federal income taxes paid in the prior three years. This recovery is permitted under the loss-carry-back provisions of the Internal Revenue Code. In addition, estimated tax payments made during the year in excess of the tax liability for the year are admitted assets. Any such amounts that are recoverable but have not yet been received are shown on line 13 of the asset page.

Electronic Data Processing Equipment. Most kinds of office equipment owned by a property-liability insurer are treated as nonadmitted assets and do not appear on the balance sheet. The major exception is mainframe computers and related equipment. The value of these items, after depreciation, is shown on line 14 of the asset page.

Interest, Dividends, and Real Estate Income Due and Accrued. Line 15 of the asset page is for investment income, such as rents, interest, or dividends, that was earned on or before the statement date but had not been received by the statement date.

Accrued investment income is a *nonledger asset* because such income is not recorded on the ledger of the company until received. The amount of such income to be shown on the Annual Statement is compiled by reviewing the investment records of the company and determining for each investment whether all the income due has been received. At one time, this was a long process. With computers, it can be done quickly and easily. Details of the accrued income are shown in Part 1 of the Underwriting and Investment Exhibit on page 6 of the Annual Statement.

Other Asset Lines. The remaining asset lines are largely self-explanatory, except for line 17, "Equities and deposits in pools and associations." An insurer may belong to many pools and associations, some voluntary and some required by law. An example of a voluntary pool is an aviation insurance pool, in which several insurers join together to write insurance on aircraft and related exposures, with the insurance being divided by formula among the members. If an insurer has an equity position in such a pool or funds deposited with such a pool, the value of the equity or funds is shown on line 17 of the Annual Statement. Involuntary pools, such as FAIR Plans, are handled in the same way.

Liabilities

The liabilities of the insurer are listed at the top of page 3 of the NAIC Annual Statement blank, with the surplus to policyholders (the statutory accounting equivalent of net worth) shown below them. The largest liability of most property-liability insurers is the reserve for incurred but unpaid losses. The reserve is shown on the first line of the liability section of the balance sheet. The line is labeled simply "Losses," and the word reserve does not appear.

Losses. The loss reserve shown on the first line of the liability section is for claims that have happened but have not been paid. (Loss payments are reflected on the income statement.) The loss reserve does not include any amount for claims that will happen in the future or for the expenses involved in adjusting losses.

Three classes of losses are included within the reserve:

1. Losses that had happened, had been reported and adjusted, but had not been paid on the statement date
2. Losses that had happened, had been reported, and were in the course of adjustment on the statement date
3. Losses that had happened but had not yet been reported to the insurer on the statement date (IBNR losses)

Annual Statements are completed on a calendar-year basis. The statement date (also known as the "as-of-date") is December 31 of that year. The first loss category consists of claims for which a settlement has been agreed, and all that remains is to send a check or draft in payment. These are included in the reserve at the agreed settlement amount. The amount included for the other two categories must be estimated. The methods of estimating such amounts were discussed in Chapters 8 and 9.

The loss reserves by line of insurance are shown in the Underwriting and Expense Exhibit, Parts 3 and 3A. Further details of loss reserves, both current and historical, are shown in Schedules H for accident and health insurance, and P for all other lines.

Loss Adjustment Expenses. The second line of the liability section of the balance sheet shows the estimated cost of adjusting losses shown on line 1. The methods of estimation for loss adjustment expenses were also discussed in Chapters 8 and 9.

There are two major categories of loss adjustment expense: allocated and unallocated. As explained in Chapter 8, allocated loss adjustment expenses are those that can be identified with a specific claim, such as fees for independent adjusters, fees for defense counsel, fees for expert witnesses, and court costs. Unallocated loss adjustment expenses are those that cannot be charged to a specific claim, such as rent for office space occupied by the claims department, salaries of claims department personnel, and similar expenses. Loss adjustment expense reserves by line of insurance are shown in the Underwriting and Investment Exhibit, Part 3A, column 6 on page 10 of the Annual Statement. The total of that column should equal the reserve shown on the balance sheet.

Contingent Commissions. Many insurers pay additional commissions to their agents if the agents sell specified amounts of business or achieve specified loss ratios on the business they sell. These additional commissions are known as contingent commissions (or sometimes as profit-sharing commissions). Any amounts of such commissions due to agents, but not yet paid, are shown as a liability on line 3, page 3 of the Annual Statement. Profit-sharing commissions owed to primary companies under reinsurance treaties also are included in this item.

Other Expenses. Other expenses, shown on line 4, excludes those items shown on lines 3, 5, 6, and 8. This category includes items such as accrued salaries, accrued rent, and similar expenses.

Taxes, Licenses and Fees. Amounts due in payment of taxes, licenses, and fees appear on line 5. These are amounts due to state and local governments for such things as premium taxes, licenses for insurers, licenses for agents, and—in some states—its claims adjusters, as well as fees for insurance department examinations (audits). Federal and foreign income taxes are *not* reported on line 5, but on line 6.

Federal and Foreign Income Taxes. Amounts due for federal and foreign income taxes are separated from other taxes and shown on line 6.

Interest. Liability for any interest payable by the company, including interest on borrowed money, is shown on line 8.

Borrowed Money. Although a line for borrowed money (line 7) is shown on the balance sheet, it is not a common practice for property-liability insurers to borrow money. Consequently, this line is blank in most cases.

Unearned Premium. Line 9 represents the second largest liability of most property-liability insurers, the unearned premium reserve. The unearned premium reserve is frequently thought of as a provision for return premiums on canceled policies. While it serves that purpose, the principal function of the unearned premium reserve is to recognize the obligation of the insurer to provide insurance in the future. The loss reserve is a measure of the obligation of the insurer to pay claims that have happened while the unearned premium reserve can be viewed as a recognition of the obligation of the insurer to pay claims that will occur in the future.

The unearned premium reserve calculation by line of insurance is shown in the Underwriting and Investment Exhibit, Part 2A, column 5. The total of that column, on line 32, should equal line 9 of page 3.

Dividends Declared and Unpaid. Lines 10(a) and 10(b) of the liability section of the balance sheet show the liability of the company for dividends declared and unpaid. Line 10(a) is for dividends to stockholders, and line 10(b) is for dividends to policyholders.

Funds Held by Company under Reinsurance Treaties. This item is the reverse side of the Funds Held by or Deposited with Reinsured Companies asset shown on line 10 of page 2 of the Annual Statement. The asset shows funds belonging to the filing company that are held by companies it reinsures. This liability reflects funds held by the company filing the statement under reinsurance agreements where the filing company is the reinsured and is shown on line 11 of page 3.

Amounts Withheld or Retained by Company for Account of Others. This liability (line 12) could include any amounts that the company withheld or retained from one party for payment to another party. However, the principal items are income taxes and other taxes withheld from employee wages and salaries for payment to governmental agencies and group insurance premiums withheld for payment to insurers.

Liability for Unauthorized Reinsurance. Lines 13(a) through 14 show a liability for amounts recoverable under reinsurance from unauthorized reinsurers. This liability relates to reinsurance recoverables included elsewhere in the balance sheet, primarily on line 12 of the asset page and lines 1, 2, and 9 of the liability section. Since most states restrict the credits for unauthorized reinsurance, this liability offsets the assets previously established. Line 13(d) reduces the liability by the amount of any funds withheld or retained by the company under reinsurance agreements with the unauthorized reinsurers. Thus, the reinsured company is allowed full credit for recoverables owed to it by unauthorized reinsurers if the recoverables are fully collateralized. Acceptable letters of credit or trust funds also may be used to collateralize the reinsurance recoverables. Line 13(e) established a liability for reinsurance payments due the filing company from reinsurers when such payments are ninety days overdue.

Excess of Statutory Reserves over Statement Reserves ("Schedule P Reserves"). The various states require insurers to carry loss reserves at least equal to statutory minimum reserves for liability insurance, workers compensation insurance, and credit insurance. The statutory minimum reserve is 60 percent (for liability) or 65 percent (for workers compensation) of earned premiums less any losses and loss adjustment expenses already paid. These percentages may be increased based on the loss ratios of the insurer in the five years immediately preceding the most recent three years. The minimum reserves for applicable lines of insurance are contained in the instructions to Schedule P. The method of calculation for these lines is also shown in the instructions to Schedule P.

If the statutory minimum reserve for each year standing on its own for any line is greater than the loss reserve shown for that line in the Underwriting and Investment Exhibit, part 3A, column (5), only the excess is included on this line. If the statutory minimum reserve is less than the actual loss reserve, this line is zero.

Adjustments for Foreign Exchange Rates. If any company assets or liabilities are denominated in foreign currencies, their dollar value may fluctuate, either upward or downward, because of changes in the value of dollars relative to the foreign currencies. Any adjustments required to reflect such changes are shown on line 16 of page 3 of the Annual Statement. The line is entitled "Net adjustments in assets and liabilities due to foreign exchange rates."

Drafts Outstanding. Some insurers use drafts, rather than checks, to pay claims. Unlike checks, drafts must be presented to the insurer for approval before payment by the bank. This liability reflects the value of drafts that have been issued but not yet paid.

Other Liabilities. The remaining liabilities are minor and self-explanatory. They include the following:

- Payable to parent, subsidiaries, and affiliates
- Payable for securities
- Liability for amounts held under uninsured accident and health plans (for employees)
- Other liabilities, to be written in on line 21, "Aggregate write-ins for liability," and explained in the appropriate schedule at the bottom of the page.

Surplus and Other Funds

The liabilities occupy lines 1 through 22 of page 3 of the Annual Statement. Lines 23 through 26 are for surplus to policyholders, the net worth of the company. The first line (23) is for miscellaneous surplus items that are itemized in the appropriate table at the bottom of the page. These items consist of surplus funds that have been set aside for some special purpose. They are sometimes called *voluntary reserves.* Such voluntary reserves may be established for many purposes. Some insurers maintain a reinsurance reserve, to which they add funds in good years and subtract funds in bad years to even out its reported profits and surplus.

Common Capital Stock. Common capital stock is used and outstanding is reported on line 24A. It is reported at its par value. If common stock is repurchased and retired, it is deducted from this account. If it is repurchased and held as treasury stock, it is shown on 25C(1) and deducted from surplus to policyholders.

Preferred Capital Stock. Preferred capital stock is reported on line 24B at par. Retired preferred stock and treasury preferred stock are treated in the same manner as common stock.

Aggregate Write-ins Other Than Special Surplus Funds. Line 24C, "Aggregate write-ins for other than special surplus funds," will be blank in most cases. When it is not blank, the most likely item to be found on it is the amount of surplus notes issued and outstanding. Some insurers, especially mutual insurers, may increase their surplus to policyholders by issuing and selling surplus notes, a debt security junior to all other debts of the company. The principal and interest under a surplus note can be repaid only from retained earnings (unassigned funds), and only with the prior approval of the state regulatory authorities.

Gross Paid-In and Contributed Surplus. Paid-in surplus arises when a stock (usually common stock) issued by the company is sold for an amount greater than its stated par value. The amount in excess of par is credited to paid-in surplus. For example, if a share of common stock with a par value of $100 is sold for $150, the $50 in excess of the par value would be added to paid-in surplus. Contributed surplus usually arises when a parent company contributes funds to its wholly owned subsidiary company without changing the amount of stock outstanding.

Unassigned Funds (Surplus). Line 25B shows the unassigned funds of the company, also known as surplus. There are three significant sources of surplus:

1. Underwriting profit
2. Investment profit (including realized capital gains)
3. Unrealized capital gains

A loss in any of these categories results in a reduction of surplus. Also, any dividends declared to stockholders reduce surplus.

Surplus is the balancing item on the balance sheet in that the total of liabilities, surplus, and other funds (page 3, line 27) equals total assets (page 2, line 21). Those two lines must be equal in order for the balance sheet to balance. A reconciliation of policyholders' surplus from the last year to the current year is shown on page 4 of the Annual Statement under the heading "Gains and Losses in Surplus" within the Underwriting and Investment Exhibit Statement of Income.

UNDERWRITING AND INVESTMENT EXHIBIT

The balance sheet shows a snapshot of the financial status of the company at one moment in time, the close of business on December 31. The income statement shows the financial results of operations for an entire year between balance sheets. The income statement, called the Underwriting and Investment Exhibit Statement of Income, appears on page 4 of the NAIC Annual Statement.

Underwriting Income

This section of the income statement shows the profit or loss of the insurer from its insurance operations. It does not include any investment profit or loss.

Premiums Earned. The first line on the income statement shows net earned premiums (net premiums written, plus any decrease or minus any increase in net changes in unearned premiums ceded) for all lines of insurance combined. Supporting details by line are shown in the Underwriting and Investment Exhibit, Part 2, column 4.

Losses Incurred. Line 2 of the income statement shows net incurred losses [net losses paid (direct plus assumed minus ceded) plus any increase or minus any decrease in net loss reserves] for all lines of insurance combined. Supporting details by line of insurance are shown in the Underwriting and Investment Exhibit, Part 3, column 7.

Loss Expenses Incurred. Line 3 of the income statement summarizes loss adjustment expenses incurred (net of reinsurance). The adjustment expenses incurred are shown by kind of expense in the Underwriting and Investment Exhibit, Part 4, column 1. The Insurance Expense Exhibit, a document that is physically separate from the

Annual Statement blank but closely related to it, categorizes the adjustment expenses by line of insurance.

Other Underwriting Expenses. Line 4 of the income statement is entitled "Other underwriting expenses incurred." Other underwriting expenses, as used here, means expenses other than loss adjustment expenses and investment expenses. This number is taken from the Underwriting and Investment Exhibit, Part 4, column 2, line 22. Lines 1 through 21 of the same exhibit show the other underwriting expenses segregated by category of expense. Expenses by line of insurance are shown in the Insurance Expense Exhibit.

Other Underwriting Deductions. Line 5 of the income statement is labeled "Aggregate write-ins for underwriting deductions." It usually is blank, but it can be used for any underwriting deduction not included in the lines above it. Line 6 is the total of lines 2 through 5.

Underwriting Gain or Loss. The underwriting gain or loss is shown on line 7 of the income statement. It is calculated by deducting lines 2 through 5 from 1. It represents the insurer's profit or loss on its insurance operations. It does not include any investment gain or loss, which is shown in the following section of the income statement.

Investment Income

This section of the income statement shows the profit or loss of the insurer from:

1. Investment income, such as interest, dividends, or rents
2. Realized capital gains

Realized capital gains arise when an asset is sold for a price greater than its cost. This difference is reported together with investment income less investment expenses. (Unrealized capital gains are not included in the income statement. They arise when the NAIC value of an invested asset is greater than its cost but the asset has not been sold. Unrealized capital gains and losses go directly to surplus without passing through the income statement.)

Net Investment Income Earned. Line 8, the first line in the investment income section of the income statement, shows net investment income earned. The detailed statement of investment income earned appears in the Underwriting and Investment Exhibit, Part 1. This item includes interest income, rents, dividends, and similar income items of investment income. All investment expenses have been deducted, including depreciation on real estate when appropriate.

Realized Capital Gains or Losses. Realized capital gains arise when an asset is sold for more than its cost. A realized capital loss arises when an asset is sold for less than its cost. The net amount, after offsetting realized capital losses against realized capital gains, is shown on line 9 of the income statement. An analysis of net realized capital gains and losses appears in the Underwriting and Investment Exhibit, Part 1A. Net investment gain or loss, the sum of lines 8 and 9, is shown on line 9A.

Other Income

The third section of the income statement shows other income not related to underwriting or investment activities. The dollar amounts of other income usually are small and frequently are negative. This section includes the following:

- Net gain or loss from agents' balances charged off and recoveries on agents' balances charged off in prior years
- Finance and service charges not included in premiums
- Miscellaneous other income

The final category is very broad, encompassing any income item not included on any of the preceding lines. One company included on this line in its 1987 statement the proceeds of a tort liability suit against one of its suppliers.

Net Income

The sum of net underwriting income (or loss), net investment income (or loss), and other income (or loss) equals net income (or loss) before dividends to policyholders and before federal and foreign income taxes. This figure appears on line 14 of the income statement.

Dividends to policyholders are deducted on line 14A, yielding net income before federal and foreign income taxes, shown on line 14B. Federal and foreign income taxes incurred are deducted on line 15, leaving after-tax net income on line 16.

Capital and Surplus Account

The capital and surplus account begins with the surplus to policyholders (policyholders' surplus) on December 31 of the preceding year. It traces all changes in the capital and surplus account during the year and ends with the surplus to policyholders at the end of the year. These are the principal sources of change in the policyholders' surplus:

- Net income (from line 16 of the Underwriting and Investment Exhibit)
- Net unrealized capital gains (from the Underwriting and Investment Exhibit, Part 1A, line 12)
- Cash dividends to stockholders

Other sources of change in surplus to policyholders, some of which may be large at times, are the following:

- Issuance of additional corporate stock
- Remittances to or from home office (primarily for U.S. branches of alien companies)
- Changes in nonadmitted assets
- Changes in the excess of statutory loss reserves over statement reserves
- Changes in the liability for unauthorized reinsurance
- Changes in foreign exchange adjustments
- Changes in treasury stock
- Extraordinary changes in taxes from prior years
- Excess of life insurance premiums over increase in cash surrender value of life insurance

Changes in surplus (unassigned funds) also may result from stock dividends or the reduction of the par value of the stock of the company. However, these events do not change the total amount of surplus to policyholders, since the resulting changes in the capital account exactly offset changes in capital and unassigned funds (surplus).

The Capital and Surplus Account is used to verify the value shown for policyholders' surplus in the balance sheet. It reconciles policyholders' surplus for the current year with the comparable figure from the preceding year and with all pertinent changes during the year. This reconciliation virtually eliminates the possibility of unintentional misstatement of policyholders' surplus. Intentional misstatements would require manipulation of other schedules and exhibits in the statement. For instance, any misstatement of loss or loss expense reserves could result in a misrepresentation of net profit, with a resulting understatement or overstatement of policyholders' surplus. The schedules for verification of loss reserves are discussed later.

Cash Flow

The cash flow statement on page 5 of the Annual Statement lists all receipts and expenditures of cash for the year. The following are principal sources of cash inflows:

- Premiums collected (less reinsurance premiums paid)

- Investment income
- Proceeds from the sale or redemption of matured securities
- Paid-in capital and surplus
- Transfers from affiliates
- Borrowed funds

Principal outflows are as follows:

- Loss and adjustment expense payments, less subrogation recoveries and salvage
- Underwriting expenses paid
- Dividends paid to policyholders
- Dividends paid to stockholders
- Taxes
- Cost of investments acquired
- Transfers to affiliates
- Borrowed funds repaid

The purpose of the cash flow statement is to test the ability of the company to generate a sufficient inflow of cash to meet its necessary outflows without borrowing money or liquidating investment securities. Large amounts of borrowed funds (line 12.2) might indicate that cash inflows are inadequate. Proceeds from investment sales (line 11.9) substantially in excess of the cost of investments acquired (line 14.8) also might be cause for concern. A decline in cash and short-term investments (line 17) also may indicate a need for further analysis.

Line 17 of the cash flow statement shows the net cash flow (cash inflows minus cash outflows). The net cash flow (line 17) should equal the difference between the value of cash and short-term investments on December 31 of the prior year (line 18.1) and the value of cash and short-term investments on December 31 of the current year (line 18.2).

Underwriting and Investment Exhibit Supporting Information

Supporting information for the Underwriting and Investment Exhibit consists of four parts. These four parts summarize the Annual Statement schedules that relate to the income statement. These four parts of the Underwriting and Investment Exhibit also develop information that appears on the balance sheet.

Part 1—Interest, Dividends, and Real Estate Income. Part 1 of the Underwriting and Investment Exhibit provides support for the net investment income figure reported in the income statement. It summarizes the detailed information concerning cash and invested assets contained in schedules A, B, BA, C, D, DA, DB, and N. These schedules are discussed later.

Part 1 shows investment income categorized by the type of investment from which the income was derived. Column 3 shows the amount of income collected from each class of investment during the year. Column 4 shows investment income received during the current year in advance (before it was due). Column 5 shows investment income received in advance in the preceding year. Column 6 shows the investment income due and accrued but not collected on December 31 of the current year. Column 7 shows the comparable figure for the preceding year. The gross investment income earned during the year [shown in column 8] equals column 3 plus column 5 plus column 6 minus column 4 minus column 7. Investment expenses line 11, depreciation on real estate line 12, and other appropriate deductions are subtracted from this gross investment income to calculate the net investment income shown on line 8 of the income statement. The investment expenses shown in Part 1 are reflected in Part 4, column 3, line 22 of the Underwriting and Investment Exhibit.

Part 1 also provides some support for the balance sheet. The figure for interest, dividends, and real estate income due and accrued, shown on line 15 of the assets page, should equal the figure at Part 1, column 6, line 10.

Part 1A—Capital Gains and Losses on Investments. Like Part 1, Part 1A also provides support for both the balance sheet and the income statement. It provides a detailed analysis of realized capital gains and losses, which appear in the income statement, and unrealized capital gains and losses, which do not appear in the income statement but are a part of the surplus account (line 19).

Part 1A categorizes capital gains and losses according to the class of investment that produced them. Stocks and real estate are more likely than other investments to produce large capital gains or losses.

The data in Part 1A are shown in columns 2 through 7, with the following titles:

(2) Profit on Sales or Maturity
(3) Losses on Sales or Maturity
(4) Increases by Adjustment in Book Value
(5) Decreases by Adjustment in Book Value
(6) Net Gain (+) or Loss (−) from Change in Difference Between Book Value and Admitted Value
(7) Total

Column 2 minus column 3 constitutes net realized capital gains or losses, which appears on line 9 of the income statement. Column 4 minus column 5 plus column 6 is net unrealized capital gains or losses, which appears on line 19 of the Capital and Surplus Account on page 4 of the statement. The "admitted value" of a security is based on market rates shown for it in the NAIC *Valuation of Securities* manual. The gains or losses shown in columns 4, 5, and 6 are only those that occurred during the current year. The gains reported in columns 2 and 3 may have occurred at any time so long as the actual sale or maturity of the investment occurred during the current year.

Parts 2, 2A, and 2B—Premiums. These three schedules are treated here as a unit because they are closely related and the order of presentation in the Annual Statement blank is not the most logical order for explanatory purposes. These parts provide support for both the balance sheet and income statement. They develop the unearned premium reserve, shown on line 9 of the liabilities section of the balance sheet. They also develop earned premiums, shown on line 1 of the income statement.

The beginning point for explaining these parts is Part 2B, which is used to calculate net written premiums. Column 1, labeled "Direct Business," shows the direct written premiums. Direct premiums are premiums on policies and endorsements written with effective dates during the year for the general public, including business firms and governmental bodies. This amount does not include reinsurance. Column 2 shows written premiums for reinsurance assumed from other insurance companies. Column 3 shows the premiums for reinsurance ceded to other insurers. Both columns 2 and 3 are split between "affiliates" and "non-affiliates" of the reporting company. Column 1 + column 2 − column 3 equals net written premiums, shown in column 4. Each of the columns shows premiums categorized by line of insurance.

The unearned premium reserve is determined in Part 2A. The starting point, columns 1 and 2, is the amount unearned plus advance premiums and reserves for rate credits and retrospective adjustments. The actual calculation is not shown in the Annual Statement, but a footnote indicates the method used. Most insurers now use the monthly pro-rata method. That method assumes that all premiums written during a month are spread evenly over the month, so that, on the average, they are effective on the fifteenth of the month. Consequently (for one-year policies) a policy written in January has one-half of a month (1/24 of a year) remaining to run on December 31. A policy written in February would have 3/24 of a year remaining, and so on. Comparable fractions can be developed for policies with terms longer or shorter than one year.

Under the monthly pro-rata method, the in-force premiums for each month are multiplied by the appropriate fraction and totaled. Premiums paid in advance and a reserve for refunds under retrospective rating plans are added to this total. The result is the unearned premium reserve, shown in column 5 of Part 2A and on line 9 of the liability page of the balance sheet.

Some companies with increased computer capability compute unearned premiums on a daily basis, which in essence would equal the pro-rata return premiums for all in-force policies if they were canceled on the balance sheet date.

Some insurers still use the annual pro-rata method for calculating the unearned premium reserve. Under that method, premiums written during the year are assumed to be evenly spread over the year, so that, on the average, they are effective on July 1. Consequently, for annual policies, the unearned premium reserve would be one-half of the in-force premiums. Comparable fractions can be developed for policies with periods less than or greater than one year.

Premiums earned for the year are determined in Part 2. The starting point for this calculation is net premiums written, from Part 2A, column 5. The unearned premium reserve from the previous year is added, and the unearned premium reserve for the current year, from Part 2B, column 7, is deducted. The result is the earned premiums for the current year, shown in column 4 and on line 1 of the income statement.

The statutory method of calculating the unearned premium reserve is mathematically precise, and the resulting reserve accurately represents the potential liability of the insurer for return premiums on canceled policies. Whether it accurately represents the liability of the insurer to provide future coverage depends on the accuracy of the underlying rates and premiums. If the rates and premiums are inadequate for the coverage provided, the unearned premium reserve will not be adequate for future coverage.[3]

Parts 3 and 3A—Losses. These two parts are also treated together because of their similarities. They are used to develop the loss and loss adjustment expense reserves for the balance sheet and the incurred losses for the income statement. The explanation of these parts is more understandable if Part 3A, which develops loss reserves, is explained first. Losses and loss reserves are shown separately for each line of insurance in both Part 3 and Part 3A. The nature of the data contained in each column of Part 3A is listed below:

(1a) Reserve for losses adjusted (but not paid) or in the process of adjustment for direct business

(1b) Same as (1a) except for reinsurance assumed (from Schedule F, Part 1A, Sec. 2, Col. 2)

(2) Reinsurance recoverable on losses in (1a) and (1b), (from Schedule F, Part 1A, Sec. 1, Col. 2)

(3) Net losses, excluding losses incurred but not reported (IBNR);

$$[(3) = (1a) + (1b) - (2)]$$

(4a) Direct IBNR

(4b) IBNR for reinsurance assumed

(4c) Reinsurance recoverable on IBNR in (4a) and (4b)

(5) Reserve for net losses unpaid, exclusive of loss adjustment expenses:

$$(5) = (3) + (4a) + (4b) - (4c)$$

(6) Reserve for unpaid loss adjustment expenses

The loss reserves in column 5 of Part 3A also are shown on line 1 of the liabilities section of the balance sheet and are used in Part 3 to calculate incurred losses. The loss adjustment expense reserves shown in column 6 of Part 3A are also shown on line 2 of the liabilities section of the balance sheet.

Losses incurred during the current year on the income statement are calculated in Part 3. The first four columns of Part 3 deal with losses paid during the year. Direct losses paid (column 1) plus losses paid on reinsurance assumed (column 2) minus loss recovered or recoverable on reinsurance ceded (column 3) equals net losses paid (column 4). Column 5 shows the loss reserves for the current year (from Part 3A), and column 6 shows the loss reserves from the Annual Statement of the previous year. Column 7 shows the incurred losses from the year, calculated by the formula:

$$(7) = (4) + (5) - (6)$$

The incurred losses from Part 3, column 7 also appear on line 2 of the income statement.

Column 8 of Part 3 shows, for each line and for all lines combined, the incurred-earned loss ratio. It is calculated by dividing the incurred losses from column 7 by the earned premiums from Part 2, column 4, and multiplying the result by 100.

Part 4—Expenses. Part 4 provides support primarily for the income statement. It allocates expenses by three major functional areas (loss adjustment, other underwriting, and investment) and by numerous expense groupings, such as claim adjustment services, commissions and brokerage, advertising, salaries, and others. There is no analysis of expenses by line of insurance in Part 4. That analysis is found in the Insurance Expense Exhibit.

The amount of net loss adjustment expenses from Part 4, column 1, line 22 also appears on line 3 of the income statement. The other underwriting expense from Part 4, column 2, line 22 appears on line 4 of the income statement. Investment expenses from Part 4, column 3, line 22 appears at line 11 of Part 1 of the Underwriting and Investment Exhibit. Thus investment expenses are reflected as a reduction of net investment income at line 8 of the income statement.

OTHER EXHIBITS AND SCHEDULES

The remainder of the Annual Statement consists of further exhibits and schedules that support the balance sheet and Underwriting and Investment Exhibit.

Analysis of Assets

Exhibit 1 lists assets of the company by category (bonds, stocks, mortgages, and so forth). It includes both admitted and nonadmitted assets, and both ledger and nonledger assets. The column headings in the exhibit are listed here:

(1) Ledger assets
(2) Nonledger assets including excess of market (or amortized) over book value
(3) Assets not admitted including excess of book over market (or amortized) value
(4) Net admitted assets

The value of net admitted assets is calculated by the formula:

$$(4) = (1) + (2) - (3)$$

The total net admitted assets from Exhibit 1 (column 4, line 21) should equal the total assets shown on the asset page of the balance sheet (page 2, line 21).

Analysis of Nonadmitted Assets

The purpose of Exhibit 2 is to determine the change in nonadmitted assets for the year. The amount of change is then entered directly to the Capital and Surplus Account, at page 4, line 20. This change does not pass through the income statement. An increase in nonadmitted assets directly reduces the policyholders' surplus of the company. A reduction in nonadmitted assets directly increases policyholders' surplus.

Reconciliation of Ledger Assets

Exhibit 3 is a reconciliation of ledger assets. Lines 1 through 7 list transactions that tend to increase ledger assets, and line 8 totals such items. The transactions listed include premiums written, investment income, realized capital gains, and other income transactions.

Lines 9 through 16 list transactions that tend to reduce ledger assets, and line 17 is the total of such transactions. The transactions included within this group are net losses paid, expenses paid, realized capital losses, dividends paid to stockholders, and similar expenditures.

The difference between lines 8 and 17 is the change in ledger assets during the year. If the change is added to the total ledger assets reported in Exhibit 1, column 1, line 21 for the previous year, the sum should equal Exhibit 1, line 21 for the current year, another check on the accuracy of the balance sheet.

Exhibit of Premiums and Losses—Per State

A separate exhibit is prepared for each state in which the company is licensed, unlike the remainder of the statement that is an aggregate for all states. The Exhibit of Premiums and Losses provides premiums, losses, and policyholder dividends for each line of insurance for the state listed at the top of the page. The columns show, by line, direct premiums written, direct premiums earned, dividends paid or credits to policyholders on direct business, direct unearned premium reserve, direct losses paid (deducting salvage), direct losses incurred, and direct losses unpaid. All of these figures are for direct business. No reinsurance information is included in the exhibit. Net losses unpaid are equivalent to loss reserves.

The statistics on the exhibit are used to calculate FAIR Plan participations, and state regulatory authorities use them to assess premium taxes, calculate assessments for guaranty (insolvency) funds, and for other state regulatory purposes. The exhibit is not used to verify entries in either the balance sheet or the income statement.

Medicare Supplemental Insurance Experience Exhibit

Like the Exhibit of Premiums and Losses, this exhibit is filed for each separate state in which the company sells Medicare supplemental insurance. Experience is separated for individual and group policies and by date of issue within each type. Earned premium, incurred claims, and the percentage of claims to premium are reported for the specific state as well as nationally.

Deposit Schedules

There are three deposit schedules in the Annual Statement. Schedule N shows bank deposits. The other two schedules list the value of the securities on deposit with governmental bodies. These deposits usually are required by state regulatory authorities as a condition of licensing. The schedule at the top of the page, entitled Special Deposit Schedule, is for deposits for the exclusive protection of citizens of the governmental unit holding the deposit, a single state for example, and not for the protection of all of the policyholders of the company. This restriction on the use of these assets must be considered in determining the financial security of the company.

The second schedule is for securities deposited for the benefit of all policyholders. The existence of deposits in both schedules is verified when the company is audited.

Securities reflected in both schedules usually are also included in Schedule D (or other investment schedules) of the company and accordingly reflected as assets of the company in its financial statements.

Five-Year Historical Data

Pages 21 and 22 of the Annual Statement are exhibits of five-year historical data taken from the Annual Statements of the current year and the four immediately preceding years. This exhibit is important because it shows trends in the business and financial status of the company over a longer period. This historical data may provide a warning of unfavorable future developments. For example, the surplus for the current year may seem adequate for the needs of the company when viewed alone. However, if the five-year historical data show a steady downward trend, there may be reason for concern about the future adequacy of surplus. Also, a steady increase in the expense ratio of the company may indicate that it is becoming inefficient and that its ability to be competitive and profitable may be impaired.

Many items from both the balance sheet and the income statement are included in the exhibit of five-year data. The exhibit also includes several operating ratios, such as the expense ratio, loss ratio, ratio of net written premiums to policyholders' surplus, and others.

Investment Schedules

Pages 23 through 46 of the Annual Statement consist of investment schedules. The schedules are shown in Exhibit 11-1.

All of these schedules provide support for the balance sheet, the income statement, or both. Space does not permit a detailed discussion of all of them, but a more detailed discussion of Schedule D, Part 1 indicates the kinds of information provided. Schedule D provides

Exhibit 11-1
Investment Schedules

Schedule A, Part 1	Real estate owned on December 31 of the current year
Schedule A, Part 2	Real estate acquired during the current year
Schedule A, Part 3	Real estate disposed of during the current year
Schedule B	Mortgages owned on December 31 of the current year and mortgages acquired or disposed of during the current year
Schedule BA, Part 1	Other long-term invested assets owned on December 31 of the current year
Schedule BA, Part 2	Other long-term invested assets acquired during the current year
Schedule BA, Part 3	Other long-term assets disposed of during the current year
Schedule C, Part 1	Long-term collateral loans in force in December of the current year
Schedule C, Part 2	All long-term collateral loans made during the current year
Schedule C, Part 3	All long-term collateral loans discharged during the current year
Schedule C, Part 4	All substitutions of collateral during the current year
Schedule D	Summary by country, long-term bonds, and stocks owned on December 31 of the current year
Schedule D, Part 1A	Maturity distribution of long-term bonds owned on December 31 of current year
Schedule D, Part 1B	Quality distribution of all bonds owned on December 31 of the current year
Schedule D, Part 1	All long-term bonds owned on December 31 of the current year
Schedule D, Part 2	Section 1—All preferred stocks owned on December 31 of the current year
Schedule D, Part 2	Section 2—All common stocks owned on December 31 of the current year
Schedule D, Part 3	All long-term bonds and stocks acquired during the current year

Schedule D, Part 4	All long-term bonds or stocks sold, redeemed, or disposed of during the current year
Schedule D, Part 5	All long-term bonds and stocks acquired and disposed of during the current year
Schedule D, Part 6	Section 1—Questionnaire relating to the valuation of shares of certain subsidiary, controlled, or affiliated companies
Schedule D, Part 6	Section 2—All investments in companies owned or controlled by another company
Schedule DA, Part 1	All short-term investments owned on December 31 of the current year
Schedule DA, Part 2	Verification of short-term investments between years
Schedule DB, Part A	Section 1—All financial options owned on December 31 of the current year
Schedule DB, Part A	Section 2—All financial options acquired during the current year
Schedule DB, Part A	Section 3—All financial options terminated during the current year
Schedule DB, Part A	Section 4—Verification between years of book value of all options owned
Schedule DB, Part B	Section 1—All financial options written and in force on December 31 of the current year
Schedule DB, Part B	Section 2—All financial options written during the current year
Schedule DB, Part B	Section 3—All financial options written and terminated during the current year
Schedule DB, Part B	Section 4—Verification between years of consideration received for options written
Schedule DB, Part C	Section 1—All financial futures contracts open on December 31 of the current year
Schedule DB, Part C	Section 2—All financial futures contracts opened during the current year
Schedule DB, Part C	Section 3—All financial futures contracts that were terminated during the current year
Schedule DB, Part C	Section 4—Verification between years of deferred gain (loss) on financial futures contracts

specific detail on the investments held at the beginning of the year, the investments bought and sold during the year, and those held at the end of the year. Its subordinate schedules also provide details on interest and dividends, capital gains or losses, and financial statement valuation relating to certain investments.

Schedule D, Part 1 is for long-term bonds. It provides information to support both the balance sheet and income statement. The first column lists each bond and provides the CUSIP number, a code number provided on the purchase confirmation that identifies the specific bonds for year-to-year comparisons and identification. The information is contained in the columns shown in Exhibit 11-2.

Columns 17 and 18 need not be completed by companies that use amortized value as book value, since they would, in that case, duplicate columns 10 and 11. Column 4, book value, is the source of the value for bonds shown on Exhibit 1, column 1, "Ledger Assets."

The total of column 9.1 is included in line 15 of the asset page, which shows interest, dividends, and real estate income due and accrued. The totals of columns 9.1 and 9.2 are included in the amount shown on line 8 of the income statement, net investment income earned. The other investment schedules provide similar data.

Reinsurance Schedules

Schedule F begins with reinsurance purchased by the company, called ceded reinsurance in the schedule. Part 1A, Section 1 lists the purchased reinsurance contracts in effect on December 31 of the current year. It identifies the reinsurer and shows the amount of (1) an aged schedule of reinsurance recoverable on paid (ceded) losses, (2) reinsurance recoverable on unpaid losses, (3) estimated unearned premiums on reinsurance, and (4) reinsurance premiums paid. There is a column for a coded indication of reinsurance amounts with reinsurers in the process of rehabilitation or liquidation.

Schedule F, Part 1A, Section 1 does not include any information regarding the nature of the reinsurance contracts or their retentions or limits. This portion of Schedule F does, however, provide some important insights into the reinsurance operations of the company. It identifies potential collection problems by showing whether any reinsurers are in liquidation or rehabilitation and by showing which reinsurers are slow in paying reinsurance recoverables. By providing the names of the reinsurers and the amounts due, this listing enables others to evaluate the soundness of the reinsurance program. Comparing the current reinsurers with those on prior statements also suggests which reinsurers might be potentially liable for long-tail losses.

This listing includes certain reinsurance recoverable on losses in

Exhibit 11-2
Information Contained in Schedule D—Part 1

Column	Information
1	CUSIP Number and description of bond
2	Coupon interest rate and initial letters of months in which interest is paid
3	Maturity date, year callable, if any, and call price
4	Book value, which usually is amortized
5	Par value
6	Rate used to obtain market value (rate is the dollar value for each thousand dollars of par value)
7	Market value excluding accrued interest (determined by multiplying the rate by per thousand of holdings)
8	Actual cost excluding accrued interest
9.1	Interest due and accrued on December 31 of the current year
9.2	Interest received during the current year
10	Increase by adjustment in book value during the current year (usually the increase from amortization)
11	Decrease by adjustment in book value during the current year (usually the decrease by amortization)
12	Amount of interest due and accrued on bonds in default on December 31 of the current year
13	NAIC designation, a code found in the NAIC Valuation of Securities Manual
14	Year acquired
15	Effective rate of interest at purchase
16	Amortized value or interest on December 31 of the current year
17	Increase in amortized value during the year
18	Decrease in amortized value during the year

dispute. If any one amount exceeds 5 percent of the surplus of the reinsured company or if the total in dispute exceeds 10 percent of the surplus of the reinsured company, then such amounts are identified in this listing. A recoverable is considered in dispute if the reinsured company has been notified by the reinsurer that coverage for amounts submitted has been denied. Typically these amounts are then the subject of arbitration or litigation. For each disputed amount shown, the schedule indicates whether the amount is (1) the subject of notification, (2) in arbitration, or (3) in litigation.

Schedule F, Part 1A, Section 2, deals with assumed reinsurance. It provides similar information to Section 1, except for an aging schedule. It is subject to the same limitations.

Part 1B of Schedule F list portfolio reinsurance purchased and assumed. It shows the date of the contract, the original premium for the business purchased or assumed or ceded, and the reinsurance premium. This schedule also is of limited usefulness in assessing the financial condition of a company except to the extent that the existence of portfolio reinsurance may indicate a problem. Most uses of portfolio reinsurance involve reinsuring all the business from one state, a line of business, all business of one agent, or reinsuring loss reserves. While any of the first three may be for valid business reasons, some believe that any insurer that is reinsuring its loss reserves may be disguising a deteriorating financial condition.

Schedule F, Part 2A is a schedule of funds withheld by the company under reinsurance contracts with unauthorized reinsurers. It is the source for the data on line 13d of the liabilities section of the balance sheet. The schedule compares the funds withheld with the amounts recoverable from the reinsurer. It is important as an indicator of the security of unauthorized reinsurance, which is important to the solvency of many insurers.

In Schedule F, Part 2B, Sections 1 and 2 develop the provision for overdue authorized reinsurance as of the end of the year. It is entered on line 13e of the liabilities section of the balance sheet. Essentially the schedule sums all amounts estimated as due and overdue from authorized reinsurers that have overdue balances, subtracts any deposits or other balances due the reporting company, and reports 20 percent of the difference as the provision for overdue authorized reinsurance.

Loss Schedules

Most of the remaining schedules of the Annual Statement deal with losses. They provide supporting information for both the balance sheet and the income statement. Accounting for paid losses and adjustment expenses is a straightforward process and subject to only minor error. Accounting for reserves for outstanding losses and adjustment expenses, especially for liability lines, is a major challenge of the insurance business. Depending upon the lines of insurance written, the loss and loss-expense reserves may be three or four times as great as the surplus of policyholders of the company. The various loss schedules in the Annual Statement are intended to disclose any significant errors in loss reserving, although their efficacy in that regard is in doubt.

The principal loss schedules in the Annual Statement are Schedule H for accident and health business and Schedule P for all other lines. Exhibit 11-3 lists the lines of insurance covered by the various subparts of Schedule P, Part 1.

Schedule H provides backup for both the balance sheet and the income statement, but it relates to a line that accounts for a very minor part of the business of most property-liability insurers. Consequently, it is not discussed in detail here.

Schedule P is a comprehensive analysis of earned premium, losses, and loss expenses by earned or incurred year. It has been made elaborate in an effort to detect errors in loss reserves as early as possible. The contents of Schedule P appear below:

- Part 1—detailed information on earned premium, losses, and loss expenses
- Part 2—history of incurred losses and allocated loss expenses
- Part 3—history of paid loss and allocated expense payments
- Part 5—schedule for claims-made policies
- Part 6—history of bulk and incurred but not reported reserves
- Schedule P interrogatories

There is no Part 4 in Schedule P. Each Part, except Part 5, has a summary and supplemental schedule labeled with letters A through Q. The summaries and supplemental schedules are the same in each part, except that the supplemental schedules address individual lines of insurance.

Schedule P, Part 1.   Each part in Part 1 of Schedule P has the same physical layout, differing only with regard to the line of insurance detailed and the length of time over which losses are developed.

The Part 1 schedules develop the information in categories consisting of premiums earned, loss and loss expense payments, number of claims reported, losses unpaid, allocated loss expenses unpaid, unallocated loss expenses unpaid, total net losses and expenses unpaid, number of claims outstanding, total losses and

Exhibit 11-3

Schedule P, Part 1 Listing of Lines of Insurance

Part	Years	Line of Insurance
1	10	Summary
1A	10	Homeowners/Farmowners
1B	10	Private Passenger Auto Liability/Medical
1C	10	Commercial Auto/Truck Liability/Medical
1D	10	Workers Compensation
1E	10	Commercial Multiple Peril
1F	10	Medical Malpractice
1G	10	Special Liability (Ocean Marine, Aircraft, Boiler and Machinery)
1H	10	Other Liability
1I	2	Special Property (Fire, Allied Lines, Inland Marine, Earthquake, Glass, Burglary, and Theft)
1J	2	Auto Physical Damage
1K	2	Fidelity, Surety, Financial Guaranty, Mortgage Guaranty
1L	2	Other (Credit, Accident and Health)
1M	10	International
1N	2	Nonproportional Property Reinsurance (1988 and subsequent)
1O	2	Nonproportional Liability Reinsurance (1988 and subsequent)
1P	2	Financial Lines Reinsurance—Financial Guaranty, Fidelity, Surety, Credit and International (1988 and subsequent)
1Q	10	Prior years' reinsurance (not reported in Parts 1N, 1O, or 1P)

expenses incurred, loss and loss expense percentage, discounts, intercompany pooling, and net balance sheet reserves after discount.

Each column in Schedule P, Part 1 relates to ten identified years plus a line for all years prior to the earliest identified year. For example, on the 1989 Schedule, years 1980 to 1989 are specifically identified and data for each appear. The "Prior" year line would be for all years prior to 1980.

Premiums Earned. Earned premium is the sum of all direct and assumed earned premium for the line of insurance reported less any ceded earned premium.

Loss and Loss Expense Payments. Columns 5 through 11 develop the loss and loss expense amounts actually paid during the periods indicated. Loss payments are for direct and assumed business less losses reinsured. Allocated loss expense payments are for direct and assumed business less reinsured business. Salvage and subrogation amounts reported are actual amounts received once salvage and subrogation activity result in cash. Unallocated loss expense payments are the final figure in this section. Net loss payments plus net unallocated loss expense payments plus unallocated loss expense payments are summed in column 11, "Total Net Paid."

Number of Claims Reported. The total number of claims reported on direct and assumed business is reported in column 12. These numbers are reported only for those supplemental schedules of Schedule P where such information is meaningful.

Losses Unpaid and Allocated Loss Expenses Unpaid. Losses and allocated loss expenses that are unpaid are segregated into case losses and bulk plus IBNR losses. For all categories, direct and assumed unpaid amounts are reported separately from reinsured unpaid amounts.

Unallocated Loss Expenses Unpaid. Any unallocated loss expenses unpaid are reported in column 21.

Total Net Losses and Expenses Unpaid. All unpaid losses and unpaid allocated loss expenses are netted (direct and assumed less ceded). The netted amounts are added to unpaid unallocated loss expenses to determine column 22, "Total Net Losses and Expenses Unpaid."

Number of Claims Outstanding. Column 23 reports the number of claims from direct and assumed business outstanding for each reported year where appropriate.

Total Losses and Loss Expenses Incurred. Column 24 sums all direct and assumed losses and loss expenses incurred (paid or unpaid). Column 25 sums all ceded losses and loss expenses incurred. Ceded figures are subtracted from direct and assumed figures for a net total loss and loss expenses incurred figure (placed in column 26). Therefore, column 24 less column 25 should equal column 11 ("Total Net Paid Losses and Loss Expenses") plus column 22 ("Total Net Losses and Expenses Unpaid").

Loss and Loss Expense Percentage. Ratios of incurred losses and loss expenses to earned premium are calculated for each of the (1) direct and assumed, (2) ceded, and (3) net figures from columns 24, 25, and 26.

Discount for Time Value of Money. Generally the information in Schedule P is for undiscounted loss and loss adjustment expenses and should reflect the estimate of management as to the ultimate amounts that will be paid on claims. Where any reserve is discounted (other than tabular reserves such as workers compensation or on other losses if allowed in any given state) the discount is reconciled in column 30 for loss amounts and column 31 for loss expenses. The amounts of the discounts are netted in columns 33 and 34 under the general heading "Net Balance Sheet Reserves After Discount."

Inter-Company Pooling Participation Percentage. If the reporting insurer reports results as pooled with other companies (typically in the same fleet or group of insurers under a common ownership), its percentage of the pool is reported in Column 32. If not all business is pooled, this column left blank and the pooling arrangement is explained in an interrogatory.

Schedule P, Part 2. The schedules in Part 2 display the net losses and allocated loss expenses incurred data reported in Part 1. The alphabetical designation following the Part number in the supplemental schedules, for example Part 2D, is exactly the same as for Part 1 (Part 2D would, for example, refer to data for workers compensation).

The figures reported are net of salvage and subrogation and unallocated loss adjustment expenses are not included. As with all Schedule P exhibits, losses and expenses reported are undiscounted. The format should provide the ability to test the adequacy of reserves over time by showing the loss development. For example, if incurred losses (including reserves) for 19X6 were estimated at $10,000,000 on December 31, 19X6, and, at $12,000,000 on December 31, 19X7, then the adverse loss development during 19X7 was $2,000,000 or 20 percent of the 19X6 estimate.

A positive development figure is assumed to indicate that the reserves of the company were inadequate in the past, and may be inadequate in the present, at least for the current year. That potential can be examined only with access to the internal records of the company. The usefulness of these Part 2 Schedules is reduced by the fact that they can be internally manipulated by management, and such manipulation, if well done, is difficult or impossible to detect using only Annual Statement data.

As with Part 1 Schedules, certain lines are reported for 10 years and others for two years (see Exhibit 11-3). For those with only two years of reporting, loss development can be determined only for (1) the last year prior to the current year and (2) the combined results of all earlier years. However, this limited scope is adequate for the lines of insurance concerned. If more years are necessary for a longer period of time to create a loss development triangle, estimates can be taken from the Annual Statements from prior years. This may even be necessary in extremely long-tail lines such as medical malpractice (Schedule P, Part 2F) that do report ten years of data.

Schedule P, Part 3. Part 3 reports paid net losses and allocated loss adjustment expenses as shown in Part 1 net of subrogation and salvage. Unallocated loss adjustment expenses are not included.

The number of claims closed (with and without payments) are reported for the years in which the losses were incurred for all lines except homeowners/farmowners, special liability, special property, financial guarantees, international, and reinsurance lines.

Part 3 is helpful in establishing cash flow patterns, since the majority of cash payments by insurers are for losses and their related expenses. It is also helpful for certain actuarial projections.

Schedule P, Part 5. (There is no Part 4 for Schedule P.) Part 5 is a report on the experience for claims-made policies. This part is completed only if current year-earned premium is more than $100,000 or exceeds 15 percent of the earned premium for the current year in that line. Question 2 in Schedule P Interrogatories provides the format to determine whether Part 5 must be completed.

Part 5 has no summary schedule and contains only supplemental schedules for Commercial Multiple Peril (Part 5E), Medical Malpractice (Part 5F), and Other Liability (Part 5H). Each, if required, reports premiums earned, loss payments, claims closed with and without payments for each year, allocated and unallocated loss expenses and their ratio to total loss payments, total loss and loss expense payments and its percentage to earned premium, the number of outstanding claims, the amount of unpaid losses, the amount of unpaid loss expenses, total losses and loss expenses incurred, and the ratio of total losses and loss expenses incurred to earned premium.

Schedule P, Part 6. Part 6 is a report on the bulk and IBNR loss reserves and allocated loss expenses as reported in Part 1. These are typically the actuarially determined reserves. They do not include a provision for unallocated loss expenses.

A limitation of this information is that it is a historical report of the bulk and IBNR reserves and cannot be used by itself to test the adequacy of the reserves. Adequacy of these reserves is usually tested by actuarial techniques based on earned premium or incurred losses (Schedule P, Part 2 information).

The reserves are reported for a ten- or two-year period as with other schedules to Schedule P.

Schedule P Interrogatories. There are eight questions relating to information in Schedule P in the interrogatories. The first is the computation of excess statutory reserves over statement reserves. The second relates to claims-made business (Part 5). Questions three and four define certain terms and cost allocation methods and ask whether information reported is in compliance with those definitions. Question five relates to discounting of reserves. The sixth question asks for net premiums in force for fidelity and surety business and the seventh asks whether claim count information provided is per claim or per claimant. The eighth, and last, question asks for any significant events that may have occurred and should be taken into consideration when using Schedule P to estimate the adequacy of loss and loss expense reserves.

Supplemental Exhibits and Scheduled Interrogatories

Page 87 of the Annual Statement includes eleven interrogatories concerning whether certain schedules will be filed by certain dates. All of the interrogatories require only a yes or no answer and an explanation of any "no" answer.

Schedule Y

Schedule Y provides information about companies that are a part of a holding company group. It has space for an organization chart of interrelated companies and a summary of transactions with affiliated companies.

General Interrogatories

The general interrogatories of the Annual Statement elicit information that does not require an extensive exhibit. Many of the interrogatories require only a yes or no answer. In all, there are forty interrogatories, some of them with subparts. Some of them are not pertinent to the discussion here. This discussion will be limited to those that are pertinent to the financial strength of the company.

Interrogatory 4 deals with the capital stock of the company. It includes both common and preferred stock, though few insurers have preferred stock. For both classes of stock, it shows the number of shares authorized, the number issued and the par value. For preferred stock, it also shows the call price if it is callable, whether dividends are limited, and whether dividends are cumulative.

Interrogatory 5 asks whether the company owns any stock of a real estate holding company or otherwise owns any real estate indirectly. If so, an explanation is required.

Interrogatory 11 asks for the largest amount insured by the company on any one risk (exclusive of workers compensation) net of reinsurance.

Interrogatory 12 asks about catastrophe reinsurance.

Interrogatory 13 asks if the company has guaranteed any premium finance accounts.

Interrogatory 14 asks about surplus relief reinsurance.

Interrogatories 15 and 16 ask whether the company has reinsured any risks from another company or guaranteed any policies issued by another company.

Interrogatories 17, 18, and 19 deal with the possession of securities owned by the company.

Interrogatories 32 through 40 constitute a ceded reinsurance report. These interrogatories are intended to indicate possible effects on the financial condition of the insurer that might result from various changes in its reinsurance program.

Notes to Financial Statements

The notes to the financial statements also should be reviewed. They may contain important financial information, such as methods of valuing assets, contingent liabilities, lease obligations, unsecured reinsurance recoverables, loss reserve discounting practices, interest rate swaps, put options, and other information.

Insurance Expense Exhibit

The Insurance Expense Exhibit is a separate document from the Annual Statement but is a supplement to it. Its principal purpose is to provide expense data by line of insurance. It also provides loss data by line of insurance, but those data largely duplicate the data found in the Underwriting and Expense Exhibit in the Annual Statement.

For each line of insurance, the Insurance Expense Exhibit (IEE) shows the following:

(1) Net written premiums

(2) Net earned premiums
(3) Net losses incurred
(4) Loss adjustment expenses incurred
(5) Commissions and brokerage incurred
(6) Other acquisition, field supervision and collection expenses incurred
(7) General expenses incurred
(8) Taxes, licenses and fees incurred
(9) Total expenses incurred
$$[(4) + (5) + (6) + (7) + (8)]$$
(10) Net investment gain or loss and other income
(11) Dividends to policyholders
(12) Net income before federal and foreign income taxes

Each of the above items is shown as a dollar amount. In addition, items (3) through (12) are shown as percentages of net earned premiums.

The items listed above are shown net of reinsurance, where applicable. The following items also are shown on a direct basis, not affected by reinsurance:

(13) Direct premiums written
(14) Adjusted direct premiums written
(15) Adjusted direct premiums earned
(16) Adjusted direct losses incurred
(17) Adjusted direct loss adjustment expenses incurred
(18) Direct commissions and brokerage incurred
(19) Adjusted direct commissions and brokerage incurred

The items indicated as "adjusted" have been recalculated to remove any distortion resulting from the pooling of premiums, losses, and expenses among companies under common ownership and management.

The data contained in the IEE are useful for two primary purposes. They can be used for ratemaking purposes and for monitoring the effectiveness of rate regulatory measures. Also, when compared to similar figures for other companies, they can be used to indicate the ability of the company to compete effectively in the marketplace.

SUMMARY

The NAIC Annual Statement and the Insurance Expense Exhibit provide a substantial amount of information about the financial condition of an insurance company with which to measure the financial strength and competitive ability of the insurer.

The major weakness of the Annual Statement is in the valuation of loss and loss adjustment expense reserves. Although many pages of the Annual Statement are devoted to loss schedules, it is not possible to verify the adequacy of loss and adjustment expense reserves from Annual Statement data alone.

Chapter Notes

---

1. The liability to transfer bonds under put options relates to the practice of certain insurers who sell bonds and provide the buyer with a "put" option that allows the buyer to sell the bond back to the insurer at a specified price within a specified time period. This material is beyond the scope of this text.
2. In some instances, such as a wholly owned subsidiary that does not have separate audited financial statements, stocks not valued by the Securities Task Force may be considered a nonadmitted asset.
3. GAAP accounting rules suggest that a deficiency reserve be established in such cases to compensate for the deficiency in the statutory unearned premium reserve.

CHAPTER 12

Financial Analysis

Financial analysis is a key aspect of the reinsurance business. Just as a primary insurance company underwrites applicants for insurance, reinsurers underwrite primary insurance companies. In either case, financial condition is a major consideration in the underwriting decision. It is also important from the opposite perspective. Neither a primary insured nor a reinsured company gains much protection by dealing with a company in shaky financial condition. In addition, financial condition reflects the quality of a company's overall management. Thus financial evaluation plays an important role in both placing and underwriting reinsurance.

The accounting process tracks financial developments within a company. Since it deals with numbers, frequently to the penny, many view accounting as a precise, inflexible process. In fact, the accounting process may be flexible, with substantial variations in some figures reported, depending upon the purposes for which the financial statements will be used. Thus any analysis of the financial statements must begin with a recognition of the accounting principles underlying the presentation.

While the numbers stated on a company's financial statements are important measures of its financial condition and profitability, the relationships between various elements of the financial statements often are even more revealing. Thus ratio analysis provides an important tool for financial analysis. Computing the ratio of one element to another greatly facilitates the evaluation of a company's financial condition.

Trend analysis is still another tool used for financial evaluation. Changes over time may indicate the direction in which the company is moving. Several factors, however, can affect the surplus and the ratios of a company. This chapter, therefore, reviews the most important factors to consider in interpreting the financial statements of an insurance or reinsurance company.

ACCOUNTING METHODS

Virtually all insurers and reinsurers in the United States must prepare two sets of financial statements. Publicly held stock insurers must also prepare a third set. These three sets of financial statements include the following:

1. The NAIC Annual Statement filed with the insurance regulatory authorities in each state in which the company is licensed or accredited to conduct business as a nonadmitted insurer
2. Federal income tax returns
3. Stockholder annual reports and Form 10-K as required by the federal Securities and Exchange Commission (SEC).

The NAIC Annual Statement, sometimes called the Convention Statement or "Blank" and described in the previous chapter, is completed according to statutory accounting principles prescribed by state laws and regulations. The stockholder and SEC statements are prepared according to Generally Accepted Accounting Principles (GAAP) prescribed by The American Institute of Certified Public Accountants (AICPA), and the Financial Accounting Standards Board (FASB). The federal income tax returns are based on the NAIC Annual Statement, but with modifications required by the Internal Revenue Code and regulations.

Liquidating Versus Continuity Concept

Statutory accounting principles and generally accepted accounting principles are used to depict two different accounting concepts. As regulators are vitally concerned with solvency, statutory accounting principles emphasize this concept. Insurance regulators seek an accurate statement of the liquidation value of the company. In a forced sale that usually accompanies the involuntary liquidation of a company, assets (other than readily marketable assets like investment stocks and bonds) are likely to bring less than their normal market value, leaving the company with less net worth than anticipated. Statutory accounting principles recognize this potential shrinkage in net worth by conservative valuation of both assets and liabilities. This tendency to understate assets and overstate liabilities results in an understatement of net worth when compared to GAAP accounting.

Generally accepted accounting principles stress the continuity or "going concern" concept. The overriding goal is an accurate statement of the value of the company as a going concern, one that will continue to operate into the foreseeable future. Thus, assets tend to be valued at their use value to the company, without reduction for possible forced sale, and liabilities tend to be valued at the cost to discharge them.

Statutory Accounting Principles Versus GAAP

State regulatory authorities use insurance company accounting data for many purposes, but their foremost concern is protecting the public against financial loss from insurer insolvency. Consequently, most of the statutory accounting principles stress stringent solvency testing and the preservation of value in liquidation. To accomplish this purpose, statutory accounting principles tend to understate assets and earnings and to overstate liabilities. Earnings are understated under statutory accounting, in part, by recognizing income as earned, but recognizing expense as paid. In other words, revenue or income is treated by accrual rules and expense by cash accounting rules. However, some notable exceptions to this general rule exist. Generally accepted accounting principles, on the other hand, are designed to provide investors and potential investors with a more realistic indication of the net worth and operating profit of the company than statutory accounting principles, although this is not always the result.

Understatement of Assets. Several statutory accounting rules promote the conservative valuation of assets and liabilities:

- Nonrecognition of nonadmitted assets (no value assigned to them as assets)
- Nonrecognition of unauthorized reinsurance
- Requirement of statutory minimum loss reserves
- The treatment of prepaid expenses
- Requirement of a gross unearned premium reserve
- Deferred income taxes

There are also some additional differences:

- Consolidation of financial statements
- Premium deficiency
- Valuation of bonds

A comparison of statutory accounting principles to GAAP in regard to these issues follows.

Nonadmitted Assets. Nonadmitted assets are assets with questionable liquidation value, or for which the liquidation value is difficult to determine. They may have substantial use value in the operations of the insurer, but there is substantial uncertainty as to their selling price in the forced sale that would accompany the liquidation of the company. Following are some items classified as nonadmitted:

- Office equipment and supplies (other than mainframe computers)
- Automobiles used in the company's business
- Agents' balances over ninety days past due
- Securities in default on principal, interest, or both

These assets, although they may have some value, are not shown on the balance sheet of the insurer and are not considered when calculating policyholders' surplus. Surplus as regards policyholders (sometimes called policyholders' surplus) is the statutory accounting equivalent of net worth in GAAP accounting. Although nonadmitted assets are not shown on the balance sheet, they are listed elsewhere in the NAIC Annual Statement.

The concept of nonadmitted assets is unique to statutory insurance accounting. The concept does not exist in GAAP accounting. GAAP accounting recognizes all assets that have value, and all such assets are included on the balance sheet and used in calculating the net worth of the firm.

Unauthorized Reinsurance. Unauthorized reinsurance is reinsurance purchased from a reinsurer that is not licensed or accredited to do business in the home state of the reinsured. Insurance companies that reinsure with authorized or accredited reinsurers can reduce current year paid losses by the amounts recovered from such reinsurers. They can also show an asset for expected recoveries from the reinsurer for outstanding losses, including IBNR losses. These reinsurance credits often are essential to the solvency of the ceding company.

The reinsured company cannot show an asset or reduce its reserves to reflect unauthorized reinsurance unless the reinsurer has (1) provided to the ceding company acceptable letters of credit at least equal to the receivables and reserve credits taken, (2) deposited with the ceding company money or acceptable securities at least equal to the receivables and reserve credits, or (3) established a trust fund with a U.S. bank at least equal to all of its U.S. obligations, but generally for not less than $25 million. For a letter of credit to be acceptable, it must (1) be unconditional, (2) be irrevocable, and (3) contain an "evergreen" clause that automatically renews the credit in the absence of prior written notice of nonrenewal. Thus, under statutory accounting rules, a primary company may not be able to show as an asset amounts receivable from unauthorized reinsurers or take reserve credits even though the reinsurer is financially able and willing to meet its obligations. GAAP accounting does not distinguish between authorized and unauthorized reinsurance, but recognizes amounts recoverable from all solvent reinsurers if in the opinion of the primary company's management, the reinsurer is willing *and* able to meet its obligations.

Statutory Minimum Reserves. In pursuit of solvency, state laws require insurers to establish minimum loss reserves for some lines of insurance. These laws were originally intended to curb the practice of some insurers that used optimistic estimates of losses on long-tail lines to increase reported profits in the early years. The minimum loss reserve for general liability insurance for the most recent statement year would range from 60 percent of earned premiums to 75 percent of earned premiums, depending on the loss experience of the insurer. Losses already paid would be deducted. If the statutory minimum reserve is greater than the estimated losses of the insurer, the difference is shown as a liability entitled "Excess of statutory reserves over statement reserves" on the balance sheet of the insurer. GAAP accounting does not provide for a minimum loss reserve. The estimate of the insurer for the amount of outstanding losses would be used.

Prepaid Expenses. Under statutory accounting, all expenses are charged to the year in which they are paid. For example, if a three-year prepaid policy is written with the full agent's commission payable at the inception, the full commission would be charged to expenses in the year the policy was issued, rather than being spread evenly over the term of the policy as under GAAP accounting.

Under GAAP accounting rules, expenses incurred in obtaining a contract that extends beyond its calendar year would be prorated over the life of the contract. An asset entitled "prepaid expenses," or some similar title, would be shown on the balance sheet for that portion of the expenses allocated to future years. Consequently, under statutory accounting, an insurer would not show an asset for prepaid expenses, as would be shown under GAAP accounting.

Gross Unearned Premium Reserve. The U.S. is one of only a very few countries where insurers are required to show a gross unearned premium reserve as a liability on their statutory balance sheets. In most other countries, and on GAAP statements, the unearned premium reserve is shown net, after deduction of prepaid expenses. The prepaid expenses in the unearned premium reserve are sometimes referred to as the "equity in the unearned premium reserve" of the company. This term reflects the fact that the insurer should recover that amount as the premiums are earned, assuming that losses are as anticipated. Some of the prepaid expenses, most notably agents' commissions and premium taxes, are recoverable by the insurer from others if the policies underlying the unearned premium reserve are canceled. Thus the gross unearned premium reserve statutory rule results in the overstatement of the liability from unearned premiums.

Deferred Income Taxes. Deferred income taxes arise when profit is realized more quickly for stockholder reports (GAAP) than for income tax purposes (IRS rules). There are several perfectly legal and acceptable reasons that this difference in realization might occur. For example, a company might use straight line depreciation for stockholder reports and accelerated depreciation for income tax purposes, resulting in higher profits for stockholder reports than for tax purposes. GAAP requires that a deferred tax liability be shown for the difference in profits, recognizing that the tax will be payable at some future time when the additional profit is realized for income tax purposes. Statutory accounting principles do not provide for this liability. In this instance, statutory accounting principles as compared to GAAP result in an overstatement of current net worth.

Consolidation of Financial Statements. It is common for one corporation to own one or more other corporations, or to own sufficient stock to exercise control over other corporations. Although statutory accounting requires a consolidated statement for all controlled property or liability insurers, it does not permit consolidation of property or liability insurers with noninsurance corporations. GAAP accounting requires that all corporations under common control file a single, consolidated financial statement including all of the assets, liabilities, revenues, and expenses of all the controlled companies. This requirement applies even if the corporations are in different businesses.

Premium Deficiency. Statutory accounting principles require the establishment of an unearned premium reserve, based on the premium actually charged for the policies in force. The unearned premium reserve is sometimes viewed as a provision for return premiums on policies canceled. However, since only a few policies are canceled, the reserve is more accurately characterized as a recognition of the obligation of the insurer to provide insurance in the future. The recognition of this liability is essential to the proper realization of premium revenue in the calculation of operating profits and losses.

In periods of intense competition, some insurers may charge premiums that are foreseeably inadequate to cover the claims and expenses related to the corresponding policies. Under those circumstances, the unearned premium reserve, based on inadequate initial premiums, is not an adequate reflection of the obligation of the insurer to provide future insurance protection. Under these inadequate premium circumstances, GAAP accounting would require that the unearned premium reserve be calculated on the basis of an estimated adequate premium, or that a separate premium deficiency reserve be shown. However, this type of GAAP adjustment to statutory accounting statements does not appear frequently.

Valuation of Bonds. There is one notable exception to the general rule that statutory accounting principles tend to understate assets. Investment bonds in good standing are valued at their amortized value, which may be more or less than market value, depending on trends in interest rates. There is a logical reason for this inconsistency. Insurers should match the maturities of their bonds with the expected payout of their losses. Because they can usually hold their bonds until maturity, adjusting the value to market would only result in large "paper" losses when interest rates are high and large "paper" gains when interest rates are low—neither of which would probably ever be realized. The effects of such "paper" gains and losses on the year-to-year surplus would not be meaningful.

An explanation of amortized value may help clarify the statutory valuation of bonds. Bonds are issued with a coupon interest rate, the rate that is paid throughout the life of the bond. If market interest rates rise above the coupon rate, the market price of the bond falls below its face value. If the market interest rate falls below the coupon rate, the market price of the bond rises. A bond that is purchased for less than its face value is said to have been purchased at a discount. If the purchase price is higher than the face amount, it is purchased at a premium. The purpose of amortization is to write off the premium or discount over the remaining life of the bond so it will be shown on the books of the company at its face amount at maturity. The holder of the bond is entitled to receive its face amount from the organization that issued the bond when it reaches maturity.

Bonds usually are issued with a face amount in a multiple of $1,000. If a $1,000 bond with ten years remaining before maturity is purchased for $900, the $100 discount will be written off at the rate of $10 per year, using the least complex method of amortization. That is, the book value of the bond would increase $10 each year until it reaches $1,000 on maturity. If the bond had been purchased at a $100 premium, its book value would have been reduced $10 each year until it reached $1,000 at maturity.

Other, more complex, methods of amortization are acceptable. They do not provide for an equal write-up or write-down each year, but they do result in a book value equal to the face on maturity.

Realization Concepts

In accounting, "realization" means recognition of the impact of revenues, expenses, losses, and gains on the financial status of the corporation. Statutory accounting principles and GAAP differ substantially regarding the realization of expenses, but they are similar with regard to the realization of revenues. They also differ with regard to the realization of gains and losses on investments. Because of these differences in realization, reported profit (or loss) of an insurer under statutory accounting principles may be greater or less than its reported profit under GAAP, but they will seldom, if ever, be equal. The following example illustrates the differences.

Assume that Quaking Casualty Company (QCC) was organized on December 31, 19X1. On that date, it issued one million shares of its common stock with a par value of $10 per share, and it received $23 per share for the stock. Assume further the QCC did not have any organizational expenses or any expenses related to the sale of its stock. Its initial balance sheet is shown in Exhibit 12-1. In this case, the statutory balance sheet and the GAAP balance sheet are identical.

On January 1, 19X2, QCC issued 1,000 policies with total premiums of $6 million. All of the policies were three-year prepaid policies. QCC immediately paid $1 million in commissions to agents, representing the full commissions for the three-year period. Other prepaid expenses incurred at the inception of the policies amounted to $500,000. Exhibit 12-2 shows the statutory balance sheet of QCC on January 1, 19X2; immediately after the policies were issued, the premiums were received, and the expenses were paid. Recognizing all of the prepaid expenses immediately causes a drain on the policyholders' surplus of QCC. It also creates an "equity" of $1.5 million in the unearned premium reserve, since the prepaid expenses were not deducted in calculating the unearned premium reserve.

The statutory balance sheet in Exhibit 12-2 can be contrasted with the GAAP balance sheet for the same date in Exhibit 12-3. In the GAAP balance sheet, an asset of $1.5 million for prepaid expenses has been established. This asset will be amortized evenly over the three-year life of the policies. Also, QCC's policyholders' surplus has not been reduced from its December 31 balance sheet. While the unearned premium reserve is still shown gross, it has been offset by the asset for prepaid expenses.

To simplify the presentation, assume that QCC did not write any more business or incur any additional expenses in 19X2. Losses of $1.5 million were incurred and paid so that QCC showed a statutory accounting principles underwriting loss of $1 million. Also assume that QCC kept all of its funds in cash, so there were no capital gains or

Exhibit 12-1
Statutory and GAAP Balance Sheet
Quaking Casualty Company

December 31, 19X1

ASSETS

Cash	$23,000,000
Total Assets	$23,000,000

LIABILITIES

Total Liabilities	0

POLICYHOLDERS' SURPLUS

Common Capital Stock	$10,000,000
Gross Paid in Surplus	13,000,000
Unassigned Surplus	0
Total Policyholders' Surplus	$23,000,000
Total Liabilities and Policyholders' Surplus	$23,000,000

losses, investment income, or investment expenses. However, since one year of the three-year policy term had elapsed on December 31, 19X2, one-third of the premiums had been earned and one-third of the prepaid expense asset in the GAAP balance sheet would have been amortized. Exhibit 12-4 shows QCC's statutory balance sheet for December 31, 19X2. At the end of the first year, QCC's policyholders' surplus increased by $500,000 during the year even though it had an underwriting loss and did not have any investment profit, capital gains, or any additional capital or paid-in surplus. The increase in policyholder surplus resulted from reclaiming $500,000 of the equity in the unearned premium reserve. The GAAP balance sheet in Exhibit 12-5 presents a more even picture of the operations of QCC for 19X2, using the same assumptions. Under GAAP, there is no change in QCC's policyholders' surplus during 19X2, a more appropriate result for the assumptions used.

Exhibit 12-2
Statutory Accounting Principles Balance Sheet
Quaking Casualty Company

January 1, 19X2

ASSETS

Cash	$27,500,000
Total Assets	$27,500,000

LIABILITIES

Unearned Premium Reserve	$6,000,000
Total Liabilities	$6,000,000

POLICYHOLDERS' SURPLUS

Common Capital Stock	$10,000,000
Gross Paid in Surplus	13,000,000
Unassigned Surplus	(1,500,000)
Total Policyholders' Surplus	$21,500,000
Total Liabilities and Policyholders' Surplus	$27,500,000

QCC's operating statements for 19X2 are equally instructive. QCC's statutory operating statement appears in Exhibit 12-6 and its GAAP statement in Exhibit 12-7. The statutory operating statement shows an underwriting loss of $1 million, resulting entirely from the full realization of the prepaid expenses in 19X2 as required by statutory accounting rules. Only one-third of the prepaid expenses were realized in the GAAP statement, since the policies were all three-year prepaid policies. Consequently, QCC broke even in 19X2 under GAAP.

The assumptions underlying these hypothetical financial statements are artificial. They were designed to produce extreme results in order to dramatize the differences between statutory accounting principles and GAAP accounting results. Such extreme differences would seldom, if ever, be encountered in real life situations.

Exhibit 12-3
GAAP Balance Sheet
Quaking Casualty Company

January 1, 19X2

ASSETS

Cash	$27,500,000
Prepaid Expenses	1,500,000
Total Assets	$29,000,000

LIABILITIES

Unearned Premium Reserve	$ 6,000,000
Total Liabilities	$ 6,000,000

POLICYHOLDERS' SURPLUS

Common Capital Stock	$10,000,000
Gross Paid in Surplus	13,000,000
Unassigned Surplus	0
Total Policyholders' Surplus	$23,000,000
Total Liabilities and Policyholders' Surplus	$29,000,000

Tax Accounting

Tax accounting principles are established by the U.S. Internal Revenue Code and the associated regulations. The taxable income of property-liability insurers is determined on the basis of statutory accounting principles with some amendments required by the Internal Revenue Code and regulations. Prior to the Tax Reform Act of 1986, most differences between statutory accounting principles profit and taxable income were relatively small. Tax accounting is a specialized field, especially with regard to changes introduced by the Tax Reform Act of 1986. For purposes of this text, it is only important to recognize

Exhibit 12-4
Statutory Balance Sheet
Quaking Casualty Company

December 31, 19X2

ASSETS

Cash	$26,000,000
Total Assets	$26,000,000

LIABILITIES

Unearned Premium Reserve	$4,000,000
Total Liabilities	$4,000,000

POLICYHOLDERS' SURPLUS

Common Capital Stock	$10,000,000
Gross Paid in Surplus	13,000,000
Unassigned Surplus	(1,000,000)
Total Policyholders' Surplus	$22,000,000
Total Liabilities and Policyholders' Surplus	$26,000,000

that special and different accounting rules apply for federal income tax purposes than for statutory or GAAP accounting purposes.

RATIO ANALYSIS

Ratio analysis provides a valuable tool for financial evaluation. Operating ratios, for example, compare a company's losses, expenses, or both to the amount of business it writes. The ratio then can be meaningfully compared to the same ratio for another company, regardless of size, to judge the relative success of the two companies. A single company's ratio can also be compared to the industry average.

Similarly, the return on equity is a ratio that measures a company's

Exhibit 12-5
GAAP Balance Sheet
Quaking Casualty Company

December 31, 19X2

ASSETS

Cash	$26,000,000
Prepaid Expenses	1,000,000
Total Assets	$27,000,000

LIABILITIES

Unearned Premium Reserve	$ 4,000,000
Total Liabilities	$ 4,000,000

POLICYHOLDERS' SURPLUS

Common Capital Stock	$10,000,000
Gross Paid in Surplus	13,000,000
Unassigned Surplus	0
Total Policyholders' Surplus	$23,000,000
Total Liabilities and Policyholders' Surplus	$27,000,000

profitability. This ratio can be compared to another company's return on equity so long as the ratios for the two companies have been computed in the same way.

Operating Ratios

Three operating ratios are useful in analyzing insurance company financial data. The principal ones are (1) the loss ratio, (2) the expense ratio, and (3) the combined ratio.

Loss Ratios. The loss ratio is the ratio of losses to premiums. Since there are two kinds of premiums (written and earned) and two

Exhibit 12-6
Statutory Operating Statement—19X2
Quaking Casualty Company

Premiums Earned		$2,000,000
Losses Incurred	$1,500,000	
Underwriting Expenses Incurred	1,500,000	3,000,000
Underwriting Loss		($1,000,000)
Investment Income	0	
Less Investment Expenses	0	0
Realized Capital Gains		0
Loss Before Taxes		($1,000,000)
Federal IncomeTaxes		0
Loss After Taxes		($1,000,000)

Exhibit 12-7
GAAP Operating Statement—19X2
Quaking Casualty Company

Premiums Earned		$2,000,000
Losses Incurred	$1,500,000	
Underwriting Expenses Incurred	500,000	2,000,000
Underwriting Profit or Loss		0
Investment Income	0	
Less Investment Expenses	0	0
Realized Capital Gains		0
Profit Before Taxes		0
Federal Income Taxes		0
Profit After Taxes		0

kinds of losses (incurred and paid), there are four kinds of loss ratios. The most useful is the ratio of *incurred losses to earned premiums*, since it most accurately matches the losses with the premiums that were intended to pay them. A loss ratio may either include or exclude the expenses incurred to adjust losses. A loss ratio that does not include loss adjustment expenses is sometimes called a *pure loss ratio.*

Incurred losses for a given year are the losses arising out of insured events that occurred during the year. They may be paid during the same year or in later years.

Paid losses are those for which actual payment is made during the year. They may have been incurred in the same year they were paid or in an earlier year. In the Quaking Casualty Company example, the incurred and paid losses were the same ($1.5 million) for year 19X1, but that would be unusual in a real life situation.

The written premiums for a given year are the premiums entered on the books of the company for policies, endorsements, premium audits, and similar transactions during the year. In the Quaking Casualty Company example, one-third of the coverage under the three-year policies was provided in 19X2, with the remaining two-thirds to be provided in the two following years. Consequently, the earned premiums were one-third of the written premiums, or $2 million. For an older company, there would also have been some earned premium from policies written in earlier years, but 19X2 was the first year of operation for QCC.

The incurred-to-earned loss ratio for Quaking Casualty for 19X2 is:

$$\text{Incurred-to-Earned Loss Ratio} = \frac{\text{Incurred Losses}}{\text{Earned Premiums}} \times 100\%$$

$$= \frac{\$1,500,000}{\$2,000,000} \times 100\% = 75\%$$

The custom in the insurance business is to express the ratios as percentages.

The paid-to-written loss ratio is:

$$\text{Paid-to-Written Loss Ratio} = \frac{\text{Losses Paid}}{\text{Premiums Written}} \times 100\%$$

$$= \frac{\$1,500,000}{\$6,000,000} \times 100\% = 25\%$$

The paid-to-written loss ratio in this case is meaningless, since it compares losses for a one-year period to premiums for a three-year period. Even though this is an extreme example, the paid-to-written loss ratio usually does not give a good match of losses to the premiums intended to cover them. Consequently, the incurred-to-earned loss ratio is used in virtually all accounting and ratemaking functions.

The extent of the inaccuracy from using the paid-written loss ratio depends on the characteristics of the line of insurance. For a line of insurance in which losses are reported and paid promptly, and policies are issued for one year or less, the paid-written loss ratio may give a reasonable indication of the profitability of an insurer especially if the premium volume is relatively stable. For lines with a long delay in claim reporting and payment (long-tail lines), or a rapidly changing premium volume, the incurred-earned loss ratio should be used.

Expense Ratios. The expense ratio is the ratio of incurred underwriting expenses to premiums. It is a measure of the efficiency of an insurer in writing and servicing business. The expense loading may include an element for profit, especially if it is to be used for ratemaking. Two expense ratios are available. The statutory expense ratio consists of the incurred underwriting expenses divided by earned premiums. The ratio is usually written without the word "underwriting" but it is understood to be underwriting expenses.

$$\text{Statutory Expense Ratio} = \frac{\text{Incurred Expenses}}{\text{Earned Premiums}} \times 100\%$$

The trade expense ratio, sometimes called Best's expense ratio, consists of the incurred expenses divided by written premiums.

$$\text{Trade Expense Ratio} = \frac{\text{Incurred Expenses}}{\text{Written Premiums}} \times 100\%$$

The trade expense ratio is an approximation to GAAP accounting rather than statutory accounting. It recognizes the desirability of spreading prepaid expenses over the life of the policy in measuring profitability of an insurer.

Combined Ratios. The combined ratio is the sum of the loss ratio and the expense ratio. A combined ratio of 100 percent indicates that the insurer broke even on its insurance operations (assuming no profit allowance in the expense ratio). It does not reflect investment profit or loss, however.

A combined ratio less than 100 percent indicates that the insurer earned an underwriting profit. A ratio greater than 100 percent indicates an underwriting loss. There are two combined ratios. The statutory combined ratio reflects statutory accounting rules. The trade combined ratio, sometimes called the Best's combined ratio, is an approximation of GAAP accounting rules.

$$\text{Statutory Combined Ratio} = \frac{\text{Incurred Losses} + \text{Incurred Expenses}}{\text{Earned Premiums}} \times 100\%$$

$$\text{Trade Combined Ratio} = \left(\frac{\text{Incurred Losses}}{\text{Earned Premiums}} + \frac{\text{Incurred Expenses}}{\text{Writted Premiums}} \right) \times 100\%$$

The expenses used in the expense ratios and combined ratios also are only the so-called "underwriting expenses," the expenses related directly to insurance operations. They do not include investment or loss expenses.

Return on Equity

Return on equity is a ratio used to measure the financial performance of a company, either insurers or noninsurers. It is an important consideration for investors and investment advisors in selecting the companies in which they invest. Return on equity is the ratio of net after tax operating profit to net worth, with the ratio expressed as a percentage.

$$\text{Return on Equity} = \frac{\text{Net After Tax Profit}}{\text{Net Worth}} \times 100\%$$

If return on equity of an insurer is to be compared to that of noninsurance corporations, the profit and policyholders' surplus of the insurer must first be converted to their GAAP equivalents in order to make an equitable comparison. If only insurers are to be compared, the return on statutory policyholders' surplus may be an adequate measure.

$$\text{Return on Policyholders' Surplus} = \frac{\text{Net After Tax Profit}}{\text{Policyholders' Surplus}} \times 100\%$$

The necessary changes to convert statutory accounting principles profit and policyholders' surplus to approximate GAAP profit and net worth are discussed later in this chapter.

FACTORS AFFECTING SURPLUS AND STATUTORY RATIOS

Four factors in the interpretation of insurance company statutory financial statements may cause stated surplus and ratios to be misleading: (1) growth or decline in premium volume; (2) adjustment to reserves for outstanding claims; (3) changes in the values of investments; and (4) some reinsurance transactions.

Changes in Premium Volume

Statutory accounting requires insurers to recognize all expenses in the year incurred, even if prepaid expenses are more properly related to future accounting periods. Also, statutory accounting requires a gross unearned premium reserve, without deduction for prepaid expenses. These two rules result in the accumulation of the "equity in the unearned premium reserve," which is withdrawn from the unearned premium reserve as premiums are earned. If premium volume is growing, more is added to the equity from newly written premiums than is withdrawn for earned premiums because with a growing premium volume the written premiums exceed the earned premiums.

These additions to the equity in the unearned premium reserve result in an understatement of both statutory underwriting profit and policyholders' surplus, when compared to GAAP profit and surplus. Consequently, the ratio of premiums to policyholders' surplus is overstated when compared to the comparable GAAP ratio.

A declining premium volume has the opposite effect. More is withdrawn from the equity in the unearned premium reserve than is added because earned premiums exceed written premiums. Consequently, the statutory underwriting profit of the insurer is overstated when compared with GAAP profit. Surplus also is increased, so the ratio of premiums to policyholders' surplus falls further than it would fall from the decrease in premiums alone.

If premium volume of an insurer remains stable, other things remaining equal, statutory underwriting profit will closely approximate the GAAP underwriting profit, since the withdrawals from, and additions to, the equity in the unearned premium reserve will be equal. The statutory premium to policyholders' surplus ratio will still be higher than the comparable GAAP figure, since there will still be some prepaid expenses in the unearned premium reserve, but the difference will not be as great as in the case of an increasing premium volume.

Changes in Loss Reserves

Based on reported claims, an insurer may determine it is under-reserved for previous years, that is, its estimation of losses in prior years was too low. Changes in loss reserves affect profits of an insurer. Assume that an insurer in the accounting year 19X5 decides to increase its loss reserves for 19X4 and earlier years by $150 million. To do this, the insurer deducts the reserve increase for prior years from the income of the current year. Other things being equal, the increase in loss reserves causes a $150 million drop in the underwriting profit of the insurer for 19X5, even though the increase was to reserves for earlier years. To illustrate this effect, assume that the 19X5 underwriting results of Quaking Casualty Company would have been as shown in Exhibit 12-8 if QCC had not increased its loss reserves for 19X4 and earlier years.

Exhibit 12-8
Quaking Casualty Company Underwriting Gain for the Year
Ending December 31, 19X5 Before Increase in Loss Reserves

Premiums Earned		$750,000,000
LESS:		
Incurred Losses	$400,000,000*	
Loss Adjustment Expense	100,000,000	
Underwriting Expense	100,000,000	
Total Deductions		600,000,000
Underwriting Gain		$150,000,000

*Incurred Losses = Year End Loss Reserve + Paid Losses for Year
 − First of Year Loss Reserve

= 900,000,000 + 350,000,000 − 850,000,000

= 400,000,000

Exhibit 12-9 shows the calculations of underwriting results after $150 million has been added to the reserves for 19X4 and earlier years. Nothing else has been changed. QCC's year-end policyholders' surplus would fall by the same amount. A reduction in the reserve for outstanding losses would have the opposite effect: an increase in profit and surplus.

Changes in loss reserves occur frequently, and the effect on profit and surplus should be reviewed carefully when evaluating the financial position of an insurer. The necessary information to determine the magnitude of such prior year reserve changes can be found in the NAIC Annual Statement in Schedule P.

Changes in Investment Values

Changes in the values of investments result in capital gains or losses. If the investments are sold, the capital gains or losses are *realized*. If the investments are not sold, the capital gains or losses are *unrealized*.

Exhibit 12-9

Quaking Casualty Company Underwriting Gain for the Year
Ending December 31, 19X5 After Adding $150,000,000 to Loss
Reserves for 19X4 and Earlier Years

Premiums Earned		$750,000,000
LESS:		
Incurred Losses	$550,000,000*	
Loss Adjustment Expense	100,000,000	
Other Underwriting Expense	100,000,000	
Total Deductions		750,000,000
Underwriting Gain		$ 0

*Incurred Losses = Year End Loss Reserve + Paid Losses for Year
− First of Year Loss Reserve

$$= 1,050,000,000 + 350,000,000 - 850,000,000$$

$$= 550,000,000$$

Realized capital gains or losses appear on the income statement of the insurer in the NAIC Annual Statement. They flow through profit into surplus, and thus do not create any problem in interpretation. Unrealized capital gains or losses, on the other hand, flow directly to surplus and must be accounted for in analyzing the financial position of the insurer. The adjustment of surplus to reflect unrealized capital gains or losses is shown on page 4, line 19, of the NAIC Annual Statement in the Capital and Surplus Account Statement. In 1974, the property-liability insurance business lost much of its policyholders' surplus because of unrealized capital losses resulting from the stock market decline of that year. Later, the bull market of the 1980s brought substantial increases in the policyholders' surplus of many insurers as a result of unrealized capital gains. Unrealized capital gains and losses are the least stable of the elements contributing to insurer earnings and surplus, and they must be weighed carefully in the evaluation of the financial results of an insurer.

Reinsurance Transactions

Reinsurance transactions and the methods of accounting for them have caused puzzling figures to appear in insurer financial statements. For example, one insurer showed a negative expense ratio for many years, although its actual expenses were not very different from those of other similar insurers. Its negative expense ratio resulted from the method of accounting for reinsurance ceding commissions.

Because the statutory method of accounting for reinsurance transactions causes problems in interpreting insurer financial statements, some explanation here may be beneficial. Reinsurance transactions affect several items in the financial statements of an insurer. Among them are net written premiums, net earned premiums, net incurred losses, net loss reserves, and expenses, especially commission and brokerage expenses.

Commission and Brokerage Expenses. Under quota share and surplus treaties, reinsurers usually pay a ceding commission to the ceding company. The ceding company shows the ceding commissions as a reduction in its account for commission and brokerage expenses. If the ceding commissions exceed the brokerage and commission expenses of the ceding company, the commission and brokerage expense account balance becomes negative. In fact, if the ceding commissions are sufficiently large, the total expense ratio of the ceding company may become negative, although this does not occur frequently. This information appears in the Underwriting and Investment Exhibit of the NAIC Annual Statement.

Net Written Premiums. Direct premiums written consist of the premiums on policies and endorsements issued directly by an insurer to consumers, either personal or commercial. Neither ceded nor assumed reinsurance premiums are included in direct premiums.

Net premiums written are calculated by the following formula:

Net Premiums Written = Direct Premiums Written
+ Reinsurance Premiums Assumed
− Reinsurance Premiums Ceded

Net premiums written is used in the premium-to-surplus ratio, one of the key tests in the NAIC Insurance Regulatory Information System (IRIS). Consequently, reinsurance, both ceded and assumed, may have a substantial effect on that ratio, which is indicated by the following formula:

$$\text{Premiums-to-Surplus Ratio} = \frac{\text{Net Written Premiums}}{\text{Policyholders' Surplus}}$$

According to the IRIS standards, the above ratio should not exceed 3 to 1.

Reinsurance can also, indirectly, have a substantial effect on policyholders' surplus. Policyholders' surplus is calculated by deducting total liabilities from total admitted assets. Reinsurance can affect several liabilities of an insurer, and these, too, may have a substantial effect on policyholders' surplus.

Loss Reserves and Net Incurred Losses. Loss reserves and the unearned premium reserve, the two largest liabilities of a property-liability insurer, are affected by reinsurance transactions. The unearned premium reserve is calculated in the Underwriting and Investment Exhibit in the NAIC Annual Statement.

The effect of reinsurance on loss reserves is shown in the Underwriting and Expense Exhibit of the Annual Statement. Amounts recoverable from reinsurers are deducted in calculating the reserve for losses in the course of adjustment and the IBNR reserve (losses incurred but not reported).

Surplus Effects. Both authorized and unauthorized reinsurance are deducted in calculating the loss and unearned premium reserves. Unauthorized reinsurance is shown as a liability on the balance sheet. The total liability for unauthorized reinsurance is offset by any funds, securities, or letters of credit held by the insurer. Also, an asset for amounts recoverable from reinsurers for losses already paid is shown in the Annual Statement. The net effect of all of these entries, especially for authorized reinsurance, frequently is an increase in policyholders' surplus. The amount of the increase, if any, depends on (1) the kinds and amounts of reinsurance purchased, (2) the premium paid for the reinsurance, and (3) the amount of the ceding commission.

Quota Share. Under a quota share reinsurance treaty, the direct insurer agrees to cede, and the reinsurer agrees to accept, an agreed percentage of the amount of insurance on each eligible risk insured by the direct insurer. Premiums and losses are split between the ceding company and the reinsurer in the same percentages as the amount of insurance. The reinsurer usually pays a ceding commission to the direct insurer under a quota share treaty. Because of the ceding commission, the ceding company pays to the reinsurer a net premium (after commission) less than the ceded premium shown on the books of the ceding company. The ceding company's unearned premium reserve, a liability, is reduced by the gross premium ceded while its assets are reduced only by the net premium paid. Consequently, policyholders' surplus of the ceding company is increased by the difference between the gross premium ceded and the net premium paid, which is the ceding commission.

Among the traditional forms of reinsurance, quota share is used most often by direct insurers that need to augment their policyholders' surplus. It also is effective in reducing the premium-to-surplus ratio. Loss portfolio reinsurance, discussed below, also has been used frequently in recent years to augment surplus.

Surplus Share. Surplus share reinsurance is similar to quota share. The only significant difference is in the way the retention of the ceding company is stated. Under a quota share treaty, the retention is stated as a percentage of the amount insured, with the same percentage applying to all policies regardless of the magnitude of the amount insured. Under a surplus share treaty, the retention is stated as a dollar amount. If the amount of insurance on a risk is less than or equal to the retention amount, no reinsurance is ceded under the treaty. If the amount of insurance is greater than the retention, the amount over and above the retention (but not over the treaty limit) is ceded to the reinsurer. Like the quota share treaty, the premiums and losses of policies reinsured under a surplus share treaty are split in the same proportion as the amount of insurance.

A ceding commission usually is paid to the ceding company under a surplus share treaty. Consequently, it is effective in augmenting the surplus of the ceding company and in reducing the premium-to-surplus ratio of the ceding company.

Excess of Loss Reinsurance. Excess of loss reinsurance has a less consistent effect on the surplus of the reinsured than the quota share and surplus share treaties. Excess treaties usually do not provide a ceding commission for the direct insurer. Consequently, the effect on surplus depends on the relationship between the reinsurance premium and covered losses. If the losses recoverable under a treaty exceed the premium paid for it, the effect on surplus will be positive. If the premium exceeds the losses, the effect on surplus will be negative. These relationships cannot be predicted accurately for any given year, but, if the treaty is properly rated, it is likely that the premiums will exceed the losses in the long run.

Loss Portfolio Reinsurance. Under the reinsurance forms discussed at this point in the chapter, the ceding company is protected against losses that occur while the treaty is in force. Loss portfolio reinsurance covers losses that occurred before the inception of the treaty but had not been paid on the inception date. Loss portfolio reinsurance may be of a proportional or excess of loss form. Some types of loss portfolio reinsurance are not recognized as true reinsurance by some state insurance regulators and by the IRS.

Proportional. Under a proportional loss portfolio reinsurance contract, the direct insurer cedes all or a fixed percentage of its loss reserves for the specified kinds of losses. The premium for the reinsurance usually equals the present value of the loss reserves (discounted for future investment income), plus an allowance for expenses and profit of the reinsurer. The reinsurer may, but does not always, assume the risk that the reinsured reserves are inadequate. The ceding company may be required to reimburse the reinsurer for lost investment income if the reinsured losses are settled more quickly than anticipated when the treaty was negotiated.

Statutory Accounting Effects

The accounting effect of loss portfolio reinsurance is not constant. For statutory accounting principles statements, the usual procedure is to reduce loss reserves by the amount of reserves ceded. Some suggest that the reinsurance premium be shown as a reduction in premiums written, while others suggest that it be shown as an increase in losses paid.[1] The effects of these two methods are different. Showing the transaction as a reduction of premiums written reduces the premiums-to-surplus ratio of the ceding company. However, it results in a higher expense ratio, since it reduces premiums without reducing expenses. Showing the reinsurance premium as an increase in losses paid does not change either the expense ratio or the ratio of premiums-to-surplus.

Since the premium is usually less than the loss reserves ceded, the purchase of such a treaty, under either accounting method outlined, usually results in an increase in the surplus of the ceding company and, consequently, a reduction in the premium-to-surplus ratio. If the reinsurance premium is shown as a reduction of premiums written, the change in the premium-to-surplus ratio is even greater. The gain in surplus is approximately equal to the expected future investment income from the reserves, so proportional loss portfolio reinsurance is most effective in augmenting surplus when used with long-tail lines such as medical malpractice liability insurance.

This presentation according to statutory accounting principles also increases the profit of the ceding company. Incurred losses under statutory accounting principles are estimated by the formula:

Incurred Losses = Year End Loss Reserves + Paid Losses
— First of Year Loss Reserves

If the year end loss reserves are reduced by loss portfolio reinsurance, the incurred losses for the year are reduced by the same amount, resulting in an increase in underwriting gain (or a reduction in underwriting loss).

GAAP Effects

GAAP accounting for loss portfolio reinsurance varies widely. One survey of the treatment of loss portfolio reinsurance on the U.S. Securities Exchange Commission form 10-K showed two distinct and contradictory methods of treatment.[2] One group of ceding companies treated proportional loss portfolio reinsurance contracts as financial arrangements, apparently on the assumption that no risk was transferred to the reinsurer. Under this method of treatment, the loss portfolio transaction did not affect either the GAAP surplus or the GAAP profit of the ceding companies. This treatment is in keeping with generally accepted accounting principles as adopted by the Financial Accounting Standards Board and promulgated in Financial Accounting Standard No. 5:

> To the extent an insurance contract or reinsurance contract does not, despite its form, provide for indemnification of the insured or the ceding company by the insurer or reinsurer against loss or liability, the premium paid less the amount of the premium to be retained by the insurer or reinsurer shall be accounted for as a deposit by the insured or the ceding company. Those contracts may be structured in various ways, but if, regardless of form, their substance is that all or part of the premium paid by the insured or the ceding company is a deposit, it shall be accounted for as such.[3]

A second group of insurers treated loss portfolios for their GAAP presentations in the same manner outlined above for statutory accounting, with the resulting increase in profit and surplus. It is not clear whether these differences in the treatment reflect differences in the treaties or merely differences in accounting theories.

The effect of such transactions on profit and surplus can be dramatic. One insurer reported a reduction of $79.7 million in loss reserves in exchange for a reinsurance premium of $21.9 million. The result was an increase of $57.8 million in reported profit for the year.[4]

Effects on the Reinsurer

For the reinsurer, it would seem appropriate to increase loss reserves by the undiscounted amount of loss portfolio coverage assumed, and to book the premium for the treaty as written premiums. However, this method would result in a loss to the reinsurer in the year the treaty is written, since the undiscounted losses usually exceed the premium by a substantial amount.

Some reinsurers follow the method outlined, except that they increase their loss reserves by the discounted amount of the assumed loss reserves. This practice avoids the initial loss shown under the above method.

One reinsurer reported on its 10-K form that it had recorded the assumed loss reserves at their full, undiscounted amount, and had offset them by equal amounts of "negative paid losses."[5] This method avoids the initial loss when the coverage is written. It also avoids increasing the ratio of premiums to surplus.

Under an excess of loss portfolio treaty, the reinsurer protects the ceding company against inadequacy of its loss reserves. The retention of the ceding company may be stated as either a loss ratio or a dollar amount, but normally will equal or exceed the loss reserves established. The reinsurer may pay only a part, such as 90 percent, of the losses in excess of the retention.

Unlike many proportional loss portfolio reinsurance agreements, the excess contracts usually involve substantial risk transfer. The premiums for them are determined accordingly and do not involve a simple discounting of reserves. The transaction should appear on the books of the ceding company as a reduction in an asset (cash or investments) and decrease in premiums written. The reinsurer should show it as an increase in an asset (cash or investments) and an increase in written premiums. Excess of loss portfolio contracts are used when the ceding company wants to put a final cap on its incurred losses, to guard against future increases in loss reserves. This cap is especially helpful if the ceding company is withdrawing from a line of insurance. For example, one large insurer had been plagued by repeated increases in its reserves for medical malpractice losses. It decided to discontinue writing the line and to limit its losses by entering into an excess of loss portfolio reinsurance contract with another insurer. By this transfer, it was able to convince investors and regulators that losses from medical malpractice would not continue to depress its earnings.

SUMMARY

Accounting is a flexible process. Most insurance companies are required to keep three sets of books: one for the state insurance departments, another for the SEC and stockholders, and a third for the internal revenue service. There are significant differences among the three sets of books, mostly with regard to the profits reported. However, there also are differences regarding the valuation of assets and liabilities.

The accounting procedures for proportional loss portfolio reinsurance are especially inconsistent among reinsurers, with essentially the same transaction being booked as premiums written by some reinsurers and as "negative losses paid" by others. The ceding company part of the same transaction may be shown either as a reduction in net premiums written or as losses paid.

The kinds and amounts of reinsurance purchased and the accounting techniques adopted may have a substantial influence on policyholders' surplus, underwriting profit or loss, loss ratio, expense ratio, combined ratio, ratio of premiums to surplus, and other financial measures of company solidity and success for both insurers and reinsurers. For these reasons, great care must be taken in interpreting financial statements of insurers and reinsurers.

Chapter Notes

---

1. See, for example, Inzerillo, James, "The Security of the Reinsurance Industry—Qualitative Issues," *The Examiner* (Winter 1984), pp. 21-28. See also, Casualty Actuarial Society, *Transcript: 1983 Casualty Loss Reserve Seminar* (New York: Casualty Actuarial Society, 1983), pp. 673-722.
2. Ernst & Whinney, *Property/Casualty Loss Reserve Disclosures Required of Public Companies* (New York: Ernst & Whinney, 1985), pp. 46-51.
3. Financial Accounting Standards Board, *Statement of Financial Accounting Standards No. 5: Accounting for Contingencies* (Stamford, CT: Financial Accounting Standards Board, 1975), pp. 20, 21.
4. *Statement of Financial Accounting Standards No. 5*, p. 48.
5. *Statement of Financial Accounting Standards No. 5*, p. 50.

CHAPTER 13

Financial Security

The value of a reinsurance relationship depends on the financial security underlying that relationship. During the 1980s, several major insolvencies resulted in uncollectible reinsurance for many insurance companies and disputed or delayed recoveries for others. These events convincingly demonstrated that an essential component of any reinsurance program is a systematic procedure for managing the financial security of that program.

Such a systematic procedure involves collecting information that relates to the financial security of current and potential reinsurance partners. While such information is available from many sources, certain kinds of information are especially significant. When information regarding a particular reinsurer involves a comparison to some established standards, that information has more value in managing the financial security of a reinsurance program. One set of standards is imposed by regulatory authorities. More stringent standards are used in determining the financial ratings issued by independent rating services. But the most stringent and most specifically relevant standards should be those established at the outset of any reinsurance program. While the other information sources are helpful, the ultimate responsibility for the financial security of a reinsurance program cannot be left to others.

INFORMATION SOURCES

Information sources concerning insurers and reinsurers include regulatory authorities, the Securities and Exchange Commission (SEC), informal sources, the Reinsurance Association of America (RAA),

155

A. M. Best, Insurance Solvency International (ISI), and Standard & Poor's Corporation (S&P).

Insurance Regulatory Authorities

The primary sources of information about insurers and reinsurers are the financial statements, audit reports, and other reports required or produced by state insurance regulatory authorities. This information can be obtained from the insurers or from the state insurance regulatory authorities that require or produce them. Because the information is filed with regulators, some organizations obtain the information from regulators and make it available to their clients. Much of the data shown in the financial statements, for example, can be purchased from the A. M. Best Company or from the National Association of Insurance Commissioners (NAIC). Other sources of such information for reinsurers are the reinsurance intermediaries (most of whom provide such information to their clients) and the rating agencies, A. M. Best, ISI, and S&P. Regulatory reports for each insurer include:

- NAIC Annual Statement
- NAIC Quarterly Statement (if required)
- License or authorization status in each state (For property-liability insurers this is partially reported in Schedule T of the Annual Statement. It is more fully reported in *Best's Insurance Reports* and *Best's Key Rating Guide*. It is also available from each pertinent state, and, for reinsurers, from reinsurance intermediaries.)
- NAIC Insurance Regulatory Information System (IRIS) Report, which shows various ratios pertinent to solvency for the previous year
- Holding Company registration statements and biographies of officers and directors

Securities and Exchange Commission (SEC)

These reports may be obtained from publicly held insurers that produce them or from the SEC. Some of this data is widely available from data bases through time-sharing computer networks. Such reports for each insurer are made up of the following:

- Annual financial statement (10K)
- Quarterly financial statement (10Q)
- Reports to stockholders
- Annual report of independent accountants

Informal

Much information is available through contacts with appropriate business relationships, including insurers, reinsurers, intermediaries, agents, brokers, competitors, and investors. Such information may include the following:

- Types, terms, and conditions of direct business and reinsurance assumed
- Terms, conditions, and participants of ceded reinsurance
- Management and ownership—strategies, business methods, and reputation

Reinsurance Association of America (RAA)

The RAA produces at least two informative reports. Usually these reports are widely publicized. They include the following:

- *Reinsurance Underwriting Review*, annual and quarterly (summary data for each reinsurer, and totals)
- *Loss Development Study*, annual

A. M. Best

A. M. Best Company publishes a variety of books containing a wealth of information. These publications, which are useful in analyzing insurers and reinsurers include:

- *Best's Insurance Reports*, annual
- *Best's Insurance Reports International*, semi-annual
- *Best's Key Rating Guide*, annual with two quarterly supplements
- *Best's Aggregates and Averages*, annual
- *Best's Insurance Management Reports*, weekly
- *Best's Review*, monthly
- *Best's Executive Data Services*, hard copy
- *Best's Data Base Services*

Insurance Solvency International

ISI publishes reports dedicated to examining solvency of insurers and reinsurers. These publications include the following:

- *International Reports Service* (analyzes over 1,100 reinsurers and insurers worldwide excluding the U.S.)

- *International Confidential Rating Service* (ratings and evaluations for over 750 reinsurers and insurers worldwide excluding the U.S.)
- *Classic Data Base Service* (financial data and text on over 1,300 insurers worldwide including the U.S.)

Standard & Poor's

S&P uses a unique system to gather and report its data on insurers and reinsurers, discussed later. The following are major S&P reports:

- *Standard & Poor's Insurance Rating Service* (worldwide insurer ratings, financial analysis, and information)
- *Standard & Poor's Insurance Digest* (quarterly abbreviated analyses and ratings for over 300 leading insurers)

REGULATION

Insurance and reinsurance entities are regulated primarily at the state level, although there are aspects of federal laws that apply to the insurance business. State regulation of insurance in the United States began early in the nineteenth century. However, state regulation as it exists today arose largely out of events that took place in the middle of the twentieth century.

The purposes of state regulation are (1) to assure financial solvency of an insurance company so that money will be available to pay claims and to refund unearned premiums, (2) to protect the public from unfair business practices, and (3) to raise revenue for states through premium taxation.

For many years the business practices of insurers were not regulated, nor was there any federal oversight to the insurance business. In 1869, in the landmark case of *Paul* v. *Virginia*, the U.S. Supreme Court held that insurance was not interstate commerce and therefore was not subject to federal laws. This ruling held until 1944, when the court's decision in the South-Eastern Underwriters Association case, alleging price-fixing, held that insurance was interstate commerce and subject to federal laws. Insurance companies were concerned by this finding because the Sherman Act of 1890 and the Clayton Act of 1914 could be construed to preclude activities such as combining loss data of insurance companies for purposes of generating rates. This prohibition could force smaller companies out of business.

As a result of lobbying by insurers, Congress passed Public Law 15, the McCarran-Ferguson Act, in 1945. This act recognizes that insurance is interstate commerce and is generally subject to federal regulation, but it exempts the business of insurance from certain federal antitrust laws, particularly as they relate to the rates used by insurance companies, as long as states had legislation in place by 1948 to regulate rates and forms. (The McCarran-Ferguson Act does not exempt insurance entities from the Sherman Act's prohibiting boycott, coercion, or intimidation.) All states developed rules and regulations for governing insurance rates and forms in that three-year time period. Many of these adapted the so-called "Model Bills" developed by the National Association of Insurance Commissioners, an association of the insurance commissioners, directors, and superintendents of the various state insurance departments. While many of these laws have been modified or changed in the years since the passage of McCarran-Ferguson, they are the basis for current rules and regulations governing insurance company activity.

Within a state, the insurance business is regulated in several ways. The principal regulatory authority is the Insurance Department or the Bureau or Division of Insurance, by whatever name it may be called. The Insurance Department is headed by a commissioner, director, or superintendent, who is either appointed by the Governor (or in some few cases the Legislature) or elected. Individual department organizations may vary, but in general there are two major kinds of activity: regulation of financial condition of the companies and market conduct regulation.

Exhibit 13-1 shows the organization chart of one state regulator.

Other state offices overseeing the insurance business include the Department of the Attorney General, which has the responsibility in most states for enforcing consumer protection laws outside of the insurance code, and the Department of Revenue, which collects the premium taxes, either directly from the companies or indirectly by means of collection by the Insurance Department.

The Insurance Department and the other state agencies are granted power by law to ensure compliance with the various rules and regulations established to control the insurance business. State laws generally provide that an insurance company must be licensed in order to conduct business in that state, and the Insurance Department has the authority to revoke or request a court hearing to revoke the license of any insurance company violating its requirements. Similarly, the attorney general has broad powers to regulate the criminal activity of insurance companies, their officers, and agents. Other enforcement activities of a lesser degree include fines and imposition of cease and desist orders.

Exhibit 13-1
Organizational Chart of Regulator—Bureau of Insurance

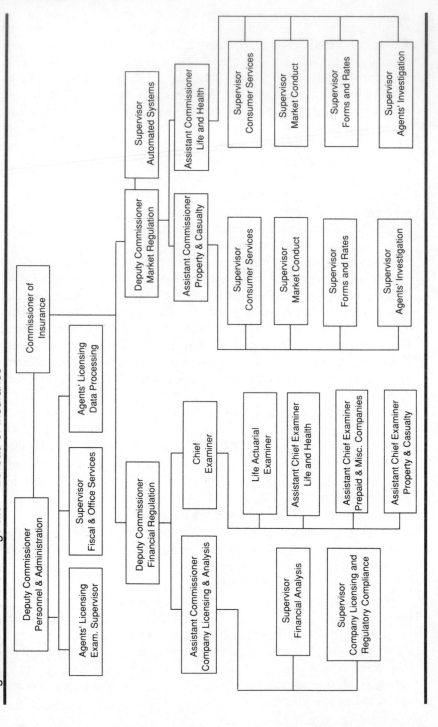

Aspects of Regulation

Although they are treated differently in some respects, both primary insurers and reinsurers are regulated by state insurance departments.

Primary Insurers. Primary insurers are regulated in areas of licensing, business history, rates and forms, investments, operating practices, and solvency.

Licensing. One principal regulatory activity is the licensing of insurance companies. Admitted primary insurers are those that hold a license from the state to conduct insurance business. All state insurance laws require that companies obtain a license before they begin any insurance activity. In order to obtain the license, minimal financial requirements must be met. While these financial requirements vary from one state to another, a typical law requires that there be $2 million of policyholders' surplus before a company may be licensed to write property and liability insurance business. In the case of a stock company, it may also require that $1 million of that policyholders' surplus be paid-in capital stock. For a company writing only one line of business, the surplus requirement may be less; for a company to write a very large portion of long-tail liability business, the requirements may be greater. Not only must a company meet these minimum surplus requirements to be licensed initially; it must also maintain a specific amount of surplus (which may be less than initially required) to have its license renewed from year to year.

Business History. In addition to financial requirements, the state insurance department examines the operating results of the insurance company in states in which it is licensed in order to determine whether it has acted properly in those states. It also reviews the experience of the officers of the corporation and inquires about them through a section of the licensing form known as the "general interrogatories."

Rates and Forms. Once a company has been licensed, most states provide for oversight of its rates for its products and the policy forms or contracts under which it provides coverage.

In the case of rates, most insurance rating laws provide that rates may not be excessive, inadequate, or unfairly discriminatory. An excessive rate is one that produces premiums in excess of those necessary to cover anticipated losses, expenses, and a reasonable allowance for profit. An inadequate rate is one that does not allow a company to cover its operating costs and losses, thus endangering the solvency of the company. A rate deemed unfairly discriminatory is one that does not reflect the true risk presented by the exposure.

More than half of the states require that rates for personal lines of insurance (homeowners and private passenger automobile, for example) be filed with the insurance department and approved by the department prior to use, while most other states permit the companies to use the rates once they have been filed but do not require prior approval of the rate before it is used. In a few states, rates are not filed, but they are subject to the review of the insurance department upon request. In the commercial lines of property and liability insurance, it is more common to require the rates to be filed with the insurance department prior to use by the insurer. In most states such commercial rates are subject to subsequent disapproval of the insurance department. All rating laws require an insurance company to use the rates it has on file.

Regarding the wording used in the insurance contracts and endorsements, states may have a different requirement than for the insurance rates. Many states that allow rates to be used without prior approval require that the policy form be approved before it can be used. Other states reserve the right to disapprove the policy form but do allow any form to be used once it has been filed. In certain personal lines in some states (such as automobile in Massachusetts), all insurers must use a policy form provided in a statute. Many state laws prohibit a certain type of exclusion or wording in regard to policy forms, deeming it in the public interest not to permit such restricted coverage. Insurance departments review policy forms to ascertain that they are consistent with the general forms of insurance usually used and are not misleading or unduly restrictive when compared to the standard expected by the insurance buying public. Some policy provisions, such as those dealing with cancellation and nonrenewal, are prescribed in state laws or department regulation. It is the duty of the insurance department to see that the policy forms filed in the state comply with those statutes.

Investments. Because of a concern for liquidity, state insurance departments also analyze the investment practices of the insurance company in question. A company is required to disclose to the insurance department a detailed listing of all of its assets. If these assets include investments that are risky or of questionable value, they may be disallowed (nonadmitted) in computing the policyholders' surplus of the company. Assets are also analyzed to make sure that their value is not overstated in financial statements.

Operating Practices. Insurance departments are also concerned with the operating practices of primary insurers and regulate these primarily through the unfair trade practices acts in the various insurance codes. These laws provide standards for the handling of claims, underwriting, rating, marketing, and advertising activities.

Typical state laws prescribe a minimal amount of time in which to respond to claims and provide guidelines for claim handling behavior. Similarly, certain underwriting restrictions, such as declining to insure individuals solely because of age, race, creed, or location of the risk, are prohibited by law. While many times these activities are brought to the attention of the insurance department through filed complaints, at other times they are uncovered through field investigations made by the insurance department's market conduct examiners.

Solvency. Primary insurers are regulated for solvency to determine whether they continue to have the capacity to honor future obligations presented against the company. Solvency regulation depends heavily on the statutory accounting rules under which the Annual Statement (described in Chapter 11) is prepared and filed.

Reinsurers. Reinsurers are treated somewhat differently from primary insurers. Reinsurers are regulated for solvency, but the international nature of the reinsurance business makes solvency review as well as rate and form regulation difficult. In regard to solvency, reinsurers generally are not as widely regulated as are primary insurers. A primary insurer can be examined by each state in which it is licensed, and the finding of insolvency can be reached by a state other than the state in which the insurer is domiciled. If a state finds the primary insurer to be in precarious financial condition, it can suspend or revoke the license to operate in that state. Reinsurers, on the other hand, are generally not required to be licensed in states where they only conduct reinsurance business, except for their domiciliary (home) state. Therefore, the primary regulatory responsibility for reinsurer solvency rests with the home state of the reinsurer. However, the financial condition of reinsurers is of concern to all insurance regulators, since a failure to honor claims of primary insurers by a reinsurer could cause the demise of a domestic primary insurer. Such an event can have a domino effect because of the multitude of reinsurance contracts that may be in place.

International Nature of Business. Another factor that affects the regulation of reinsurers is the international nature of the business. So great is the demand for reinsurance capacity in the United States that it cannot be met exclusively by United States reinsurers. At the same time, demand for reinsurance is worldwide. The net result of this international need for reinsurance is an increase in the number of reinsurers located overseas, as well as an increase in the number of reinsurance placements by United States primary insurance companies and United States reinsurers with overseas reinsurers. When a reinsurance company itself runs out of capacity, it looks for additional capacity through reinsurance of its own business (retrocessions).

Frequently these retrocessions are placed with alien (non U.S.) reinsurers. This international reinsurance activity makes it more difficult to track the financial condition of reinsurers. Alien reinsurers are not subject to individual state reporting laws. Their financial reports frequently represent different time intervals, state values in different currencies, and present results in different formats. The NAIC is taking steps to gather information from these international companies that is consistent with the financial disclosure required of domestic reinsurers. These international companies now make an annual reporting to the NAIC on its prescribed form.

Rates and Forms. Reinsurance forms and rates are not required to be filed for approval. The reinsurance business, being intrastate, interstate, and international, and necessarily limited to unique situations of the primary companies reinsured or the individual risks reinsured, does not lend itself to strict regulation of forms and rates. This lack of regulation of rates and forms creates problems in analyzing the financial solvency of reinsurers, since it is more difficult to know of all of the obligations and pricing of the reinsurer under its tailor-made reinsurance contracts.

The net result of these differences in regulation between reinsurers and primary insurers is that regulators conduct more detailed analyses to be assured that the reinsurance backing a primary insurer is in fact valid and collectible. This analysis relies on regulatory compliance tools.

Compliance Tools

Insurance regulations are enforced by different means, depending on whether the insurance company under consideration is an admitted company (licensed in the state involved) or nonadmitted (not licensed in the state involved, such as a surplus lines company or some reinsurance companies).

Admitted Companies. Admitted companies are subject to both market conduct and financial examinations.

Market Conduct Examinations. In regard to matters involving rates, policy forms, employee practices, underwriting, and market conduct activity, field examinations (called market conduct examinations) are conducted by state insurance department personnel. Market conduct examiners visit the home office or the branch office of admitted companies in their state to ascertain compliance with the various insurance rules and regulations. In general, the market conduct examination looks at four major areas: sales, underwriting, claims, and rating.

In examining the sales function, the examiner reviews the advertising materials used by the company to detect statements that are false, misleading, or otherwise not in compliance with state law. They also check to see that all of the sales personnel conducting business on behalf of the insurer are licensed as agents in compliance with state agency licensing law. (Employees of direct writers may not be required to be licensed.)

In the area of underwriting, both new and renewal policies as well as declined applications are reviewed to determine whether there has been any kind of behavior considered unfairly discriminatory or in violation of the various statutes governing cancellation or nonrenewal of insurance policies.

Market conduct examiners review claims activity to determine that companies are fairly paying amounts owed in a timely manner under the policies in force and that they are not violating any unfair claims settlement acts. Most states require the maintenance of a complaint register. Insurance department personnel examine these registers to see that they have been properly handled.

Finally, examiners look at new and renewal policies as well as at changes to those policies to determine that the companies used the rates in effect at the time the policy was issued. Analysis of these rates and their application to insureds shows whether the company has competed fairly or has unfairly discriminated among insureds of equal exposure by charging rates not consistent with the company's rate schedule filed with the insurance department.

Financial Examinations. In addition to market conduct examinations, financial examiners of insurance departments visit the home office of companies domiciled in their state and, often although less frequently, companies domiciled in other states to determine their financial condition. These financial examinations involve a detailed analysis of all of the financial transactions of the insurance company and generally take longer to complete than a market conduct examination (a market conduct examination may take anywhere from three to eight weeks while financial examinations can take anywhere from a month to over a year to conclude).

Financial examinations confirm the information provided to the insurance departments in the Annual Statement. This confirmation includes verifying that assets listed actually exist and are properly valued, as well as determining that all liabilities have been listed and are properly valued. Examiners audit and verify underwriting and investment income and capital gains and losses on investments, delineated by type of investment. They also examine, on a line of business basis, premiums earned, losses and loss adjustment expenses paid and incurred, changes in unpaid loss and loss adjustment expense reserves, and all reinsurance in force. Much of the operating data is collected for a five-year period. With this data on all the business written by the company in each state in the United States and its territories, deteriorating trends can be examined and analyzed on a state-by-state basis. Examinations also cover a review of the board of directors meeting minutes and provide for general interrogatories designed to show any unusual activity in the organizational structure or financial foundation of the company examined.

Results of Examination. Once market conduct or financial examinations have been concluded, they are translated into a written format known as an examination report. These reports are generally provided to the insurance company in draft form so that items of disagreement between the insurance department and the company concerning findings of the insurance examiners can be identified and discussed prior to the printing of the final report. The final report becomes a public document available to other insurance departments for review or for members of the public who may have an interest in the report. If these examinations have uncovered violations of the insurance rules and regulations in that state, the insurance departments may take any of a range of actions to correct a situation. These actions can vary, from a general agreement that the insurance company will take every step not to conduct such activities in the future, to the imposition of a financial penalty as punishment for the improper activity, to the most severe, and least employed penalty, suspension or revocation of the license of the insurance company to do the business of insurance in that state. If the examination reveals impairment of capital, liquidation or rehabilitation of the insurer may result.

Other Compliance Tools. Other means also promote compliance with financial and market conduct regulations. These include a review of Annual Statements filed with the insurance department or through a monitoring of complaint activity. In the case of financial condition, by reviewing Annual Statements filed with the insurance department, financial examiners can determine a change in the financial status of an insurance company. Because the format of the Annual Statement is devised to reveal unfavorable trends in the financial results of the company, a thorough review of the statement can identify companies that need closer attention. Some states require audited financial statements, certifications of reserves, or both. Where required, they may be reviewed for financial compliance.

In the case of market conduct, a review of the monthly statistics provided by the complaint department of most insurance departments generally indicates when one company's market behavior triggers a disproportionate number of complaints.

In addition, certain steps can be taken to provide some additional security for policyholders in each of the states through the provision of deposit funds. Many states require as a condition of licensure that a company deposit with the state treasurer funds available for the policyholders of that company should the company become insolvent. Once a company has been licensed for several years, it may be permissible for those funds to be withdrawn from the state as long as they are deposited in a policyholders fund in the home state of the insurance company and as long as verification of the deposit is provided annually to the insurance department. In addition, most state laws provide that additional deposit funds may be required as a condition for continuing the license of an insurance company when the insurance department has reason to believe that the financial condition of an insurer is worsening. These funds are held on deposit in the state treasury, and policyholders are given first priority on distribution of these funds should the company become insolvent. Most states also require licensed companies to participate in guaranty funds that are available to pay claims if an insurer is insolvent.

Nonadmitted Insurance Companies. Because of the differences of licensing and form and rate regulation of nonadmitted companies, the compliance tools are somewhat different, although not necessarily less effective. Nonadmitted reinsurance companies and surplus lines companies generally are required to be licensed in their home states or countries. In addition, some reinsurance companies also act as primary insurers in some states, as do some surplus lines companies. In those states where they are primary insurers, they are subject to all of the requirements for admitted companies. Therefore, the results of examinations by those states in which they are licensed are available to regulators in states where they are acting as surplus lines or reinsurance companies only.

There is a similarity in the way surplus lines companies and reinsurance companies are treated by states in which they are not directly regulated, since they are both indirectly regulated by control of other insurance entities licensed in the states. However, the approaches to this indirect regulation vary between the types of nonadmitted companies.

Surplus Lines Insurers. Since a surplus lines company is not licensed to do business in the state, it is permitted to operate in an unlicensed capacity on the assumption that it is providing coverage for exposures that cannot be readily obtained in the market provided by admitted insurance companies. Regulation is accomplished by regulating the in-state broker who places the business with the nonadmitted surplus lines company. Most state regulations provide that a surplus lines broker placing business with an unlicensed surplus lines company must have a special license and that the company with which the business is placed, although unlicensed, be on a list of companies approved to do surplus lines business in the state (called a "white list"). Approval is primarily conditioned upon the financial status of the surplus lines company. It is common to have minimum surplus requirements for surplus lines insurers higher than those for licensed companies to compensate for the inability of direct review of the records of the company. Surplus lines brokers are also generally required to file a form called an affidavit with the state insurance department every time business is placed with an unlicensed company and, through a review of these forms, the regulator can monitor compliance with the surplus lines laws.

In order for a surplus lines company to remain on the approved list, the surplus lines broker sponsoring such a company may be required to provide financial information about the insurer to the insurance department. Surplus lines brokers who place business with a company not on the approved list or who place business with a surplus lines company when such a placement may be prohibited subject themselves to monetary penalties or suspension or revocation of their surplus lines license. Some states do not have an approved list of surplus lines insurers. In these states, the broker is responsible to exercise care in selecting the insurer.

Nonadmitted Reinsurers. Similarly, direct regulation of primary insurance companies has an indirect effect on activities of reinsurance companies with which they do business in states in which the reinsurers are not licensed. State financial laws governing insurance companies require a reinsured to hold dedicated funds under its control to assure sufficient capital to (1) return premium should all in-force policies be canceled at any given point in time (the unearned premium reserve) or (2) collect reinsurance recoverables on loss payments. When business is reinsured, the amount of premium ceded to the reinsurer is released from the unearned premium reserve of the primary company, and those dedicated funds that remain with the primary insurer (principally the ceding commission) may be used by the primary insurance company elsewhere in its operations. In order to receive credit against this unearned premium reserve for cessions with reinsurance entities, the reinsurer must be approved by the insurance department, or other acceptable security must be available. This approval depends on the financial condition of the reinsurance entity involved. Credit is also taken on loss reserves for amounts ceded. The approval and security requirements can be effective deterrents to the placement of insurance with financially troubled nonadmitted reinsurers.

Also, there have been recent movements by the NAIC and several states to regulate the activities of managing general agents or reinsurance intermediaries somewhat similar to that of surplus lines brokers.

Other Regulations Applying to Nonadmitted Reinsurers. Deposit funds may also be required of surplus lines companies or reinsurance companies in order to be approved as accredited reinsurers or unlicensed insurance companies. In the case of alien surplus lines companies, trust funds are required to be on deposit in the United States for the protection of policyholders. The same requirement can also apply to alien reinsurance companies. In addition, the National Association of Insurance Commissioners collects information concerning all companies licensed in any state so that there is a central repository of information of a financial nature on every company licensed in the United States. Not only does the NAIC collect this data, but it also evaluates the financial statements of these companies and publishes results for members of the NAIC to review.

As an adjunct to the National Association of Insurance Commissioners, the Non-Admitted Insurers Information Office has been formed. It compiles information on insurers located abroad. This office does an analysis of the financial condition of these companies, analyzing their financial structure as well as their present financial results converted from their domestic currency to U.S. currency. This analysis provides a valuable service to state regulators who otherwise would not have the adequate resources to make these determinations.

Future of Reinsurance Regulation

Recent insolvencies of some large insurance companies have focused increased attention on reinsurance regulation. Some insolvencies of primary insurers were caused, in part, by uncollectible reinsurance due to the insolvency of a reinsurer. Poor management of the primary insurers also contributed to the insolvency, but the role played by uncollectible reinsurance in the demise of these companies attracted the attention of insurance commissioners among others. As a result, regulators sense the need for more detailed information concerning the financial condition of all reinsurance companies with which a licensed company does business. New statutory accounting requirements reduce the primary insurers stated policyholders' surplus when a reinsurance recoverable has not been collected within a specified time. Additional demands have come for licensing of all reinsurers, managing general agents, and brokers involved in any facet of the reinsurance business.

Regulation of the reinsurance business may become more intense in the years ahead and those transacting the reinsurance business will be held to a much higher standard. Attention must be given to the unique and worldwide nature of the reinsurance business as additional regulation is proposed to ensure a balance between regulation and commercial viability. Stricter regulation of reinsurance could diminish the availability of reinsurance capacity when it is needed the most on a worldwide basis.

RATINGS OF REINSURERS

The criteria that reinsureds use in selecting reinsurers include the ratings published by rating agencies. A reinsured that selects only highly rated reinsurers in conjunction with other criteria is likely to have fewer problems with uncollectible reinsurance and spend less time and resources evaluating its reinsurers. Nevertheless, a knowledge of how the rating agencies rate reinsurers is helpful in fully understanding the ratings, in evaluating the significance of changes that may occur in the reinsurers, and in evaluating information that a reinsured may possess and that may not yet be available to the rating agencies.

One important limitation of ratings is that their reports are delayed. For example, because the rating service considers an insurer's 1990 results that are not available until the end of the first quarter of 1991, the resultant rating may not be available until the third quarter of 1991.

A. M. Best Company

The A. M. Best Company rates all significant insurers and reinsurers licensed in the United States but so far has not rated insurers in other countries. Best's uses nine ratings and ten "Not Assigned" classifications. It also publishes a Financial Size Category based on the size of the "adjusted policyholders' surplus" for the insurer.

Best publishes its ratings annually in August, with advance releases in batches from April through July in its weekly and monthly publications. About October and December, Best's publishes a few rating changes in its weekly and monthly publications, reflecting changes in ownership and pooling arrangements, and so forth, and a few based on a review of quarterly results for the quarters ending in June and September. Also, throughout the year, Best's publishes changes in ratings that reflect regulatory actions such as appointment of receivers.

Best's publishes an explanation of its rating system in the preface of the publications that contain its ratings.

The rating system developed by the A. M. Best Company attempts to evaluate the factors that affect the financial performance of insurance companies in order to determine whether each company has the ability to meet the obligations of its contracts. Best's uses both quantitative and qualitative tests in analyzing the ability of a company to perform its future obligations.

Best's Quantitative Measures. Financial tests have been established over the years by the A. M. Best Company. These quantitative measures have been developed to analyze operating performance and financial condition of a company. These tests include measures of profitability, leverage, and relative liquidity.

Profitability Tests. For a property-liability company to continue as a viable entity, profit from operations is necessary. It is a measure of the ability of management to provide attractive insurance products and services to policyholders at competitive prices. At the same time the company must remain efficient and control costs in order to compare favorably with the competition. Profitability tests include the combined ratio, operating ratio, net operating income to net premium earned, yield on investments, change in policyholders' surplus, and return on policyholders' surplus. Exhibit 13-2 defines each of these ratios, among others.

Leverage Tests. Use of leverage increases return on capital and increases the risk of variation on that return. Best's uses seven leverage tests: (1) change in net premiums written, (2) net premiums written to policyholders' surplus, (3) net liabilities to policyholders' surplus, (4) net leverage, (5) ceded reinsurance leverage, (6) gross leverage, and (7) surplus aid to policyholders' surplus. These ratios are shown in Exhibit 13-3.

Liquidity Tests. An insurer must meet its obligations in the short run and in the long run. This liquidity requires holding cash and sound investments that are diversified yet readily convertible to cash. With a high degree of liquidity, an insurer has the flexibility to restrict its unprofitable lines and expand into more profitable ones. Best's liquidity tests include quick liquidity, quick assets, current liquidity, agents' balances to policyholders' surplus, premium balances to policyholders' surplus, and investment leverage. Exhibit 13-4 describes these tests.

Best's Qualitative Measures. Qualitative measures are judgments rather than mathematical measures.

Spread of Risk. The book of business is analyzed on both a geographic and a by-line of business basis. Geographic location can

Exhibit 13-2
Best's Profitability Tests

Combined ratio is the sum of the loss ratio, expense ratio, and dividend ratio. It does not reflect investment income or income taxes.

$$\text{Loss ratio} = \frac{\text{Incurred losses} + \text{Loss adjustment expenses}}{\text{Net premiums earned}}$$

$$\text{Expense ratio} = \frac{\text{Underwriting expenses}}{\text{Net premiums written}}$$

$$\text{Dividend ratio} = \frac{\text{Dividends to policyholders}}{\text{Net premiums earned}}$$

$$\text{Operating ratio} = \text{Combined ratio} - \text{net investment income ratio}$$

$$\text{Net investment income ratio} = \frac{\text{Net investment income}}{\text{Net premiums earned}}$$

Does not reflect capital gains or income taxes

$$\text{NOI to NPE} = \frac{\text{Net operating income}}{\text{Net premiums earned}}$$

Does not reflect capital gains

$$\text{Yield on investments} = \frac{\text{Net investment income}}{\begin{array}{c}\text{(Mean cash \& invested assets}\\\text{+ accrued investment income}\\\text{− borrowed money)}\end{array}}$$

Does not reflect capital gains or income taxes

$$\text{Change in PHS} = \frac{\text{Policyholders' surplus, year end}}{\begin{array}{c}\text{Policyholders' surplus (current)}\\\text{− Policyholders' surplus (prior)}\end{array}}$$

$$\text{Return on policyholders' surplus} = \frac{\text{Operating income after taxes} + \text{other investment gains}}{\text{Prior year policyholders' surplus}}$$

Exhibit 13-3
Best's Leverage Tests

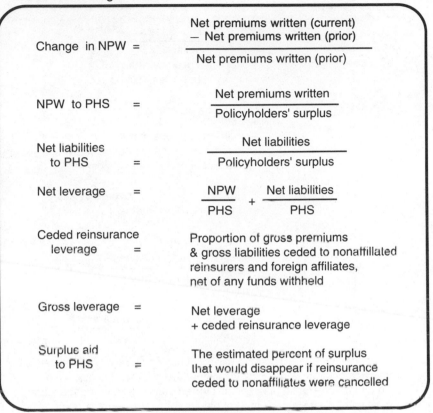

$$\text{Change in NPW} = \frac{\text{Net premiums written (current)} - \text{Net premiums written (prior)}}{\text{Net premiums written (prior)}}$$

$$\text{NPW to PHS} = \frac{\text{Net premiums written}}{\text{Policyholders' surplus}}$$

$$\begin{array}{l}\text{Net liabilities} \\ \text{to PHS}\end{array} = \frac{\text{Net liabilities}}{\text{Policyholders' surplus}}$$

$$\text{Net leverage} = \frac{\text{NPW}}{\text{PHS}} + \frac{\text{Net liabilities}}{\text{PHS}}$$

Ceded reinsurance
leverage = Proportion of gross premiums
& gross liabilities ceded to nonaffiliated
reinsurers and foreign affiliates,
net of any funds withheld

Gross leverage = Net leverage
+ ceded reinsurance leverage

Surplus aid
to PHS = The estimated percent of surplus
that would disappear if reinsurance
ceded to nonaffiliates were cancelled

have a great impact on the extent of its exposure to various hazards such as hurricanes, tornadoes, earthquakes, and so forth.

Amount and Soundness of Reinsurance. Reinsurance is essential and plays an important role in risk spreading and financial security of insurers. Both the amount of reinsurance purchased and the quality of reinsurers are examined.

Quality and Estimated Market Value of Assets. Assets are reviewed to determine the potential impact on policyholders' surplus if the assets need to be sold quickly. The higher the liquidity or quality of the assets, or both, the more certain the value to be received on the sale of these assets. The market value of nonequity assets depends on their yield and maturity, particularly with bonds. For this reason, the impact

Exhibit 13-4
Best's Liquidity Tests

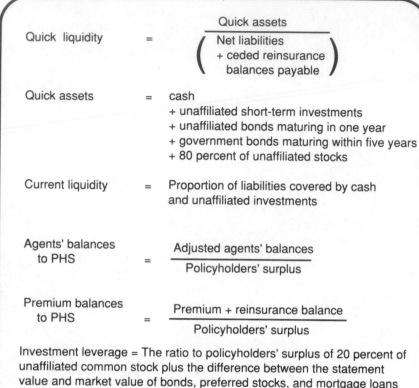

Quick liquidity $= \dfrac{\text{Quick assets}}{\left(\begin{array}{l}\text{Net liabilities} \\ \text{+ ceded reinsurance} \\ \text{balances payable}\end{array}\right)}$

Quick assets $=$ cash
+ unaffiliated short-term investments
+ unaffiliated bonds maturing in one year
+ government bonds maturing within five years
+ 80 percent of unaffiliated stocks

Current liquidity $=$ Proportion of liabilities covered by cash
and unaffiliated investments

Agents' balances to PHS $= \dfrac{\text{Adjusted agents' balances}}{\text{Policyholders' surplus}}$

Premium balances to PHS $= \dfrac{\text{Premium + reinsurance balance}}{\text{Policyholders' surplus}}$

Investment leverage = The ratio to policyholders' surplus of 20 percent of unaffiliated common stock plus the difference between the statement value and market value of bonds, preferred stocks, and mortgage loans that would occur if yields at market values rose 2 percentage points (200 basis points), expressed as a percent. This measures the effect on surplus of a 20 percent decline in common stock prices and a 2 percent rise in interest rates. Statutory surplus is not affected by a change in bond values, but if it were, this ratio measures what the effect would be.

on policyholders' surplus due to changes in interest rates on interest sensitive assets is estimated.

Adequacy of Loss Reserves. Loss reserves are essential to evaluating profitability, leverage, and liquidity. Policyholders' surplus is what is available to policyholders after reported reserves have been established. Thus if loss reserves are inadequate, then the surplus position is less favorable than it appears. Similarly, if the insurer has not established adequate reserves for losses during the period, then its reported net income is overstated.

Management. The integrity, competence, and experience of management, although difficult qualities to assess, are important factors for success in the insurance industry, where financial integrity and security are more critical than in many other types of business endeavors.

Best's Rating. The 1989 edition of *Best's Trend Report for Property-Casualty Insurance Companies* reported that of the 2,070 companies reported on in *Best's Insurance Reports*, approximately 66 percent were assigned a Best's rating ranging from A+ (superior) to C− (fair). The remaining 34 percent carried a "Not Assigned" rating. Assigned ratings appear as follows:

A+	Superior
A and A−	Excellent
B+	Very Good
B and B−	Good
C+	Fairly Good
C and C−	Fair

These ratings are assigned according to Best's opinion of overall performance of the company compared to the norms of the property-liability insurance business. The A+ (superior) rating means that insurers generally have demonstrated their strongest ability to meet respective policyholder and other contractual obligations. A C− (fair) rating means that the company has demonstrated only a fair ability to meet its obligations.

Rating Modifications for Performance. Each of these companies may also be assigned a *rating modifier* to qualify the status of an assigned rating. The modifier appears as a lower-case suffix to the rating (for example, Ac, Be, or Cg). The rating modifiers are as follows:

c—Contingent Rating
e—Parent Rating
g—Group Rating
p—Pooled Rating
q—Qualified Rating
r—Reinsured Rating
s—Consolidated Rating
w—Watch List
x—Revised Rating

Four rating modifiers are based on the performance of the company to which the modifier is assigned.

Contingent Rating. A Contingent Rating, "c," is temporarily assigned to a company when there has been decline in performance (profitability, leverage, liquidity, or a combination of these). Although the decline may not be significant enough to warrant a reduction in the overall rating, unless corrective action is taken, or more current adverse information becomes available, the rating may be reduced.

Qualified Rating. A Qualified Rating, "q," is assigned to a company that might be adversely affected by (1) pending state legislation that would mandate rate restrictions or (2) the possibility of payments due from mandated state residual market programs which are equal to, or in excess of, its policyholders' surplus.

Watch List Rating. A Watch List, "w" assignment may be given because of a downward trend in performance based on profitability, leverage liquidity, or a combination of these. However, the trend may not be significant enough to deserve an actual reduction in the assigned rating.

Revised Rating. The Revised Rating, "x," is given when the assigned rating of the company was revised during the year in which the rating is shown.

Rating Modifications Based on Affiliations. Five rating modifiers may be assigned to a company whose rating is based on an affiliation with one or more other property-liability insurers in the industry.

Parent Rating. An "e" Parent Rating may be received by a subsidiary company if the parent ownership exceeds 50 percent. The rating is based on the consolidated performance of the parent and subsidiary.

Group Rating. A "g" Group Rating may be given to a group of companies if they are related by either common management or ownership. Pooling a substantial portion of net business and having only minor differences in underwriting and operating performance would permit this Group Rating.

Pooled Rating. A "p" Pooled Rating is assigned to companies under common management or ownership that pool 100 percent of their net business. All premiums, expenses, and losses must be reasonably prorated in relationship to the policyholders' surplus of each member of the group.

Reinsured Rating. The "r" Reinsured Rating indicates that the Rating and Financial Size Category assigned to the company is that of an affiliated carrier that reinsures 100 percent of the written net business of the company.

Consolidated Rating. The "s" Consolidated Rating is assigned to a parent company and is based on the consolidated performance of the company and its domestic property-liability subsidiaries in which it owns 50 percent or greater ownership interest.

Not Assigned Rating. Approximately 34 percent of companies appearing in the Property-Casualty Edition of *Best's Insurance Reports* carry a "Not Assigned" rating. This designation (abbreviated NA) is divided into ten different classifications to explain why a company is not eligible for a Best's Rating.

NA-1 Special Data Filing. This rating is assigned primarily to small mutuals exempt from the requirement to file the standard NAIC Fire and Casualty Annual Statement blank. The report is based on selected financial information requested by the A. M. Best Company and received from the National Association of Mutual Insurance Companies (NAMIC) by way of a cooperative arrangement. Although the information received is reviewed and audited, and believed to be reliable, its accuracy is not guaranteed by either Best's or NAMIC.

NA-2 Less Than Minimum Size. In order to receive a Best's Rating, the following minimum size requirements must be met:

- Annual gross premiums written must exceed $3.5 million to provide a reasonable spread of risk on its book of business.
- Admitted assets must exceed $3.5 million in order to insure reasonable financial stability.
- Policyholders' surplus must exceed $1.5 million.

Exceptions to the size requirements for the company occur when:

- It is 100 percent reinsured by a rated company.
- It is a member of a group participating in a business pooling arrangement.
- It formerly was assigned a rating.
- It has a long history of consistent overall performance as compared to the norms of the industry.

A dormant company may also receive this classification, since it is associated with an active insurance company.

NA-3 Insufficient Experience. This is the classification given to a company when it has not accumulated five consecutive years of experience even though it has met the minimum financial standards. Some companies, primarily engaged in "long tail" liability lines, may require more than five years' experience to obtain a rating.

NA-4 Rating Procedure Inapplicable. This classification is assigned to a company when normal rating procedures do not apply, perhaps due to the nature of its business. Companies writing primarily financial guaranty insurance would be an example.

NA-5 Significant Change. This classification is assigned to a previously rated company that experiences a significant change in ownership, management, or book of business that alters or interrupts, or may interrupt, the general trend of the operations of the company. Depending on the nature of the change, a one-to-five-year period may be required before the company may qualify for a rating.

NA-6 Reinsured by Unrated Reinsurer. Companies with a substantial portion of their books of business reinsured by unrated reinsurers are assigned this classification. Exceptions are unrated foreign reinsurers that meet Best's financial performance standards and meet their reporting requirements.

NA-7 Below Minimum Standards. This rating is assigned to companies that do not meet the minimum standards for a Best's rating of "C-," but do meet its minimum size and experience requirements.

NA-8 Incomplete Financial Information. The classification is given to a company that fails to meet the deadline of submitting the required financial information for the current five-year period under review, but would otherwise be eligible for a rating.

NA-9 Company Request. This is assigned to a company eligible for a rating when the company requests that the rating not be published. This request also avoids the $500 rating service fee payable by each company receiving a Best's rating. Many captives operate in markets that do not require a rating, but cooperate with the A. M. Best request so that a report can be prepared. Companies not agreeing with their assigned rating or Best's procedure or both would likely appear in this category. After a company requests this classification, Best normally requires at least a two-year waiting period before issuing the rating.

NA-10 Under State Supervision. This classification is assigned when a company is under any form of supervision, restraint, or control by state regulatory authorities, including but not limited to, receivership, conservatorship, or rehabilitation.

Insurance Solvency International

Between 1986 and 1989, Insurance Solvency International (ISI) rated about 350 nonlife reinsurers and insurers in the U.S. and about 750 nonlife insurers and reinsurers outside the U.S. In 1990, ISI discontinued its ratings of U.S. companies, but it continues to rate companies outside the U.S. ISI uses four ratings, A+ (strongest), A (strong), B (acceptable for some lines of business), and C (inadequate security), as well as U for not rated. Provisional ratings (A, B, or C, enclosed in parentheses) may be assigned to insurers less than five years old.

ISI ratings are based on an analysis of the financial statements and management of the insurer or reinsurer examined. Size classifications are not used. Instead, ISI reports the policyholders surplus as well as its rating of the company. ISI considers several items:

- Underwriting exposure
- Ceded reinsurance
- Assets and liquidity
- Earnings
- Loss reserves
- Sponsorship

Underwriting Exposure.   Trends in premiums are compared to policyholders' surplus adjusted by consideration of the lines of business written and "market conditions."

Ceded Reinsurance.   ISI evaluations consider which reinsurers are used to determine any exposure to slow receivables or potential collection problems. In addition, the trend of net retention and reliance on ceding commission is examined.

Assets and Liquidity.   Solvency and liquidity trends are studied with particular attention to common stock investment and agents' balances.

Earnings.   Profitability is evaluated by the composition and trends in net income balanced against reserving practices that may distort the underwriting income portion of net income.

Loss Reserves.   Reserves and their reporting are studied with consideration given to the lines of business written, reinsurance effects, and discounting practices. The goal is to identify any reserve deficiencies or redundancies.

Sponsorship.   This factor includes the historical support the company has received, and can be expected to receive, from its owners. Both publicly held and wholly owned companies are examined for these commitments. The sponsorship category also measures the overall success of management in its ability to expand the capital base of the insurer.

ISI publishes its rating reports in loose-leaf format throughout the year in about ten batches per year. Most insurers are reported on only once per year, but significant changes for the insurer may trigger a second report.

Standard and Poor's Corporation

In 1989, Standard and Poor's Corporation published ratings indicating the claims-paying ability of about 300 major property-liability insurers and reinsurers worldwide. S&P uses four "investment grade" ratings from AAA (extremely strong) through AA and A to BBB (able) and six "speculative grade" ratings from BB (speculative) through B, CCC, CC, C, to D (under court order of liquidation).

The S&P ratings result from quantitative and qualitative examination of seven categories:

- Industry risk
- Management and corporate strategy
- Business review
- Operational analysis
- Capitalization
- Liquidity
- Financial flexibility

Industry Risk.   Based on U.S. operations, S&P evaluation of the relative risk the insurer faces considers (1) the threat of new companies entering its lines of business, (2) the bargaining power of its buyers, (3) the bargaining power of its suppliers, (4) the potential of alternate products, and (5) the rivalry among insurers in the segment.

Management and Corporate Strategy.   This subjective measure includes the organizational structure, the quality and riskiness of strategic plans, the managerial ability to carry out the plans, and the financial ability to carry out the plans.

Business Review.   This analysis considers the *revenue* impact of the type of insurance the company writes within lines of business and among its operational units. It focuses on growth in revenue, rather than on the impact of growth on profit.

Operational Analysis.   This portion of the analysis examines the impact on profit based on the ability of the company to carry out its plans. Underwriting performance, investment performance, and tax rates are studied to ascertain trends and return on assets. Loss reserves are carefully studied in this analysis.

Capitalization.   The use of and degree of both financial leverage and operating leverage are examined. S&P measures financial leverage by the traditional debt-to-capital ratio and operational leverage by the ratio of reserves to policyholders' surplus.

Liquidity.   S&P measures cash flow (1) from underwriting, (2) from investments, and (3) in total. Both sources and applications of cash are considered.

Financial Flexibility.   This area includes an examination of both capital requirements and sources. Individual items examined include sources such as new capital from the financial markets or current owners (parent corporation), potential sale of assets, reinsurance, and so forth.

S&P publishes its ratings reports in loose-leaf format throughout the year and announces its rating changes in the financial news publications. Most insurers are reported on only once per year.

Comparisons

All three rating services attempt to measure the financial security of insurers. A comparison of the methodology, however, suggests some differences. First, ISI tends to emphasize financial security in its ratings. Second, Best's and S&P emphasize both management ability and financial security. Finally, S&P appears to weight projected future results more heavily than ISI or Best's. However, none of the services reveal their exact procedures and analytical methods. In any event, if an insurer receives consistent ratings from all services, that is a strong indication of the security of that insurer.

National Association of Insurance Commissioners

In 1989, the NAIC prioritized insurers licensed in the U.S. into four categories according to the estimated need for regulatory attention: First Priority, Second Priority, Third Priority, and No Priority. In earlier years, fewer categories were used. This process of prioritizing insurers for regulatory examination was based initially (in the early 1970's) on the number of "unusual" results on eleven ratios calculated from the Annual Statement, and the recommended frequency of examination was based on the size of the insurer. Four or more unusual results was the initial criterion for prioritization.

Early studies showed that the "four or more unusual results" identified about 11 percent of all insurers and about 80 percent of the insurers that became insolvent within three years. But as this NAIC Early Warning System, later named the Insurance Regulatory Information System (IRIS), evolved, this test flagged a higher percentage of all insurers and fewer than were in fact insolvent. But by then, the system had become so widely accepted and politically sensitive that it was hard to change.

As a result, the original eleven ratios continue to be published, but they are no longer the sole basis for regulatory prioritization. The IRIS tests are now only one factor of many, and the other factors are not published. Currently, many insurers with four or more unusual results are not prioritized, and many insurers with fewer than four unusual results are prioritized.

The IRIS ratios are incomplete as a system, as they have always omitted the following factors:

- Information that required judgment, such as management, ownership, strategy, and history
- Information that was politically sensitive for regulatory bodies to use publicly, such as size (which is shown, but not counted as "unusual") and state of domicile
- Information not readily available to the NAIC, such as consolidated data (with subsidiaries), gross premiums, and liabilities (often distorted by pooling transactions with affiliates), and the amount of reinsurance with non-affiliates.

Nevertheless, because the IRIS ratios are published by regulatory bodies, they continue to be listed by the AICPA as relevant to reinsurance security, and they continue to be used by reinsureds to evaluate reinsurers.

Because the IRIS ratios are official and public, many reinsureds fear that critics will use the benefit of hindsight to allege negligence in failing to use the IRIS ratios to exclude a reinsurer that subsequently becomes insolvent after having four or more unusual IRIS results. Such critics ignore the corollary costs of excluding many solvent reinsurers as a result of using the imperfect and incomplete IRIS system. They also ignore the fact that the regulators no longer rely solely on the IRIS ratios to set priorities.

Exhibit 13-5 shows the eleven IRIS ratios and the standards used to identify unusual results used in 1989 (for 1988 data).

MANAGING REINSURANCE SECURITY

Unrecoverable reinsurance has been a prominent factor in several recent insurer insolvencies. As a result, the issue of reinsurance security now is receiving much more attention than ever. This increased scrutiny and the resulting "flight to quality" gives reinsurers an additional incentive to strengthen their balance sheets. In addition, because of the large sums involved, many reinsurance buyers and brokers have expanded the time and staff they devote to reinsurance security analysis. A careful review of this problem and the options available may help reinsurers to understand the needs of their clients and help reinsureds to reduce their risks and to allocate reinsurance purchases more wisely.

Although the complexity of managing the security of a reinsurance program varies with the type and size of that program, the security management process generally includes six basic steps:

Exhibit 13-5
IRIS Ratios and the Standards for Unusual Results

Ratio	Unusual Results Equal to or Over	Under
1. Net premium written to surplus	300	—
2. Change in net premium written	33	–33
3. Surplus aid to surplus	25	—
4. Two-year overall operating ratio	100	—
5. Investment yield	—	6
6. Change in surplus	50	–10
7. Liabilities to liquid assets	105	—
8. Agents' balances to surplus	40	—
9. One-year loss reserve development to surplus	25	—
10. Two-year loss reserve development to surplus	25	—
11. Estimated current reservo deficiency to surplus	25	—

- Selecting reinsurers for new and renewal reinsurance
- Establishing criteria for evaluating the security of reinsurers
- Limiting the amount of reinsurance placed with any one reinsurer
- Obtaining backup security for reinsurance agreements with reinsurers whose security would otherwise be inadequate
- Monitoring reinsurers selected in the past that continue to have outstanding obligations to the reinsured
- Documenting all these processes

While this description concentrates on placing reinsurance, a similar process applies in managing the security of a portfolio of reinsurance accepted.

Selecting Reinsurers

Selecting the right reinsurers for both new and renewal business is vital to the solvency and profitability of the reinsured. The four most important criteria used for this purpose are availability, price, security (financial ability to meet its obligations), and service. These factors can involve inverse relationships. For example, the weakest reinsurers in terms of security and service may be the most desirable with regard to availability and price. Reinsureds must evaluate the resulting tradeoffs. Some flexibility in selection criteria help to accommodate these tradeoffs.

Tradeoffs. Because selecting reinsurers involves tradeoffs among availability, price, security, and service, the senior officers of the reinsured are usually in the best position to evaluate which tradeoffs are most suitable. Since security is a relative concept, the role of the intermediary, if one is involved, is not to select reinsurers for the company, but to provide timely information about price, availability, service, and security.

Intermediaries, or those employees of the reinsured who buy directly, can provide better service when they understand the priorities of the reinsured. Intermediaries, for example, can use their contacts and knowledge to survey the marketplace for the best reinsurance protection available within the parameters the reinsured has set and offer advice on market conditions and expected changes in price levels and availability. That is why the responsibility for selecting reinsurers falls to the reinsured, which is the only party in the reinsurance relationship able to evaluate and determine its own preference between price and security. Reinsureds are also more likely to obtain the most appropriate reinsurance for their circumstances when they either select the reinsurers themselves or inform their intermediaries of their criteria and priorities for selecting reinsurers.

The American Institute of Certified Public Accountants has adopted a statement of position regarding the internal controls an insurance company should adopt to evaluate the financial stability of its reinsurers.[1] It defines extensive procedures for performing such an evaluation and states that a reinsured may delegate those procedures to a reinsurance intermediary. However, intermediaries normally do not accept responsibility for the evaluation or selection of reinsurers.

Unless the intermediary accepts this responsibility, it remains with the reinsured. This means that if the reinsured simply accepts whatever reinsurers an intermediary or adviser suggests, it has not truly delegated the responsibility for selecting its reinsurers. It simply has failed to define any criteria of its own, and it remains responsible for whatever reinsurers it accepts. Accordingly, a reinsured that places any priority on security specifies either a list of acceptable reinsurers or precise criteria acceptable reinsurers must meet.

Flexibility Required. Because availability, price, security, and service can involve tradeoffs, some flexibility is required in the selection process. If the reinsured sets the criteria for security too strictly, it may not be able to obtain adequate reinsurance, or the price may be too high. Similarly, if the reinsured sets the criteria for price too strictly, adequate reinsurance may not be available; or the security may be imprudently weak. How the reinsured's management handles these tradeoffs is a measure of its wisdom and skill.

It usually is beneficial to make several successive attempts to determine an optimum tradeoff. A simple and practical structure for achieving this goal is more important than engaging in a tedious and complex process of evaluating the financial security or price structure or any other aspect of a reinsurer in the selection process.

None of the components, especially security, can be measured exactly, even if unlimited resources were devoted to the task. Since a better-than-average result can be achieved simply, complex systems can be needlessly expensive, unnecessarily difficult to administer, less responsive, and less effective. A potential danger is that as a system for evaluating security becomes more complex, it becomes easier in practice for users of that system to find a way to justify choosing almost any reinsurer.

An effective system used by some reinsureds begins by setting a strict standard for both security and price. Then the reinsurers are canvassed. If adequate capacity is not available within the initial constraints, the reinsured has the option of relaxing the constraints for price or security or both, or of retaining the unplaced exposure.

If security constraints are relaxed, additional reinsurers are approached within the new constraints. If price constraints are relaxed, the reinsurers that declined to participate on the first approach are contacted again. But, this step means an increase in price for *all* reinsurers, not just those that are added, because all participants in an agreement normally require the same terms. If adequate capacity is still not available on the second attempt, the reinsured has the same options as before: it may relax the constraints for price or security or both, or it may retain its unplaced exposure. By using this procedure, the reinsured avoids overpaying for reinsurance and can control all relevant criteria (keeping in mind that uncollectible reinsurance is very expensive).

If the first attempt to place or renew reinsurance is oversubscribed, it is possible that the initial criteria were too lenient for security or price or both. It is not as easy to tighten criteria for a second attempt as it is to relax them.

Establishing Criteria for Evaluating Security of Reinsurers

The evaluation of a reinsurer's security can involve many complex considerations. To standardize this evaluation, reinsureds should establish certain initial criteria. Special circumstances may suggest some modifications of the initial criteria, but the more structured the process, the sounder the evaluation.

Initial Criteria. The most important and widely used initial criteria for security are size, rating, and ownership (and these may be interrelated).

Size. The influence of size on security is evidenced by the fact that the largest insurer in the United States to become insolvent in the past fifty years was the Mission Insurance Group (which wrote reinsurance as well as primary insurance). At this peak, Mission was the fifty-third largest property-liability insurance group in the U.S. The top fifty groups in the U.S. have about 75 percent of the market share. These facts suggest that the 400 to 500 insolvencies of property-liability insurers in the U.S. in the past fifty years have been confined to the smaller companies that overall held only 25 percent of the market share. Reinsurers have followed a similar pattern.

In light of this history, it is reasonable to establish a top category criterion for policyholders' surplus of reinsurers such as one that approximates the threshold for the top fifty U.S. insurance groups (called premier reinsurers in this discussion). In 1989 that threshold was about $300 million. This tier included about twenty-five U.S. reinsurers (including primary insurers that wrote significant amounts of reinsurance) that wrote about 65 percent of the market share for reinsurance written by U.S. reinsurers. A second tier of reinsurers includes those with a minimum of one-third as much policyholders' surplus (about $100 million in 1989) or, if they are wholly owned subsidiaries of premier insurance groups, a minimum of one-tenth as much policyholders' surplus as the first group (about $25 million in 1989).

Rating. The rating of a reinsurer by an independent source is a second security criterion that may be used in conjunction with size. The significance of high ratings as an indication of security is illustrated by a study of A. M. Best's Ratings presented in a hearing in September 1988 before the Maine Superintendent of Insurance. The study tabulated the ratings of the sixty-nine U.S. property-liability insurers whose insolvencies in the ten-year period from 1973 to 1982 resulted in a guaranty fund payment. According to the study, if the top two Best's Ratings (A+ and A) had been set as a criterion for choosing an insurer, 67 percent of all insurers would have met the criterion and 88 percent of those that became insolvent would have failed to meet it (based on the rating in effect five years before insolvency). Those failing to meet the A+ or A criterion would have been excluded.

The number of insolvencies has increased since 1982, but the proportion of insolvent insurers with Best's Ratings below A+ or A is approximately the same. It is doubtful that a reinsured with fewer resources to devote to financial analysis than Best's could improve upon the success of the rating agencies. Therefore, a second criterion for a "premier reinsurer" could be a Best's rating of A+ or A.

A reinsured that selects only premier reinsurers is likely to have fewer problems with uncollectible reinsurance and to spend less time and resources evaluating its reinsurers. This does not mean that this reinsured is a better evaluator of reinsurers than other reinsureds or the rating agencies. It means that this reinsured places a higher priority on security relative to price and availability.

Two other well-regarded rating systems became available in the 1980s. Insurance Solvency International rates about 750 of the most significant nonlife insurers and reinsurers outside the U.S. Standard & Poor's rated about 300 of the larger property-liability insurers and reinsurers worldwide. Best's rates all significant insurers and reinsurers licensed in the U.S., but none outside the U.S.

Another reasonable rating criterion for premier reinsurers is a requirement that the company have one of the top two ratings from all of the rating agencies that rate the company. (A— is the third rating for A. M. Best.) Standard & Poor's does not publish a rating for some large U.S. insurers at the request of the insurer. Accordingly, if Standard & Poor's publishes a rating of any of the affiliates of such an insurer, one should assume that it has rated the insurer but has not given it one of its top two ratings. If the insurer is assigned a rating below the top two categories of any of the three prominent rating agencies, caution is advisable. The second tier of reinsurers includes those whose ratings are in the top three ratings for each rating agency.

Ownership. A third important security criterion relates to the ownership and management of a reinsurer. They are reflected in varying degrees in the ratings published by rating agencies. A reasonable ownership criterion for a premier reinsurer could be that ownership, management, and book of business, for the group as a whole, have maintained reasonable continuity and success for at least twenty years and are well regarded by the reinsured or its peers. A second tier of reinsurers could include those whose owners have a long-term commitment to reinsurance and are well regarded, but have fewer than twenty years of continuity.

Modifications. Reinsureds often modify security criteria under three circumstances: (1) for some kinds of reinsurance, especially long-tail lines; (2) for some kinds of reinsurers, especially alien and nonauthorized; and (3) for maintaining continuity of relationships with existing reinsurers.

Long-tail Reinsurers. Long-tail reinsurance, such as excess of loss liability, involves a longer time frame and requires more expertise than property catastrophe and property pro-rata reinsurance. Accordingly, many reinsureds use stricter security criteria for long-tail reinsurance or restrict the amount of reinsurance placed with one reinsurer.

Alien and Nonauthorized Reinsurers. Alien reinsurers often are less familiar and more difficult to evaluate for reinsureds because of greater distances, national differences, fewer contacts, and the less stringent financial reporting requirements in most countries outside the U.S. Because of the distances involved and different currencies used, payments tend to be received less promptly from alien than from domestic reinsurers, diminishing the perceived quality of alien reinsurers. Further, alien reinsurers customarily expect face-to-face contact with reinsureds, which requires more travel and personal involvement by the management of the reinsured. This custom results not only from the reduced availability of financial information, but also from a greater emphasis on longer-term relationships.

But these handicaps for reinsureds are offset by the better solvency record of reinsurers in Western Europe and Japan compared with those in the U.S. For example, West Germany, which has 2,800 insurers, has had only one insolvency. Switzerland and Japan have had none in the last forty-five years. Western Europe and Japan also have much more conservative accounting practices. Accordingly, reinsureds familiar with all of those practices often require less reported capital and surplus of these reinsurers.

Nonauthorized reinsurers, which include virtually all alien reinsurers, are required to furnish letters of credit or equivalent security for recoverable balances so that reinsureds may obtain credit for such reinsurance in their Annual Statements prescribed by the National Association of Insurance Commissioners. Such letters of credit provide added security beyond that provided by the usual security criteria of the reinsured.

Long-term Relationships. Many reinsureds modify their security criteria, within reasonable limits, to include reinsurers that have served the reinsured well in the past. Continuity is an important element of good service. This is especially true for reinsurers that accommodated the reinsured during periods when availability of reinsurance coverage was a problem. Continuing such relationships helps to assure the reinsured of adequate capacity during future periods of capacity contractions.

Limiting the Amount of Reinsurance Exposure with Selected Reinsurers

Many reinsureds limit the amount of their reinsurance exposure with any one reinsurer according to the size of the reinsurer's policyholders' surplus. They do so in order to reduce the chance the reinsurer will retrocede part of its business, which often leads to delays on claim payments. Generally, a reinsurer is more likely to retrocede substantial portions of a block of business it has assumed when that block is more than 1 percent of its own policyholders' surplus.

By limiting the cessions based on the size of the reinsurer's policyholders' surplus, and the subsequent lower probability of a retrocession, the reinsured reduces its ultimate exposure to overly aggressive reinsurers. Premier reinsurers rarely expose more than 1 percent of their policyholders' surplus to any one risk. It is primarily smaller and newer reinsurers that subscribe to participations greater than 1 percent (sometimes as much as 10 percent) of their policyholders' surplus.

Also, the greater the participation in relation to the reinsurer's surplus, the greater the reliance on retrocessionaires and the greater the proportion of the reinsurer's commission income to underwriting income. A reinsurer that retrocedes a substantial portion of its business has the potential for both commission income from its cessions and underwriting income from its retentions. Too much reliance on commission income can lead a reinsurer to be more concerned about volume than profitability, thus weakening its solvency potential. In addition, if a company uses a large amount of retrocessions, the financial security of the retrocessionaires becomes as important to the primary reinsurers as the reinsurer's financial security. The failure of a retrocessionaire may cause the reinsurer to become insolvent.

Reinsureds generally need not limit the amount they cede to a premier reinsurer in relation to the policyholders' surplus of the reinsurer because premier reinsurers watch their own exposure. But, as an example, a limit of about 1 percent for second-tier reinsurers and 0.5 percent for third-tier reinsurers provides valuable security for a reinsured. It is reasonable to make an exception to this formula for wholly owned subsidiaries of premier insurers that retrocede to their parent. Other exceptions may be merited when backup security is obtained, or when price or availability considerations are more compelling.

Many reinsureds also limit the amount they cede to any one reinsurer on the basis of their own policyholders' surplus. This is especially true when ceding to other than premier reinsurers, where the risk of insolvency is more significant. The amount of exposure to any one reinsurer, especially nonpremier reinsurers, in terms of both the amount of one risk and the accumulation of balances recoverable, should not exceed the largest amount that the reinsured is willing to retain on any one primary risk or catastrophe.

Another way to reduce the credit risk is to insert a right of offset clause in the reinsurance contract. Then, to the extent that uncollectible recoverables are due to the reinsured, the reinsured can reduce any payment that may be due the reinsurer.

Backup Security

Backup security or collateral is sometimes used (1) to make acceptable a reinsurer that otherwise would not meet the security criteria of the reinsured or (2) to cede greater amounts to one reinsurer than the usual limitations of the reinsured allow. Backup security can take several forms, including letters of credit, funds withheld, and trust funds. Another form includes a guarantee from a third party, such as an affiliate of the reinsurer, or an affiliate of the insured to which the insured is directing the placement of the reinsurance.

Some guarantees are more an assurance of general support than a specific guarantee. Such guarantees often are referred to as "comfort letters." All guarantees, especially comfort letters, should be reviewed by the reinsured's attorney to verify that they are valid and sufficient. Although generally imprudent, occasionally a reinsured asks an intermediary to provide a comfort letter that serves not as a financial guarantee but rather as an assurance that the intermediary has exercised reasonable care in evaluating the financial responsibility of the reinsurer. Intermediaries normally do not supply such comfort letters because the letters may imply acceptance of the delegation of responsibility for evaluating or selecting reinsurers.

Monitoring Reinsurers

A prudent reinsured monitors its reinsurers during the life of the reinsurance agreements and for as long as any obligations remain outstanding. If a reinsurer's financial condition deteriorates during the term of the agreement, the reinsured may consider a mid-term cancellation (or delay payments as much as permissible). If such trouble develops while balances remain outstanding, the reinsured may wish to negotiate a commutation while the reinsurer is still trying to retain its active status in the marketplace.

The reinsured should follow a systematic program for monitoring changes in the ratings, surplus, assets, reserves, premium volume, ownership, and management, and for monitoring news reports, the timeliness of claim payments, and other information from miscellaneous sources. This information helps prepare the reinsured to take timely corrective action if unexpected financial problems arise with its reinsurers.

Documentation

The American Institute of Certified Public Accountants (AICPA) has issued a statement of position regarding the internal controls an insurance company should establish to evaluate the financial stability of its reinsurers. It is important that reinsureds maintain proper controls not only to minimize losses, but also to avoid litigation from stockholders and investors for errors and omissions. Material departures from the controls recommended by the AICPA would be identified as an exception in the auditor's report. Consequently, reinsureds are careful to document their compliance with the recommended control procedures.

The AICPA statement of position recommends the following, in part:

> The ceding company should have those internal accounting control procedures that it considers necessary to (a) evaluate the financial responsibility and stability of the assuming company (whether the assuming company is domiciled in the United States or in a foreign country) and (b) provide reasonable assurance of the accuracy and reliability of information reported to the assuming company and amounts due to or from the assuming company. The ceding company's control procedures to evaluate the financial responsibility and stability of the assuming company may include....[2]

There follows a comprehensive list of information sources, inquiry procedures, and analysis procedures, which include all available financial reports, regulatory reports, rating agency reports, and other sources.

The reinsured is not required to obtain all the information listed or to perform all the inquiries and analysis. To do so would be to duplicate and even go beyond the work of the rating and regulatory agencies, which in most instances would be impractical and uneconomical. AICPA standards only require the company to follow procedures that are adequate to "evaluate the financial responsibility and stability of the assuming company."

Sophistication and complexity are not the sole keys to success in evaluating security. Priority of security is more important. If priority is high, good security is easy to achieve with the criteria of size, rating, and ownership.

When the reinsured uses only premier reinsurers, it needs less information and analysis, but as the reinsured increases its use of second- and third-tier reinsurers, and especially unrated, new and little-known reinsurers, it increases its need for information and analysis. This is particularly true if the reinsured does not obtain available backup security and does not use prudent limitations. Not only will the reinsured be subject to a greater potential for loss from uncollectible reinsurance; it also will bear a greater burden of proof in any stockholder lawsuits alleging that its information and analysis were adequate.

SUMMARY

Because of the potentially devastating effects of uncollectible reinsurance, many parties have an interest in the financial condition of reinsurers. They include state regulators and independent rating services, as well as the reinsured companies. Information available from these sources facilitates management of the financial security of a reinsurance program, which includes a process for setting priorities in selecting reinsurers. By understanding the process primary insurers use in selecting reinsurers, reinsurers can adapt and better serve their clients.

The purposes of state regulations are assuring solvency of insurers, protecting the public from unfair practices, and raising revenue. Insurance is regulated by the individual states by an official who is either appointed or elected. Regulation of insurers differs for companies licensed in a state and those not licensed. Licensed companies are subject to both financial and market conduct examinations. They are regulated for minimum capital, business history, rates and forms, investments, operating practices, and solvency. Many reinsurers in most states are not licensed and are considered nonadmitted. A nonadmitted insurer is regulated differently because it is usually not licensed in each state (except its home state) and because its business is of an international nature.

Compliance tools for all U.S. companies are the financial and market conduct examinations and the publication of the results of those examinations. State regulators also examine the financial statements of admitted or nonadmitted insurers. Deposits may also be required. In the case of nonadmitted reinsurers, regulators may require dedicated funds or other security available to reinsureds.

To gather information on reinsurers, primary companies may examine documents filed with regulators and the SEC, as well as publications of the RAA, A. M. Best, ISI, and S&P. Best, ISI, and S&P

ratings provide independent evaluation of the financial condition of reinsurers.

The process used to manage security of reinsurers includes (1) selecting reinsurers, (2) selecting criteria for evaluating reinsurers, (3) limiting the reinsurance exposure to selected insurers, (4) obtaining backup security when appropriate, (5) monitoring reinsurers, and (6) documenting the process.

Selecting a reinsurer involves tradeoffs among availability of coverage, price, security (ability to meet financial obligations), and service. As some of these are inversely related, tradeoffs and flexibility are necessary in establishing the criteria.

The criteria for selection of reinsurers include size, rating, and ownership. Size and ratings are directly related to solvency. Ownership may reflect the degree of commitment to long-term relationships.

Limiting exposure to any one reinsurer helps avoid payment problems and ultimate reliance on lower tier reinsurers. Obtaining backup security or collateral helps to make an otherwise unacceptable reinsurer acceptable.

Once a reinsurance program is in place, it must be monitored to assure that selected reinsurers remain financially able to meet their obligations. For accounting and legal purposes, all parts of the process should be documented.

Chapter Notes

---

1. American Institute of Certified Public Accountants, *Auditing Property and Liability Reinsurance*, October 1982, sections 9, 20, and 21, reprinted in *Audits of Fire and Casualty Insurance Companies*, 4th ed. (New York: American Institute of Certified Public Accountants, 1982), pp. 92-93, 98-99.
2. *Auditing Property and Liability Reinsurance*, section 9.

Bibliography

Annual Statement Instructions: Property and Casualty (1989). Kansas City, MO: National Association of Insurance Commissioners.

"Auditing Property and Liability Reinsurance." *Audits of Fire and Casualty Insurance Companies.* 4th ed. New York: American Institute of Certified Public Accountants, 1982.

"Auto Insurance-1987." *Best's Review,* Property/Casualty Insurance Edition, September 1988.

Bornhuetter, R. and Ferguson, R. "The Actuary and IBNR." *Proceedings of the Casualty Actuarial Society,* Vol. LIX, 1972.

Casualty Loss Reserve Seminar Transcript (annual). Washington, DC: American Academy of Actuaries.

Din, Adel Salah el. *Reinsurance for the Professional.* London: Ocean Investment and Management, Ltd., no date.

Fisher, Gerald F. "Financial Reinsurance—Regulatory Aspects." *Research Review,* January 1987.

"Insurance Premium Distribution–1987." *Best's Review,* Property/Casualty Insurance Edition, August 1988.

Inzerillo, James. "The Security of the Reinsurance Industry—Qualitative Issues." *The Examiner,* Winter 1984.

Kwitny, Jonathan. "Brother Act: Hundreds of Insurers Search for Remnants of Missing Millions." *The Wall Street Journal,* October 12, 1976.

Langler, William J. *The Business of Reinsurance.* Hartford: Northeastern Insurance Company of Hartford, 1954.

Lanzone, Anthony M. "Analyzing Reinsurance Disputes," part one. *The National Underwriter,* Property & Casualty Insurance Edition, August 19, 1983.

_____. "Analyzing Reinsurance Disputes," part two. *The National Underwriter,* Property & Casualty Insurance Edition, August 26, 1983.

Launie, J.J.; Lee, J. Finley; and Baglini, Norman A. *Principles of Property and Liability Underwriting.* 3rd ed. Malvern, PA: Insurance Institute of America, 1986.

Loomis, Carol J. "How Fireman's Fund Stoked Its Profits." *Fortune,* 28 May 1983.

Malecki, Donald S.; Horn, Ronald C.; Wiening, Eric A.; and Donaldson, James H. *Commercial Liability Risk Management and Insurance.* 2nd ed. Malvern, PA: American Institute for Property and Liability Underwriters, 1986.

"Mentor Liquidation Hits Crisis Point." *ReActions,* June 1988.

Novik, Jay A. "The Other Side of Reinsurance or P/C Insurance for Life Actuaries." *The Actuarial Digest,* October 1987.

Peterson, T.M. *Loss Reserving Property/Casualty Insurance.* Cleveland, OH: Ernst & Whinney, 1981.

Property/Casualty Loss Reserve Disclosures Required of Public Companies. New York: Ernst & Whinney, 1985.

Reinsurance Statistics 1982-1987. London: Reinsurance Offices Association, 1988.

Rodda, William H.; Trieschmann, James S.; Wiening, Eric A.; and Hedges, Bob A. *Commercial Property Risk Management and Insurance.* 3rd ed. Malvern, PA: American Institute for Property and Liability Underwriters, 1988.

Salzmann, R.E. *Estimated Liabilities for Losses and Loss Adjustment Expenses.* Englewood Cliffs, NJ: Prentice Hall, Inc., 1984.

Statement of Financial Accounting Standards No. 5: Accounting for Contingencies. Stamford, CT: Financial Accounting Standards Board, 1975.

Statement of Principles Regarding Property and Casualty Loss and Loss Adjustment Expense Reserves. New York: Casualty Actuarial Society, 1988.

Strain, Robert W. *Property-Liability Insurance Accounting.* 4th ed. Durham, NC: Insurance Accounting and Systems Association, 1988.

Thirkill, David. "What Is Financial Reinsurance?" *Bermuda.* London: ReActions Ltd., 1987.

Tract, Harold M. "Liability of Intermediaries for Placing Reinsurance with Financially Troubled Insurers." *The Examiner,* Spring 1984.

Tract, Harold M. and Henderson, Donald B., Jr. "A Dangerous Position." *Best's Review,* Property/Casualty Insurance Edition, October 1985.

Transcript: 1983 Casualty Loss Reserve Seminar. New York: Casualty Actuarial Society, 1983.

Troxel, Terrie E.; Bouchie, George E.; and Young, Lowell C. *Property-Liability Insurance Accounting and Finance.* 3rd ed. Malvern, PA: American Institute for Property and Liability Underwriters, 1990.

Wollan, Eugene. "Caught in the Middle." *Best's Review,* Property/Casualty Insurance Edition, April 1986.

Wood, Glenn L.; Lilly, Claude C. III; Malecki, Donald S.; Graves, Edward E.; and Rosenbloom, Jerry S. *Personal Risk Management and Insurance.* 4th ed. Malvern, PA: American Institute for Property and Liability Underwriters, 1989.

"Workers' Compensation and General Liability—1987." *Best's Review,* Property/Casualty Insurance Edition, October 1988.

Index

M

N

O

P

Q

R

S

Appendix

Annual Statement
of
Fire and Casualty
Companies

Note: In the case of reciprocal exchanges and other types of insurers using special terminology, the printed items and references in this blank, if not appropriately changed, shall be construed to apply to such insurers in respect to corresponding data and information as the context may require.

ANNUAL STATEMENT
For the Year Ended December 31, 1989
OF THE CONDITION AND AFFAIRS OF THE

NAIC Group Code_____ NAIC Company Code_____ Employer's ID Number_____

Organized under the Laws of the State of_____, made to the

INSURANCE DEPARTMENT OF THE STATE OF

PURSUANT TO THE LAWS THEREOF

Incorporated _____Commenced Business _____

Statutory Home Office_____ , _____
(Street and Number)   (City or Town, State and Zip Code)

Mail Address_____ , _____
(Street and Number or P.O. Box)   (City or Town, State and Zip Code)

Main Administrative Office_____
(Area Code)   (Telephone Number)

Primary Location of Books and Records _____ ,
(Street and Number)

_____
(City or Town, State and Zip Code)   (Area Code)   (Telephone Number)

Annual Statement Contact Person and Phone Number_____

OFFICERS

President_____

Secretary_____

Treasurer_____

Vice Presidents {
_____
_____
_____
_____

DIRECTORS OR TRUSTEES

State of .... }
County of .... ss

.... President, ... Secretary, ... Treasurer of the .... being duly sworn, each for himself deposes and says that they are the above described officers of the said insurer, and that on the thirty-first day of December last, all of the herein described assets were the absolute property of the said insurer, free and clear from any liens or claims thereon, except as herein stated, and that this annual statement, together with related exhibits, schedules and explanations therein contained, annexed or referred to are a full and true statement of all the assets and liabilities and of the condition and affairs of the said insurer as of the thirty-first day of December last, and of its income and deductions therefrom for the year ended on that date, according to the best of their information, knowledge and belief respectively.

Subscribed and sworn to before me this

....................day of 1990

....

....President

....Secretary

....Treasurer

ANNUAL STATEMENT FOR THE YEAR 1989 OF THE ....
(Name)

ASSETS	1 Current Year	2 Previous Year
1 Bonds (less $ .... liability for asset transfers with put options)		
2 Stocks:		
2.1 Preferred stocks		
2.2 Common stocks		
3 Mortgage loans on real estate		
4 Real estate:		
4.1 Properties occupied by the company (less $ .... encumbrances)		
4.2 Other properties (less $ .... encumbrances)		
5 Collateral loans		
6.1 Cash on hand and on deposit		
6.2 Short-term investments		
7 Other invested assets		
8 Aggregate write-ins for invested assets		
8a. Subtotals, cash and invested assets (Items 1 to 8)		
9 Agents' balances or uncollected premiums:		
9.1 Premiums and agents' balances in course of collection		
9.2 Premiums, agents' balances and installments booked but deferred and not yet due		
9.3 Accrued retrospective premiums		
10 Funds held by or deposited with reinsured companies		
11 Bills receivable, taken for premiums		
12 Reinsurance recoverable on loss payments		
13 Federal income tax recoverable		
14 Electronic data processing equipment		
15 Interest, dividends and real estate income due and accrued		
16 Receivable from parent, subsidiaries and affiliates		
17 Equities and deposits in pools and associations		
18 Amounts receivable relating to uninsured accident and health plans		
20 Aggregate write-ins for other than invested assets		
21 TOTALS (Items 8a through 20)		
DETAILS OF WRITE-INS AGGREGATED AT ITEM 8 FOR INVESTED ASSETS		
0801		
0802		
0803		
0804		
0805		
0898 Summary of remaining write-ins for Item 8 from overflow page		
0899 TOTALS (Items 0801 thru 0805 plus 0898) (Page 2, Item 8)		
DETAILS OF WRITE-INS AGGREGATED AT ITEM 20 FOR OTHER THAN INVESTED ASSETS		
2001		
2002		
2003		
2004		
2005		
2098 Summary of remaining write-ins for Item 20 from overflow page		
2099 TOTALS (Items 2001 thru 2005 plus 2098) (Page 2, Item 20)		

NOTE: The items on this page to agree with Exhibit 1, Col. 4
The Notes to Financial Statements are an integral part of this statement

ANNUAL STATEMENT FOR THE YEAR 1989 OF THE ....
                                                                                    (Name)

			1 Current Year	2 Previous Year
		LIABILITIES, SURPLUS AND OTHER FUNDS		
1		Losses (Part 3A, Column 5, Item 32)		
1A		Reinsurance payable on paid losses (Schedule F, Part 1A, Section 2, Column 1)		
2		Loss adjustment expenses (Part 3A, Column 6, Item 32)		
3		Contingent commissions and other similar charges		
4		Other expenses (excluding taxes, licenses and fees)		
5		Taxes, licenses and fees (excluding federal and foreign income taxes)		
6		Federal and foreign income taxes (excluding deferred taxes)		
7		Borrowed money		
8		Interest including $ on borrowed money		
9		Unearned premiums (Part 2A, Column 5, Item 34)		
10		Dividends declared and unpaid		
	(a)	Stockholders		
	(b)	Policyholders		
11		Funds held by company under reinsurance treaties		
12		Amounts withheld or retained by company for account of others		
13a		Unearned premiums on reinsurance in unauthorized companies $		
13b		Reinsurance on paid losses $ and on unpaid reported losses $		
		and on incurred but not reported losses $ recoverable from unauthorized		
		companies $		
13c		Paid and unpaid allocated loss adjustment expenses recoverable from unauthorized companies $		
13d		Less funds held or retained by company for account of such		
		unauthorized companies as per Schedule F, Part 2, Column 6 $		
13e		Provision for overdue authorized reinsurance as per Schedule F, Part 2B, Section 2 $		
14		Provision for reinsurance (Items 13a + 13b + 13c + 13e − 13d)		
15		Excess of statutory reserves over statement reserves (Schedule P Interrogatories)		
16		Net adjustments in assets and liabilities due to foreign exchange rates		
17		Drafts outstanding		
18		Payable to parent, subsidiaries and affiliates		
19		Payable for securities		
20		Liability for amounts held under uninsured accident and health plans		
21		Aggregate write-ins for liabilities		
22		Total liabilities (Items 1 through 21)		
23		Aggregate write-ins for special surplus funds		
24A		Common capital stock		
24B		Preferred capital stock		
24C		Aggregate write-ins for other than special surplus funds		
25A		Gross paid in and contributed surplus		
25B		Unassigned funds (surplus)		
25C		Less treasury stock at cost		
	(1)	shares common (value included in Item 24 A $)		
	(2)	shares preferred (value included in Item 24 B $)		
26		Surplus as regards policyholders (Items 23 to 25B, less 25C) (Page 4, Item 32)		
27		TOTALS (Page 2, Item 21)		

DETAILS OF WRITE-INS AGGREGATED AT ITEM 21 FOR LIABILITIES

2101				
2102				
2103				
2104				
2105				
2198	Summary of remaining write-ins for Item 21 from overflow page			
2199	TOTALS (Items 2101 thru 2105 plus 2198) (Page 3, Item 21)			

DETAILS OF WRITE-INS AGGREGATED AT ITEM 23 FOR SPECIAL SURPLUS FUNDS

2301				
2302				
2303				
2304				
2305				
2398	Summary of remaining write-ins for Item 23 from overflow page			
2399	TOTALS (Items 2301 thru 2305 plus 2398) (Page 3, Item 23)			

DETAILS OF WRITE-INS AGGREGATED AT ITEM 24C FOR OTHER THAN SPECIAL SURPLUS FUNDS

24C01				
24C02				
24C03				
24C04				
24C05				
24C98	Summary of remaining write-ins for Item 24C from overflow page			
24C99	TOTALS (Items 24C01 thru 24C05 plus 24C98) (Page 3, Item 24C)			

ANNUAL STATEMENT FOR THE YEAR 1989 OF THE ....
(Name)

	1 Current Year	2 Previous Year
UNDERWRITING AND INVESTMENT EXHIBIT		
STATEMENT OF INCOME		
UNDERWRITING INCOME		
1 Premiums earned (Part 2, Column 4, Item 32)		
DEDUCTIONS		
2 Losses incurred (Part 3, Column 7, Item 32)		
3 Loss expenses incurred (Part 4, Column 1, Item 22)		
4 Other underwriting expenses incurred (Part 4, Column 2, Item 22)		
5 Aggregate write-ins for underwriting deductions		
6 Total underwriting deductions (Items 2 through 5)		
7 Net underwriting gain or (loss) (Item 1 minus 6)		
INVESTMENT INCOME		
8 Net investment income earned (Part 1, Item 15)		
9 Net realized capital gains or (losses) (Part 1A, Item 11)		
9A Net investment gain or (loss) (Items 8 + 9)		
OTHER INCOME		
10 Net gain or (loss) from agents or premium balances charged off		
(amount recovered $ amount charged off $)		
11 Finance and service charges not included in premiums (Schedule T Column 8 total)		
12 Aggregate write-ins for miscellaneous income		
13 Total other income (Items 10 through 12)		
14 Net income before dividends to policyholders and before federal and foreign income taxes (Items 7 + 9A - 13)		
14A Dividends to policyholders (Exhibit 3, Item 16, plus Page 3, Item 10b, Column 1 minus 2)		
14B Net income after dividends to policyholders but before federal and foreign income taxes (Item 14 minus 14A)		
15 Federal and foreign income taxes incurred		
16 Net income (Item 14B minus 15) (to Item 18)		
CAPITAL AND SURPLUS ACCOUNT		
17 Surplus as regards policyholders, December 31 previous year (Page 4, Column 2, Item 32)		
GAINS AND (LOSSES) IN SURPLUS		
18 Net income (from Item 16)		
19 Net unrealized capital gains or losses (Part 1A, Item 12)		
20 Change in non-admitted assets (Exhibit 2, Item 31, Col 3)		
21 Change in liability for reinsurance (Page 3, Item 14, Column 2 minus 1)		
22 Change in foreign exchange adjustment		
23 Change in excess of statutory reserves over statement reserves (Page 3, Item 15, Column 2 minus 1)		
24 Capital changes		
(a) Paid in (Exhibit 3, Item 6)		
(b) Transferred from surplus (Stock Divd)		
(c) Transferred to surplus		
25 Surplus adjustments		
(a) Paid in (Exhibit 3, Item 7)		
(b) Transferred to capital (Stock Divd)		
(c) Transferred from capital		
26 Net remittances from or (to) Home Office (Exhibit 3, Items 4b minus 12b)		
27 Dividends to stockholders (cash)		
28 Change in treasury stock (Page 3, Item 25C (1) and (2), Column 2 minus 1)		
29 Extraordinary amounts of taxes for prior years		
30 Aggregate write-ins for gains and losses in surplus		
31 Change in surplus as regards policyholders for the year (Items 18 through 30)		
32 Surplus as regards policyholders, December 31 current year (Items 17 plus 31) (Page 3, Item 26)		
DETAILS OF WRITE-INS AGGREGATED AT ITEM 5 FOR UNDERWRITING DEDUCTIONS		
0501		
0502		
0503		
0504		
0505		
0598 Summary of remaining write-ins for Item 5 from overflow page		
0599 TOTALS (Items 0501 thru 0505 plus 0598) (Page 4, Item 5)		
DETAILS OF WRITE-INS AGGREGATED AT ITEM 12 FOR MISCELLANEOUS INCOME		
1201		
1202		
1203		
1204		
1205		
1298 Summary of remaining write-ins for Item 12 from overflow page		
1299 TOTALS (Items 1201 thru 1205 plus 1298) (Page 4, Item 12)		
DETAILS OF WRITE-INS AGGREGATED AT ITEM 30 FOR GAINS AND LOSSES IN SURPLUS		
3001		
3002		
3003		
3004		
3005		
3098 Summary of remaining write-ins for Item 30 from overflow page		
3099 TOTALS (Items 3001 thru 3005 plus 3098) (Page 4, Item 30)		

ANNUAL STATEMENT FOR THE YEAR 1989 OF THE ....

(Name)

	1 Current Year	2 Previous Year

CASH FLOW

1. Premiums collected net of reinsurance		
2. Loss and loss adjustment expenses paid (net of salvage and subrogation)		
3. Underwriting expenses paid		
4. Other underwriting income (expenses)		
5. Cash from underwriting (Item 1 minus item 2 minus item 3 plus item 4)		
6. Investment income (net of investment expense)		
7. Other income (expenses)		
8. Dividends to policyholders paid		
9. Federal income taxes (paid) recovered		
10. Net cash from operations (Item 5 plus item 6 plus item 7 minus item 8 plus item 9)		
11. Proceeds from investments sold, matured or repaid:		
11.1 Bonds		
11.2 Stocks		
11.3 Mortgage loans		
11.4 Real estate		
11.5 Collateral loans		
11.6 Other invested assets		
11.7 Net gains or (losses) on cash and short-term investments		
11.8 Miscellaneous proceeds		
11.9 Total investment proceeds (Items 11.1 thru 11.8)		
12. Other cash provided:		
12.1 Net transfers from affiliates		
12.2 Borrowed funds received		
12.3 Capital paid in		
12.4 Surplus paid in		
12.5 Other sources		
12.6 Total other cash provided (Items 12.1 thru 12.5)		
13. Total (Item 10 plus item 11.9 plus item 12.6)		
14. Cost of investments acquired (long-term only):		
14.1 Bonds		
14.2 Stocks		
14.3 Mortgage loans		
14.4 Real estate		
14.5 Collateral loans		
14.6 Other invested assets		
14.7 Miscellaneous applications		
14.8 Total investments acquired (Items 14.1 thru 14.7)		
15. Other cash applied:		
15.1 Dividends to stockholders paid		
15.2 Net transfers to affiliates		
15.3 Borrowed funds repaid		
15.4 Other applications		
15.5 Total other cash applied (Items 15.1 thru 15.4)		
16. Total (Item 14.8 plus item 15.5)		
17. Net change in cash and short-term investments (Item 13 minus Item 16)		

RECONCILIATION

18. Cash and short-term investments:		
18.1 Beginning of year		
18.2 End of year (Item 17 plus item 18.1)		

UNDERWRITING AND INVESTMENT EXHIBIT

PART 1 — INTEREST, DIVIDENDS AND REAL ESTATE INCOME

1	2	3	Paid in Advance		Due and Accrued‡		8
	Schedule	Collected During Year Less Paid For Accrued On Purchases	4 Current Year	5 Previous Year	6 Current Year	7 Previous Year	Earned During Year 3 + 5 + 6 − 4 − 7
1 U.S. government bonds	D*						
1.1 Bonds exempt from U.S. tax	D*						
1.2 Other bonds (unaffiliated)	D*						
1.3 Bonds of affiliates	D*						
2.1 Preferred stocks (unaffiliated)	D						
2.11 Preferred stocks of affiliates	D						
2.2 Common stocks (unaffiliated)	D						
2.21 Common stocks of affiliates	D						
3. Mortgage loans	B†						
4. Real estate	A§						
5. Collateral loans	C						
6.1 Cash on hand and on deposit	N						
6.2 Short-term investments	DA**						
7. Other invested assets	BA						
8. Financial options and futures	DB						
9. Aggregate write-ins for investment income							
10 TOTALS		#					#

	DEDUCTIONS	
11. Total investment expenses incurred (Part 4, Col. 3, Item 22)		
12. Depreciation on real estate (for companies which depreciate annually on a formula basis)		
13. Aggregate write-ins for deductions from investment income		
14. Total deductions (Items 11 to 13)		
15. Net Investment Income Earned (Item 10 minus Item 14—to Page 4, Item 8)		

*Includes $ .... accrual of discount less $ .... amortization of premium. **Includes $ .... accrual of discount less $ .... amortization of premium.
†Includes $ .... accrual of discount less $ .... amortization of premium. ‡Admitted items only. State basis of exclusions ....
§Includes $ .... for company's occupancy of its own buildings #Includes for asset transfers with put options accounted for as financing arrangements: $ .... Column 3, $ .... Column 8.

DETAILS OF WRITE-INS AGGREGATED AT ITEM 9 OF PART 1

1	2	3	4	5	6	7	8
0901.							
0902.							
0903.							
0904.							
0905.							
0998. Summary of remaining write-ins for Item 9 from overflow page							
0999. TOTALS (Items 0901 thru 0905 plus 0998) (Part 1, Item 9)							

DETAILS OF WRITE-INS AGGREGATED AT ITEM 13 OF PART 1

	DEDUCTIONS
1301.	
1302.	
1303.	
1304.	
1305.	
1398. Summary of remaining write-ins for Item 13 from overflow page	
1399. TOTALS (Items 1301 thru 1305 plus 1398) (Part 1, Item 13)	

PART 1A—CAPITAL GAINS AND (LOSSES) ON INVESTMENTS

1	2 Profit on Sales or Maturity	3 Loss on Sales or Maturity	4 Increases by Adjustment in Book Value	5 Decreases by Adjustment in Book Value	6 Net Gain or (Loss) from Change in Difference Between Book and Admitted Values	7 Total (Net of Cols. 2 to 6 incl.) (2 − 3 + 4 − 5 + 6)
1. U.S. government bonds						
1.1 Bonds exempt from U.S. tax						
1.2 Other bonds (unaffiliated)						
1.3 Bonds of affiliates						
2.1 Preferred stocks (unaffiliated)						
2.11 Preferred stocks of affiliates						
2.2 Common stocks (unaffiliated)						
2.21 Common stocks of affiliates						
3. Mortgage loans						
4. Real estate				‡		
5. Collateral loans						
6.1 Cash on hand and on deposit						
6.2 Short-term investments						
7. Other invested assets						
8. Financial options and futures						
9. Aggregate write-ins for capital gains and (losses)						
10. TOTALS						

(Distribution of Item 10, Col. 7)	
11. Net realized capital gains or (losses)* (Page 4, Item 9) (Col. 2-3, Item 10)	
12. Net unrealized capital gains or (losses)* (Page 4, Item 19) (Col. 4 − 5 + 6, Item 10)	

*Attach statement or memorandum explaining basis of division. ‡Excluding $ .... depreciation on real estate included in Part 1, Item 12.

DETAILS OF WRITE-INS AGGREGATED AT ITEM 9 OF PART 1A

1	2	3	4	5	6	7
0901.						
0902.						
0903.						
0904.						
0905.						
0998. Summary of remaining write-ins for Item 9 from overflow page						
0999. TOTALS (Items 0901 thru 0905 plus 0998) (Part 1A, Item 9)						

ANNUAL STATEMENT FOR THE YEAR 1989 OF THE ....
(Name)

UNDERWRITING AND INVESTMENT EXHIBIT

PART 2 — PREMIUMS EARNED

Line of Business	1 Net Premiums Written Per Column 4, Part 2B	2 Unearned Premiums Dec 31 Previous Year — per Col 3 Last Year's Part 2	3 Unearned Premiums Dec 31 Current Year — per Col 5 Part 2A	4 Premiums Earned During Year Cols 1 + 2 − 3
1. Fire				
2. Allied lines				
3. Farmowners multiple peril				
4. Homeowners multiple peril				
5. Commercial multiple peril				
8. Ocean marine				
9. Inland marine				
10. Financial guaranty				
11. Medical malpractice				
12. Earthquake				
13. Group accident and health				
14. Credit accident and health (group and individual)				
15. Other accident and health				
16. Workers' compensation				
17. Other liability				
19. Auto liability				
21. Auto phys. damage				
22. Aircraft (all perils)				
23. Fidelity				
24. Surety				
25. Glass				
26. Burglary and theft				
27. Boiler and machinery				
28. Credit				
29. International				
30A. Reinsurance*				
30B. Reinsurance*				
30C. Reinsurance*				
30D. Reinsurance*				
31. Aggregate write-ins for other lines of business				
32. TOTALS				

DETAILS OF WRITE-INS AGGREGATED AT ITEM 31

3101.				
3102.				
3103.				
3104.				
3105.				
3198. Summary of remaining write-ins for Item 31 from overflow page				
3199. TOTALS (Items 3101 thru 3105 plus 3198) (Item 31)				

*See Line 30 Instructions

ANNUAL STATEMENT FOR THE YEAR 1989 OF THE ....

.... (Name)

UNDERWRITING AND INVESTMENT EXHIBIT

PART 2A — RECAPITULATION OF ALL PREMIUMS

†Gross premiums (less reinsurance) and unearned premiums on all unexpired risks and reserve for return premiums under rate credit or retrospective rating plans based upon experience, viz:

Line of Business	1 Amount Unearned* (Running One Year or Less from Date of Policy)	2 Amount Unearned* (Running More than One Year from Date of Policy)	3 Advance Premiums (100%)	4 Reserve for Rate Credits and Retrospective Adjustments Based on Experience	5 Total Reserve for Unearned Premiums 1 + 2 + 3 + 4
1. Fire					
2. Allied lines					
3. Farmowners multiple peril					
4. Homeowners multiple peril					
5. Commercial multiple peril					
8. Ocean marine					
9. Inland marine					
10. Financial guaranty					
11. Medical malpractice					
12. Earthquake					
13. Group accident and health					
14. Credit accident and health (group and individual)**			(b)		
15. Other accident and health			(b)		
16. Workers' compensation					
17. Other liability					
19. Auto liability					
21. Auto phys. damage					
22. Aircraft (all perils)					
23. Fidelity					
24. Surety					
25. Glass					
26. Burglary and theft					
27. Boiler and machinery					
28. Credit					
29. International					
30A. Reinsurance***					
30B. Reinsurance***					
30C. Reinsurance***					
30D. Reinsurance***					
31. Aggregate write-ins for other lines of business					
32. TOTALS					

33. Accrued retrospective premiums based on experience ....
34. Balance (Line 32 plus line 33) ....

DETAILS OF WRITE-INS AGGREGATED AT ITEM 31

3101					
3102					
3103					
3104					
3105					
3198. Summary of remaining write-ins for item 31 from overflow page					
3199. TOTALS (Items 3101 thru 3105 plus 3198) (Item 31)					

*By gross premiums is meant the aggregate of all the premiums written in the policies or renewals in force.

Are they so returned in this statement? Answer: ....

*State here basis of computation used in each case. ....

**Business not exceeding 120 months duration.

***See Line 30 Instruction.

(b) Including $............... reserved for deferred maternity and other similar benefits.

PART 2B — PREMIUMS WRITTEN

	1 Direct Business	Gross Premiums (Less Return Premiums) Including Policy and Membership Fees Written and Renewed During Year					4 Net Premiums Written 1 + 2a + 2b − 3a − 3b
		Reinsurance Assumed		Reinsurance Ceded			
		2a From Affiliates	2b From Non-Affiliates	3a To Affiliates	3b To Non-Affiliates		
1.							
2.							
3.							
4.							
5.							
8.							
9.							
10.							
11.							
12.							
13.							
14.							
15.							
16.							
17.							
19.							
21.							
22.							
23.							
24.							
25.							
26.							
27.							
28.							
29.							
30A.	XXXX						
30B.	XXXX						
30C.	XXXX						
30D.	XXXX						
31.							
32.							

01							
02							
03							
04							
05							
98							
99							

Form 2

UNDERWRITING AND INVESTMENT EXHIBIT
PART 3 — LOSSES PAID AND INCURRED

| Line of Business | Losses Paid Less Salvage | | | | 5 Net Losses Unpaid Current Year (Part 3A, Col. 5) | 6 Net Losses Unpaid Previous Year | 7 Losses Incurred Current Year 4 + 5 − 6 | 8 Percentage of Losses Incurred (Col. 7, Part 3) to Premiums Earned (Col. 4, Part 2) | |
	1 Direct Business	2 Reinsurance Assumed	3 Reinsurance Recovered	4 Net Payments 1 + 2 − 3					
1. Fire									1
2. Allied lines									2
3. Farmowners multiple peril									3
4. Homeowners multiple peril									4
5. Commercial multiple peril									5
8. Ocean marine									8
9. Inland marine									9
10. Financial guaranty									10
11. Medical malpractice									11
12. Earthquake									12
13. Group accident and health									13
14. Credit accident and health (group and individual)*									14
15. Other accident and health									15
16. Workers' compensation									16
17. Other liability									17
19. Auto liability									19
21. Auto phys. damage									21
22. Aircraft (all perils)									22
23. Fidelity									23
24. Surety									24
25. Glass									25
26. Burglary and theft									26
27. Boiler and machinery									27
28. Credit									28
29. International									29
30A. Reinsurance**	XXX								30A
30B. Reinsurance**	XXX								30B
30C. Reinsurance**	XXX								30C
30D. Reinsurance**	XXX								30D
31. Aggregate write-ins for other lines of business									31
32. TOTALS									32

DETAILS OF WRITE-INS AGGREGATED AT ITEMS 31

3101									01
3102									02
3103									03
3104									04
3105									05
3198. Summary of remaining write-ins for item 31 from overflow page									98
3199. TOTALS (Items 3101 thru 3105 plus 3198) (Item 31)									99

*Business not exceeding 120 months duration
**See Line 30 Instructions

Form 2

ANNUAL STATEMENT FOR THE YEAR 1989 OF THE ....

....
(Name)

UNDERWRITING AND INVESTMENT EXHIBIT
PART 3A — UNPAID LOSSES AND LOSS ADJUSTMENT EXPENSES

| Line of Business | Adjusted or in Process of Adjustment | | 2 Deduct Reinsurance Recoverable from Authorized and Unauthorized Companies per Schedule F, Part 1A, Sec. 1, Col. 2 | 3 Net Losses Excl. Incurred But Not Reported 1a + 1b − 2 | Incurred But Not Reported | | | 5 Net Losses Unpaid Excluding Loss Adjustment Expenses 3 + 4a + 4b − 4c | 6 Unpaid Loss Adjustment Expenses |
	1a Direct	1b Reinsurance Assumed Schedule F, Part 1A, Sec. 2, Col. 2			4a Direct	4b Reinsurance Assumed	4c Reinsurance Ceded		
1 Fire									
2 Allied lines									
3 Farmowners multiple peril									
4 Homeowners multiple peril									
5 Commercial multiple peril									
8 Ocean marine									
9 Inland marine									
10 Financial guaranty									
11 Medical malpractice									
12 Earthquake									
13 Group accident and health								(a)	
14 Credit accident and health (group and individual)**								(a)	
15 Other accident and health									
16 Workers' compensation									
17 Other liability									
19 Auto liability									
21 Auto phys. damage									
22 Aircraft (all perils)									
23 Fidelity									
24 Surety									
25 Glass									
26 Burglary and theft									
27 Boiler and machinery									
28 Credit									
29 International									
30A Reinsurance***	XXX	XXX			XXX				
30B Reinsurance***	XXX	XXX			XXX				
30C Reinsurance***	XXX	XXX			XXX				
31 Aggregate write-ins for other lines of business									
32 TOTALS									

DETAILS OF WRITE-INS AGGREGATED AT ITEM 31

3101.									01
3102.									02
3103.									03
3104.									04
3105.									05
3198. Summary of remaining write-ins for item 31 from overflow page									98
3199. TOTALS (Items 3101 thru 3105 plus 3198) (Item 31)									99

**Business not exceeding 120 months duration.

(a) Including $ .... for present value of life indemnity claims and $ .... reserved for deferred maternity and other similar benefits.

***See Line 30 Instructions

ANNUAL STATEMENT FOR THE YEAR 1989 OF THE ....
(Name)

UNDERWRITING AND INVESTMENT EXHIBIT

PART 4 — EXPENSES

	1 Loss Adjustment Expenses	2 Other Underwriting Expenses	3 Investment Expenses	4 Total
1. Claim adjustment services.				
(a) Direct				
(b) Reinsurance assumed				
(c) Reinsurance ceded				
(d) Net claim adjustment services (a + b – c)				
2. Commission and brokerage.				
(a) Direct				
(b) Reinsurance assumed				
(c) Reinsurance ceded				
(d) Contingent — net				
(e) Policy and membership fees				
(f) Net commission and brokerage (a + b – c + d + e)				
3. Allowances to managers and agents				
4. Advertising				
5. Boards, bureaus and associations				
6. Surveys and underwriting reports				
7. Audit of assureds' records				
8. Salaries				
9. Employee relations and welfare				
10. Insurance				
11. Directors' fees				
12. Travel and travel items				
13. Rent and rent items				
14. Equipment				
15. Printing and stationery				
16. Postage, telephone and telegraph, exchange and express				
17. Legal and auditing				
17A. Totals (Items 3 to 17)				
18. Taxes, licenses and fees:				
(a) State and local insurance taxes				
(b) Insurance department licenses and fees				
(c) Payroll taxes				
(d) All other (excluding federal and foreign income and real estate)				
(e) Total taxes, licenses and fees (a + b + c + d)				
19. Real estate expenses				
20. Real estate taxes				
20A. Reimbursements by uninsured accident and health plans				
21. Aggregate write-ins for miscellaneous expenses				
22. Total expenses incurred				
23. Less unpaid expenses — current year				
24. Add unpaid expenses — previous year				
25. TOTAL EXPENSES PAID (Items 22 – 23 + 24)				

DETAILS OF WRITE-INS AGGREGATED AT ITEM 21 FOR MISCELLANEOUS EXPENSES

2101.				
2102.				
2103.				
2104.				
2105.				
2198. Summary of remaining write-ins for item 21 from overflow page				
2199. Totals (Items 2101 thru 2105 plus 2198) (Part 4, Item 21)				

ANNUAL STATEMENT FOR THE YEAR 1989 OF THE ....
                                      (Name)

EXHIBIT 1—ANALYSIS OF ASSETS

	1 Ledger Assets	2 Non-Ledger Including Excess of Market (or Amortized) Over Book Values	3 Assets Not Admitted Including Excess of Book Over Market (or Amortized) Values	4 Net Admitted Assets (Cols. 1 + 2 − 3)
1. Bonds (Schedule D)				
2. Stocks (Schedule D)				
2.1 Preferred stocks				
2.2 Common stocks				
3. Mortgage loans on real estate (Schedule B)				
(a) First liens				
(b) Other than first liens				
4. Real estate (Schedule A)				
4.1 Properties occupied by the company (less $_____ encumbrances)				
4.2 Other properties (less $_____ encumbrances)				
5. Collateral loans (Schedule C)				
6.1 Cash on hand and on deposit				
(a) Cash on company's office				
(b) Cash on deposit (Schedule N)				
6.2 Short-term investments (Schedule DA)				
7. Other invested assets (Schedule BA)				
8. Aggregate write-ins for invested assets				
9. Agents' balances or uncollected premiums (net as to commissions and dividends):				
9.1 Premiums and agents' balances in course of collection (after deducting ceded reinsurance balances payable of $_____)				
9.2 Premiums, agents' balances and installments booked but deferred and not yet due (after deducting ceded reinsurance balances payable of $_____)				
9.3 Accrued retrospective premiums				
10. Funds held by or deposited with reinsured companies				
11. Bills receivable, taken for premiums				
12. Reinsurance recoverable on loss payments (Schedule F, Part 1A, Col. 1)				
13. Federal income tax recoverable				
14. Electronic data processing equipment				
15. Interest, dividends and real estate income due and accrued				
16. Receivable from parent, subsidiaries and affiliates				
17. Equities and deposits in pools and associations				
18. Amounts receivable relating to uninsured accident and health plans				
19. Other assets				
19.1 Equipment, furniture and supplies				XXXXXX
19.2 Bills receivable, not taken for premiums				XXXXXX
19.3 Loans on personal security, endorsed or not				XXXXXX
20. Aggregate write-ins for other than invested assets				
21. TOTALS				

DETAILS OF WRITE-INS AGGREGATED AT ITEM 8 FOR INVESTED ASSETS

0801.				
0802.				
0803.				
0804.				
0805.				
0898. Summary of remaining write-ins for Item 8 from overflow page				
0899. TOTALS (Items 0801 thru 0805 plus 0898) (Page 12, Item 8)				

DETAILS OF WRITE-INS AGGREGATED AT ITEM 20 FOR OTHER THAN INVESTED ASSETS

2001.				
2002.				
2003.				
2004.				
2005.				
2098. Summary of remaining write-ins for Item 20 from overflow page				
2099. TOTALS (Items 2001 thru 2005 plus 2098) (Page 12, Item 20)				

EXHIBIT 2—ANALYSIS OF NON-ADMITTED ASSETS
Excluding Excess of Book over Market (or Amortized) Values and Item 15, Col. 3, Exhibit 1

	1 End of Previous Year	2 End of Current Year	3 Change for Year (Increase) or Decrease (Col. 1 − 2)
22. Loans on company's stock			
23. Deposits in suspended depositories, less estimated amount recoverable			
24. Agents' balances or uncollected premiums over three months due:			
24.1 Premiums and agents' balances in course of collection			
24.2 Premiums, agents' balances and installments booked but deferred and not yet due			
24.3 Accrued retrospective premiums			
25. Bills receivable, past due, taken for premiums			
26. Excess of bills receivable, not past due, taken for risks over the unearned premiums thereon			
27. Equipment, furniture and supplies			
28. Bills receivable, not taken for premiums			
29. Loans on personal security, endorsed or not			
30. Aggregate write-ins for assets not admitted			
31. Total change (Col. 3) (Carry to Item 20, Page 4)	XXXXXX	XXXXXX	

DETAILS OF WRITE-INS AGGREGATED AT ITEM 30 FOR ASSETS NOT ADMITTED

3001.			
3002.			
3003.			
3004.			
3005.			
3098. Summary of remaining write-ins for Item 30 from overflow page			
3099. TOTALS (Items 3001 thru 3005 plus 3098) (Page 13, Item 30)			

EXHIBIT 3 — RECONCILIATION OF LEDGER ASSETS

INCREASE IN LEDGER ASSETS

1. Net premiums written (Part 2, Col. 1, Item 32) ....

2. Interest, dividends and real estate income received (Part 1, Item 10, Col. 3) ....

3. From sale or maturity of ledger assets (Part 1A, Col. 2, Item 10) ....

4. Other income items or increases, viz:

    (a) Agents' balances previously charged off ....

    (b) Remittances from home office to U.S. branch (gross) ....

    (c) Funds held under reinsurance treaties (net) ....

    (d) Borrowed money (gross) ....

    (e) Amounts withheld or retained for account of others (net) ....

    (f) Aggregate write-ins for increases in ledger assets ....

5. Adjustment in book value of ledger assets (Part 1A, Item 10, Col. 4) ....

6. Capital paid in (Page 4, Item 24a) ....

7. Surplus paid in (Page 4, Item 25a) ....

8.   Total (Items 1 to 7) ....

DECREASE IN LEDGER ASSETS

9. Net losses paid (Part 3, Col. 4, Item 32) ....

10. Expenses paid (Part 4, Item 25, Col. 4) ....

11. From sale or maturity of ledger assets (Part 1A, Col. 3, Item 10) ....

12. Other disbursement items or decreases, viz:

    (a) Agents' balances charged off ....

    (b) Remittances to home office from U.S. branch (gross) ....

    (c) Funds held under reinsurance treaties (net) ....

    (d) Borrowed money (gross) ....

    (e) Amounts withheld or retained for account of others (net) ....

    (f) Aggregate write-ins for decreases in ledger assets ....

13. Adjustment in book value of ledger assets (Part 1A, Item 10, Col. 5) and depreciation (Item 12, Part 1) ....

14. Federal and foreign income taxes paid ....

15. Dividends paid stockholders ....

16. Dividends to policyholders on direct business, less $................ dividends on reinsurance assumed or ceded (net) ....

17.   Total (Items 9 to 16) ....

RECONCILIATION BETWEEN YEARS

18. Amount of ledger assets as per balance December 31 of previous year ....

19. Increase or (decrease) in ledger assets during the year (Item 8 minus Item 17) ....

20.   Balance = ledger assets December 31 of current year ....

DETAILS OF WRITE-INS AGGREGATED AT ITEM 4(f) FOR INCREASES IN LEDGER ASSETS

04401. ....

04402. ....

04403. ....

04404. ....

04405. ....

04498. Summary of remaining write-ins for item 4f from overflow page ....

04499.   TOTAL (Items 04401 thru 04405 plus 04498) (Page 13, Item 4(f)) ....

DETAILS OF WRITE-INS AGGREGATED AT ITEM 12(f) FOR DECREASES IN LEDGER ASSETS

12401. ....

12402. ....

12403. ....

12404. ....

12405. ....

12498. Summary of remaining write-ins for item 12f from overflow page ....

12499.   TOTAL (Items 12401 thru 12405 plus 12498) (Page 13, Item 12(f)) ....

ANNUAL STATEMENT FOR THE YEAR 1989 OF THE

NAIC Group Code ....
NAIC Company Code ....

EXHIBIT OF PREMIUMS AND LOSSES

BUSINESS IN THE STATE OF   DURING THE YEAR

1 Line of Business	Gross Premiums, Including Policy and Membership Fees, Less Return Premiums and Premiums on Policies Not Taken		4 Dividends Paid or Credited to Policyholders on Direct Business	5 Direct Unearned Premium Reserves	6 Direct Losses Paid (deducting salvage)	7 Direct Losses Incurred	8 Direct Losses Unpaid
	2 Direct Premiums Written	3 Direct Premiums Earned*					
1. Fire							
2. Allied lines							
3. Farmowners multiple peril							
4. Homeowners multiple peril							
5. Commercial multiple peril							
8. Ocean marine							
9. Inland marine							
10. Financial guaranty							
11. Medical malpractice							
12. Earthquake							
13. Group accident and health							
14. Credit A & H (Group and Individual)							
15.1 Collectively renewable A & H							
15.2 Non-cancellable A & H							
15.3 Guaranteed renewable A & H							
15.4 Non-renewable for stated reasons only							
15.5 Other accident only							
15.6 All other A & H							
16. Workers' compensation							
17. Other liability							
19.1 Private passenger auto no-fault (personal injury protection)							
19.2 Other private passenger auto liability							
19.3 Commercial auto no-fault (personal injury protection)							
19.4 Other commercial auto liability							
21.1 Private passenger auto physical damage							
21.2 Commercial auto physical damage							
22. Aircraft (all perils)							
23. Fidelity							
24. Surety							
25. Glass							
26. Burglary and theft							
27. Boiler and machinery							
28. Credit							
31. Aggregate write-ins for other lines of business							
32. TOTALS							

DETAILS OF WRITE-INS AGGREGATED AT ITEM 31 FOR OTHER LINES OF BUSINESS

3101.							
3102.							
3103.							
3104.							
3105.							
3198. Summary of remaining write-ins for Line 31 from overflow page							
3199. TOTALS (Items 3101 thru 3105 plus 3198) (Line 31)							

Finance and service charges not included in Lines 1 to 32 $ ....
*Direct premiums earned may be estimated by formula on the basis of country-wide ratios for the respective lines of business except where adjustments are required to recognize special situations.

ANNUAL STATEMENT FOR THE YEAR 1989 OF THE ....
(Name)

MEDICARE SUPPLEMENT INSURANCE EXPERIENCE EXHIBIT

FOR THE STATE OF

ADDRESS (City, State and Zip Code)

NAIC Group Code   NAIC Company Code

PERSON COMPLETING THIS EXHIBIT ....

TO BE FILED BY JUNE 30 FOLLOWING THE ANNUAL STATEMENT FILING

| 1 | 2 | Incurred Claims | |
| | | 3 | 4 |
Classification	Premiums Earned	Amount	Percent of Premiums Earned
A Experience on individual policies			
1. Policies issued through 19			
a. Reporting State			
b. Nationwide			
2. Policies issued after 19			
a. Reporting State			
b. Nationwide			
B Experience on group policies			
1. Policies issued through 19			
a. Reporting State			
b. Nationwide			
2. Policies issued after 19			
a. Reporting State			
b. Nationwide			

The undersigned officer hereby certifies that the company named above has complied with the requirements contained in the federal Omnibus Budget Reconciliation Act of 1987, Section 4081.

Signature

Title and Name (Please type)

GENERAL INTERROGATORIES

1   (a) Does the company issue both participating and non-participating policies?   Yes [ ]   No [ ]
    (b) If yes. state the amount of net premiums in force on
            (i) Participating policies. $_____
            (ii) Non-participating policies. $_____

2   For Mutual Companies and Reciprocal Exchanges Only
            (a) Does company issue assessable policies?   Yes [ ]   No [ ]   N A [ ]
            (b) Does company issue nonassessable policies?   Yes [ ]   No [ ]   N A [ ]
            (c) If assessable policies are issued. what is the extent of the contingent liability of the policyholders?   _____%
            (d) Total amount of assessments laid or ordered to be laid during the year on deposit notes or contingent premiums $_____

3   For Reciprocal Exchanges Only
            (a) Does the Exchange appoint local agents?   Yes [ ]   No [ ]   N A [ ]
            (b) If yes. is the commission paid
                (i) out of Attorney's in-fact compensation?   Yes [ ]   No [ ]   N A [ ]
                (ii) as a direct expense of the Exchange?   Yes [ ]   No [ ]   N A [ ]
            (c) What expenses of the Exchange are not paid out of the compensation of the Attorney-in-fact?
_____
_____
            (d) Has any Attorney-in-fact compensation. contingent on fulfillment of certain conditions. been deferred?   Yes [ ]   No [ ]   N A [ ]
            (e) If yes. give full information _____
_____

4

CAPITAL STOCK OF THIS COMPANY

1 Class	2 Number Shares Authorized	3 Number Shares Outstanding	4 Par Value Per Share	5 Redemption Price if Callable	6 IS DIVIDEND RATE LIMITED?		7 ARE DIVIDENDS CUMULATIVE?	
					Yes	No	Yes	No
Preferred					[ ]	[ ]		
Common				XXXX	XXX	XXX	XXX	XXX

5   (a) Does the company own any securities of a real estate holding company or otherwise hold real estate indirectly?   Yes [ ]   No [ ]
    (b) If yes. (i) explain _____
_____
            (ii) Name of real estate holding company _____
            (iii) Number of parcels involved?
            (iv) Total book value $_____

6   (a) Is the company a member of an insurance Holding Company System consisting of two or more affiliated persons. one or more of which is an insurer?   Yes [ ]   No [ ]
    (b) If yes. did the company register and file with its domiciliary State Insurance Commissioner. Director. or Superintendent. or with such regulatory official of the State of domicile of the principal insurer in the Holding Company System. a registration statement providing disclosure substantially similar to the standards adopted by the National Association of Insurance Commissioners in its Model Holding Company System Regulatory Act and model regulations pertaining thereto. or is the company subject to standards and disclosure requirements substantially similar to those required by such Act and regulations?   Yes [ ]   No [ ]   N A [ ]
    (c) State regulating _____

7   (a) Total amount loaned during the year:
            (i) to directors or other officers $_____
            (ii) to stockholders not officers $_____
    (b) Total amount of loans outstanding at end of year:
            (i) to directors or other officers $_____
            (ii) to stockholders not officers $_____

8   (a) Did any person while an officer. director or trustee of the company receive directly or indirectly. during the period covered by this statement. any commission on the business transactions of the company?   Yes [ ]   No [ ]
    (b) Did any person while an officer. director. trustee or employee receive directly or indirectly. during the period covered by this statement. any compensation in addition to his regular compensation on account of the reinsurance transactions of the company?   Yes [ ]   No [ ]
    (c) Has the company an established procedure for disclosure to its board of directors or trustees of any material interest or affiliation on the part of any of its officers. directors. trustees. or responsible employees which is in or is likely to conflict with the official duties of such person?   Yes [ ]   No [ ]
    (d) Except for retirement plans generally applicable to its staff employees and agents and contracts with its agents for the payment of commissions. has the company any agreement with a person whereby it agrees that for any service rendered or to be rendered. he shall receive directly or indirectly any salary. compensation or emolument that will extend beyond a period of 12 months from the date of the agreement?   Yes [ ]   No [ ]

9   What amount of installment notes is owned and now held by the company? $_____

10   (a) Have any of these notes been hypothecated. sold or used in any manner as security for money loaned within the past year?   Yes [ ]   No [ ]
    (b) If yes. what amount? $_____

11   Largest net aggregate amount insured in any one risk (excluding workers' compensation). $_____

12   What provision has this company made to protect itself from an excessive loss in the event of a catastrophe under a workers' compensation contract issued without limit of loss?

13   (a) Has this company guaranteed any financed premium accounts?   Yes [ ]   No [ ]
    (b) If so. give full information _____

14   Has this company reinsured any risk with any other company and agreed to release such company from liability. in whole or in part. from any loss that may occur on the risk. or portion thereof. reinsured?   Yes [ ]   No [ ]
    (b) If so. give full information _____

15   If the company has assumed risks from another company. there should be charged on account of such reinsurances a reserve equal to that which the original company would have been required to charge had it retained the risks. Has this been done?   Yes [ ]   No [ ]

16   (a) Has this company guaranteed policies issued by any other company and now in force?   Yes [ ]   No [ ]
    (b) If yes. give full information _____

17   (a) Were all the stocks. bonds and other securities owned December 31 of current year. over which the company has exclusive control in the actual possession of the company on said date. except as shown by the schedules of special and other deposits?   Yes [ ]   No [ ]
    (b) If no. give full and complete information relating thereto: _____

18   (a) Have all private placement investments which were the subject of renegotiation or modification of their terms during the year been disclosed to the Valuation of Securities office of the NAIC. with full details as to the provisions renegotiated or modified?   Yes [ ]   No [ ]
    (b) Have filings been made with the Valuation of Securities office of the NAIC in connection with acquisition and disposition of securities as required by Section 8 of the Valuation Procedures and Instructions for Bonds and Stocks?   Yes [ ]   No [ ]

19   (a) Were any of the stocks. bonds or other assets of the company owned at December 31 of the current year not exclusively under the control of the company. or has the company sold or transferred any assets subject to a put option contract that is currently in force?   Yes [ ]   No [ ]
    (b) If yes. state the amount thereof at December 31 of the current year:
            (i) loaned to others $_____
            (ii) subject to reverse repurchase agreements $_____
            (iii) subject to dollar repurchase agreements $_____
            (iv) subject to reverse dollar repurchase agreements $_____
            (v) pledged as collateral $_____
            (vi) placed under option agreements $_____
            (vii) letter stock or other securities restricted as to sale $_____
            (viii) other $_____
    (c) For each category above. if any of these assets are held by others. identify by whom held.
            (i) _____
            (ii) _____
            (iii) _____
            (v) _____
            (vi) _____
            (vii) _____
            (viii) _____
    (d) For categories (b)(i) and (ii) above. and for any other securities that were made available for use by another person during the year covered by this statement. attach a schedule as shown in the instructions to the annual statement.
    (e) For category (b)(vi) above. do any of the option agreements involve asset transfers with put options?   Yes [ ]   No [ ]
    If yes. disclose in the Notes to Financial Statements the information specified in the instructions to the annual statement.

ANNUAL STATEMENT FOR THE YEAR 1989 OF THE ....
(Name)

GENERAL INTERROGATORIES (Continued)

20. (a) State as of what date the latest financial examination of the company was made or is being made:
(b) By what department or departments? _____

21. (a) Has any change been made during the year of this statement in the charter, by-laws, articles of incorporation, or deed of settlement of the company?   Yes [ ]   No [ ]
(b) If yes, date of change:
If not previously filed, furnish herewith a certified copy of the instrument as amended.

22. (a) Has any direct new business been solicited or written in any state where the company was not licensed?   Yes [ ]   No [ ]
(b) If yes, explain _____

23. Is the purchase or sale of all investments of the company passed upon either by the board of directors or a subordinate committee thereof?   Yes [ ]   No [ ]

24. Does the company keep a complete permanent record of the proceedings of its board of directors and all subordinate committees thereof?   Yes [ ]   No [ ]

25. Have the instructions for completing the blank required by this department been followed in every detail?   Yes [ ]   No [ ]

ONLY UNITED STATES BRANCHES OF FOREIGN COMPANIES NEED ANSWER INTERROGATORIES 26 and 27:

26. What changes have been made during the year in the United States manager or the United States trustees of the company? _____

27. Does this statement contain all business transacted for the company through its United States branch, on risks wherever located?   Yes [ ]   No [ ]   N A [ ]

28. (a) During the period covered by this statement, did any agent, general agent, broker, sales representative, non-affiliated sales/service organization or any combination thereof under common control (other than salaried employees of the company), receive credit or commissions for or control a substantial part (more than 20 percent of any major line of business measured on direct premiums) of:
(i) sales of new business?   Yes [ ]   No [ ]
(ii) renewals?   Yes [ ]   No [ ]
(b) During the period covered by this statement, did any sales/service organization owned in whole or in part by the company or an affiliate, receive credit or commissions for or control a substantial part (more than 20 percent of any major line of business measured on direct premiums) of:
(i) sales of new business?   Yes [ ]   No [ ]
(ii) renewals?   Yes [ ]   No [ ]

29. (a) If the company recorded accrued retrospective premiums on insurance contracts on line 9.3 of the asset schedule, page 2, state the amount of corresponding liabilities recorded for:
(i) Unpaid losses: $ _____
(ii) Unpaid underwriting expenses (including loss adjustment expenses) $ _____
(b) Of the amount on line 9.3 of the asset schedule, page 2, state the amount which is secured by letters of credit, collateral and other funds? $ _____
(c) If the company underwrites commercial insurance risks, such as workers' compensation, are premium or promissory notes accepted from its insureds covering unpaid premiums and/or unpaid losses?   Yes [ ]   No [ ]
(d) If yes, provide the range of interest rates charged under such notes during the period covered by this statement?
(i) From   _____ %
(ii) To   _____ %
(e) Are letters of credit or collateral and other funds received from insureds being utilized by the company to secure premium or promissory notes taken by the company, or to secure any of the company's reported direct unpaid loss reserves, including unpaid losses under loss deductible features of commercial policies?   Yes [ ]   No [ ]
(f) If yes, state the amount thereof at December 31 of the current year:
(i) Letters of Credit $ _____
(ii) Collateral and other funds $ _____

30. What interest, direct or indirect, has this company in the capital stock of any other insurance company? _____

31. (a) Has this company written any Medicare supplement insurance business?   Yes [ ]   No [ ]
(b) If yes, indicate total premium volume $ _____

Ceded Reinsurance Report — Section 1. Annual Report of Reinsurance Transactions (including facultative and pooling transactions)

32. What is the maximum amount of return commission which would have been due reinsurers if they or you had cancelled all of your company's reinsurance or if you or a receiver had cancelled all of your company's direct business and reinsurance assumed as of the end of the period covered by this Annual Statement with the return of the unearned premium reserve? For:
(a) Intercompany pooling agreement. $ _____
(b) All other reinsurance. $ _____
(c) Total: $ _____

33. What would be the amount of the reduction in surplus as shown on this Annual Statement if adjustments were made to reflect the full amount described in Question 32?
(a) Intercompany pooling agreement: $ _____
(b) All other reinsurance: $ _____
(c) Total: $ _____

34. (a) On the basis of loss experience to date, have you accrued earned additional premiums which would be payable or return reinsurance commissions which would be refundable in the future if the reinsurer or you cancelled all of your company's reinsurance as of the end of the period covered by this Annual Statement?   Yes [ ]   No [ ]
(b) If you have not so accrued, what would be the amount of such additional premium or return commission?
(i) Intercompany pooling agreement: $ _____
(ii) All other reinsurance: $ _____
(iii) Total: $ _____

35. What would be the amount of the reduction in surplus as of the end of the period covered by this Annual Statement if adjustments were made to reflect the full amount described in Question 34?
(a) Intercompany pooling agreement: $ _____
(b) All other reinsurance: $ _____
(c) Total: $ _____

36. What would be the percentage reduction in surplus as of the end of the period covered by this Annual Statement from the combined effects of the amounts described in Questions 33 and 35?
(a) Intercompany pooling agreement: _____ %
(b) All other reinsurance: _____ %
(c) Total: _____ %

37. What is the amount of additional reinsurance premiums, computed at the maximum level provided by the reinsurance contracts, in excess of amounts previously paid and presently accrued (including as accrued the amount shown in response to Question 34) on retrospective adjustment periods covering the most recent three years?
(a) Intercompany pooling agreement: $ _____
(b) All other reinsurance: $ _____
(c) Total: $ _____

38. What is the amount of return reinsurance commission, computed at the minimum level provided by the reinsurance contracts, in excess of amounts previously paid and presently accrued (including as accrued the amount shown in response to Question 34) on retrospective adjustment periods covering the most recent three years?
(a) Intercompany pooling agreement: $ _____
(b) All other reinsurance: $ _____
(c) Total: $ _____

39. What would be the percentage reduction in surplus as of the end of the period covered by this Annual Statement from the combined effects of the amounts described in Questions 37 and 38?
(a) Intercompany pooling agreement: _____ %
(b) All other reinsurance: _____ %
(c) Total: _____ %

40. What would be the percentage reduction in surplus as of the end of the period covered by this Annual Statement from the combined effects of the amounts described in Questions 33, 35, 37 and 38?
(a) Intercompany pooling agreement: _____ %
(b) All other reinsurance: _____ %
(c) Total: _____ %

ANNUAL STATEMENT FOR THE YEAR 1989 OF THE ....
(Name)

NOTES TO FINANCIAL STATEMENTS

Form 2

19

ANNUAL STATEMENT FOR THE YEAR 1989 OF THE ....
(Name)

Note: In case the following schedules do not afford sufficient space, companies may furnish them on separate forms, provided the same are upon paper of like size and arrangements and contain the information asked for herein and have the name of the Company printed or stamped at the top thereof.

SPECIAL DEPOSIT SCHEDULE

Showing all deposits or investments NOT held for the protection of ALL the policyholders of the Company

1 Where Deposited	2 Description and Purpose of Deposit (Indicating literal form of registration of Securities)	3 Par Value	4 Statement Value	5 Market Value
999999	TOTALS			

ANNUAL STATEMENT FOR THE YEAR 1989 OF THE ....
(Name)

SCHEDULE OF ALL OTHER DEPOSITS

Showing all deposits made with any Government, Province, State, District, County, Municipality, Corporation, firm or
individual, except those shown in Schedule N, and those shown in "Special Deposit Schedule"

1 Where Deposited	2 Description and Purpose of Deposit (Indicating literal form of registration of Securities)	3 Par Value	4 Statement Value	5 Market Value
999999	TOTALS			

ANNUAL STATEMENT FOR THE YEAR 1989 OF THE ....

(Name)

FIVE-YEAR HISTORICAL DATA

All Figures Taken From or Developed From Annual Statements of Corresponding Years

Show amounts in whole dollars only, no cents; show percentages to one decimal place, i.e. 17.6.

	1 1989	2 1988	3 1987	4 1986	5 1985
Gross Premiums Written (Page 8, Part 2B [2C prior to 1988] Cols. 1 & 2)					
1 Liability Lines (Items 11, 16, 17 & 19)					
2 Property Lines (Items 1, 2, 9, 12, 21, 25 & 26)					
3 Property and Liability Combined Lines (Items 3, 4, 5, 8, 22 & 27)					
4A All Other Lines (Items 10, 13, 14, 15, 23, 24, 28, 29 & 30 [and 30D, 1988 and after] [and Item 31, 1986 and after])					
4B Non-proportional Reinsurance Lines (Items 30A, 30B and 30C)					
5 Total (Item 31 [Item 32, 1986 and after])					
Net Premiums Written (Page 8, Part 2B [2C prior to 1988] Col. 4)					
6 Liability Lines (Items 11, 16, 17 & 19)					
7 Property Lines (Items 1, 2, 9, 12, 21, 25 & 26)					
8 Property and Liability Combined Lines (Items 3, 4, 5, 8, 22 & 27)					
9A All Other Lines (Items 10, 13, 14, 15, 23, 24, 28, 29 & 30 [and 30D, 1988 and after] [and Item 31, 1986 and after])					
9B Non-proportional Reinsurance Lines (Items 30A, 30B and 30C)					
10 Total (Item 31 [Item 32, 1986 and after])					
Statement of Income (Page 4)					
11 Net Underwriting Gain or (Loss) (Item 7)					
12 Net Investment Gain or (Loss) (Item 9A)					
13 Total Other Income (Item 17 [Item 13, 1986 and after])					
14 (Dividends to Policyholders (Item 18A [Item 14A, 1986 and after])					
15 Federal and Foreign Income Taxes Incurred (Item 19 [Item 15, 1986 and after])					
16 Net Income (Item 20 [Item 16, 1986 and after])					
Balance Sheet Items (Pages 2 and 3)					
17 Total Admitted Assets (Page 2, Item 22 [Item 21, 1986 and after])					
18 Agents' Balances or Uncollected Premiums (Page 2):					
18.1 In Course of Collection (Item 8.1 [Item 9.1, 1986 and after])					
18.2 Deferred and Not Yet Due (Item 8.2 [Item 9.2, 1986 and after])					
19 Total Liabilities (Page 3, Item 23 [Item 22, 1986 and after])					
20 Losses (Page 3, Item 1 [and Item 1A, 1988 and after])					
21 Loss Adjustment Expenses (Page 3, Item 2)					
22 Unearned Premiums (Page 3, Item 10 [Item 9, 1986 and after])					
23 Capital Paid Up (Page 3, Items 25A and 25B [Items 24A and 24B, 1986 and after])					
24 Surplus as Regards Policyholders (Page 3, Item 27 [Item 26, 1986 and after])					
Percentage Distribution of Cash and Invested Assets					
(Page 2) (Item divided by Page 2, Item 7a [Item 8a, 1986 and after]) x 100.0					
25 Bonds (Item 1)					
26 Stocks (Items 2.1 and 2.2)					
27 Mortgage Loans on Real Estate (Item 3)					
28 Real Estate (Items 4.1 and 4.2)					
29 Collateral Loans (Item 5)					
30 Cash and short-term investments (Items 6.1 and 6.2)					
31 Other Invested Assets (Item 7)					
31A Aggregate write-ins for invested assets (Item 8)					
32 Cash and Invested Assets (Item 7a [Item 8a, 1986 and after])	100.0	100.0	100.0	100.0	100.0
Investment in Parent, Subsidiaries and **Affiliates**					
33 Affiliated Bonds (Item 29, Col. 6, Sch. D Summary)					
34 Affiliated Preferred Stocks (Item 47, Col. 3, Sch. D Summary)					
35 Affiliated Common Stocks (Item 65, Col. 3, Sch. D Summary)					
36 Affiliated Short-Term Investments (Subtotals included in Schedule DA, Part 1, Col. 10)					
36A Affiliated Mortgage Loans on Real Estate					
36B All Other Affiliated					
37 Total of above Items 33, 34, 35, 36, 36A and 36B					
38 Percentage of Investments in Parent, Subsidiaries and Affiliates to Surplus as Regards Policyholders (Item 37 above divided by Page 3, Col. 1, Item 27 [Item 26, 1986 and after] x 100.0)					

ANNUAL STATEMENT FOR THE YEAR 1989 OF THE

FIVE-YEAR HISTORICAL DATA
(Continued)

		1 1989	2 1988	3 1987	4 1986	5 1985
	Capital and Surplus Accounts (Page 4)					
39	Net Unrealized Capital Gains or (Losses) (Item 24) (Item 25 1986 and after)					
40	Dividends to Stockholders (Cash) (Item 35) (Item 37 1986 and after)					
41	Change in Surplus as Regards Policyholders for the Year (Item 39 (Item 31 1986 and after)					
	Gross Losses Paid (Page 9 Part 3 Cols 1 & 2)					
42	Liability Lines (Items 11 16 17 & 19)					
43	Property Lines (Items 1 2 9 12 21 25 & 26)					
44	Property and Liability Combined Lines (Items 3 4 5 8 22 & 27)					
45A	All Other Lines (Items 10 13 14 15 23 24 28 29 & 30 (and 30D 1988 and after) (& Item 31 1986 and after)					
45B	Non-Proportional Reinsurance Lines (Items 30A 30B and 30C)					
46	Total (Item 31 (Item 32 1986 and after))					
	Net Losses Paid (Page 9 Part 3 Col 4)					
47	Liability Lines (Items 11 16 17 & 19)					
48	Property Lines (Items 1 2 9 12 21 25 & 26)					
49	Property and Liability Combined Lines (Items 3 4 5 8 22 & 27)					
50A	All Other Lines (Items 10 13 14 15 23 24 28 29 & 30 (and 30D 1988 and after) (& Item 31 1986 and after))					
50B	Non-Proportional Reinsurance Lines (Items 30A 30B and 30C)					
51	Total (Item 31 (Item 32 1986 and after))					
	Operating Percentages (Page 4) (Item divided by Page 4 Item 1) x 100.0					
52	Premiums Earned (Item 1)	100.0	100.0	100.0	100.0	100.0
53	Losses Incurred (Item 2)					
54	Loss Expenses Incurred (Item 3)					
55	Other Underwriting Expenses Incurred (Item 4)					
56	Net Underwriting Gain or (Loss) (Item 7)					
	Other Percentages					
57	Other Underwriting Expenses to Net Premiums Written (Page 4 Items 4 - 5 17 (Item 13 1986 and after) divided by Page 8 Part 2B (2C prior to 1988) Col 4 Item 31 (Item 32 1986 and after) - 100 0)					
58	Losses and Loss Expenses Incurred to Premiums Earned (Page 4 Items 2 + 3 divided by Page 4 Item 1 - 100 0)					
59	Net Premiums Written to Policyholders' Surplus (Page 8 (Part 2B (2C prior to 1988) Col 4 Item 31 (Item 32 1986 and after) divided by Page 3 Item 27 (Item 26 1986 and after) Col 1 - 100 0)					
	One Year Loss Development (000 omitted) Schedule "P" (Schedule O and P prior to 1989)					
60	Development in estimated losses and loss expenses incurred prior to current year (Part 2 Item 11 Col 7 less Col 6 Part 2-Summary One Year Total 1989 and after)					
61	Percent of development of loss and loss expenses incurred to policyholders surplus of previous year end (Item 60 (Item 63 prior to 1989) divided by Page 4 Item 21 (Item 17 1986 and after) Col 1 - 100 0)					
	Two Year Loss Development (000 omitted) Schedule "P" (Schedule O and P prior to 1989)					
62	Development in estimated losses and loss expenses incurred 2 years before the current year and prior (Part 2 Item 9 Col 7 less Col 5 Part 2-Summary Two Year Total 1989 and after)					
63	Percent of development of loss and loss expenses incurred to reported policyholders surplus of second previous year end (Item 62 (Item 68 prior to 1989) divided by Page 4 Item 21 (Item 17 1986 and after) Col 2 x 100 0)					

Form 2

ANNUAL STATEMENT FOR THE YEAR 1949 OF THE ....

Name ....

SCHEDULE A—PART 1

Showing all Real Estate OWNED December 31 of Current Year, the Cost, Book and Market Value thereof the Nature and Amount of all Liens and Encumbrances thereon, including Interest Due and Accrued, etc.

| No. | 1 Quantity, Dimensions and Location of Lands, Size and Description of Buildings (Nature of encumbrances, if any, including interest due and accrued) | 2 Date Acquired | 3 Name of Vendor | 4 Amount of Encumbrances | 5 *Actual Cost | 6 Book Value Less Encumbrances | 7 Market Value Less Encumbrances | 8 Increase by Adjustment in Book Value During Year | 9 Decrease by Adjustment in Book Value During Year | 10 Gross Income Less Interest on Encumbrances | 11 Expended for Taxes, Repairs and Expenses | 12 Net Income | Rental Value of Space Occupied by | | 15 Year of Last Appraisal |
													13 Company	14 Parent, Subsidiaries and Affiliates	
999999 TOTALS															x x x

*Including cost of acquiring title and, if the property was acquired by foreclosure, such cost shall include the amounts expended for taxes, repairs and improvements prior to the date on which the company acquired title
†State basis on which market value was determined

CLASSIFICATION

Showing the total amount of Real Estate owned in each State and Foreign Country

1 State	2 Market Value	1 State	2 Market Value	1 State	2 Market Value	3 Foreign Country	Market Value
					999999 TOTALS		x x x

23

Form 2

ANNUAL STATEMENT FOR THE YEAR 1989 OF THE

.... (Name) ....

SCHEDULE A—PART 2

Showing all Real Estate **ACQUIRED** During the Year and Showing also Amounts Expended for Additions and Permanent Improvements Made During said Year to **ALL** Real Estate.

No	1 Quantity, Dimensions and Location of Lands; Size and Description of Buildings. (a) Nature of Additions and Permanent Improvements made During the Year (Nature of encumbrances, if any)	2 Date Acquired	3 How Acquired	4 Name of Vendor	5 Cost to Company During the Year	6 Amount Expended for Additions and Permanent Improvements During the Year	7 Book Value December 31 of Current Year Less Encumbrances
9999999	TOTALS						

SCHEDULE A—PART 3

Showing all Real Estate **SOLD** or Otherwise Disposed of During the Year including Payments During the Year on "Sales under Contract"

No.	1 Quantity, Dimensions and Location of Lands; Size and Description of Buildings. (Nature of encumbrances, if any)	2 Date Sold	3 Name of Purchaser	4 †Cost to Company	5 Increase by Adjustment in Book Value During the Year	6 Decrease by Adjustment in Book Value During the Year	7 †Book Value at Date of Sale Less Encumbrances	8 ‡Amount Received Including Payments on Sales Under Contract	9 Profit or Sale	10 Loss on Sale	11 Gross Income Due ring the Year Less Interest on Encumbrances	12 Expended for Taxes, Repairs and Expenses During Year
9999999	TOTALS											

† Including cost of acquiring title, and, if the property was acquired by foreclosure, such cost shall include the amounts expended for taxes, repairs, and improvements prior to the date on which the company acquired title. In reporting sales under contract, include payments received during the current year only.
‡ Indicate payments on "Sales under Contract" in Part 3 by inserting the letter 'P' after the number of the parcel.
†† In case of sales under contract, include payments received during current year only, until book value per Part I is exhausted.

SCHEDULE A—Verification Between Years

1. Book value, December 31, previous year (Item 4, Col 1, Exhibit 1, prior year statement)		7 Decrease by adjustment
2. Increase by adjustment		(a) Totals, Part 1, Col 9
(a) Totals, Part 1, Col 8		(b) Totals, Part 3, Col 6
(b) Totals, Part 3, Col 5		8. Received on sales, Part 3, Col 8
3. Cost of acquired, Part 2, Col 5		9. Loss on sales, Part 3, Col 10
4. Cost of additions and permanent improvements, Part 2, Col 6		10. Book value, December 31, current year (Item 4, Col 1, Exhibit 1)
5. Profit on sales, Part 3, Col 9		
6. Total		

24

ANNUAL STATEMENT FOR THE YEAR 1989 OF THE .... (Name)

SCHEDULE B

Showing all Long-Term MORTGAGES OWNED December 31 of Current Year, and all Mortgage Loans Made, Increased Discharged, Reduced or Disposed of During the Year

Indicate by symbols FHA and VA if loans are so insured. All such FHA and VA insured loans not in process of foreclosure may be summarized by year and state of issue and combined values may be shown for land and buildings.

	Date		Record of Mortgage		Principal				Interest								Location and Description
Number	Year Given	Year Due	State	County	Book Value Dec. 31 of Previous Year	Amount Loaned During Year (A)	Amount Paid on Account or in full During Year (B)	Increase or (Decrease) in Book Value	Book Value Dec. 31 of Current Year 6 + 7 - 8 - 9	Date Due	Rate of	Amount Past Due Dec. 31 of Current Year	Am't Accrued Dec 31 of Current Year	Gross Am't Rec'd During Year	Paid for Accrued Interest on Mortgages Acquired During Year	Value of Lands Mortgaged	Value of Buildings	Amount of Fire Insurance Held by Company on the Buildings	(State if this mortgage is being foreclosed; or if there are any prior liens. State name of mortgagor if mortgage is a parent, subsidiary affiliate, officer or director.)
																			20
999999										XXXX	XXXX					XXX	XXX	XXX	XXX

TOTALS

(A) Including all mortgages purchased or otherwise acquired during the year and all increases during the year or loans outstanding december 31 of previous year
(B) Including mortgages under which Company has secured title and possession by foreclosure

CLASSIFICATION

Showing the Total Amount of Long-Term Mortgage Loans on Real Estate in Each State and Foreign Country

1 State	2 Amount	1 State	2 Amount	1 State	2 Amount	3 Foreign Country	4 Amount
999999	TOTALS					XXX	

NOTE: Any casualty company having a majority of its premium volume derived from non-cancellable accident and health policies, may report on Schedule 3 forms or the Life Blank in lieu of this schedule.

Form 2

ANNUAL STATEMENT FOR THE YEAR 1989 OF THE ....

(Name)

SCHEDULE B A—PART 1

Showing Other Long-Term Invested Assets OWNED December 31, Current Year

1	2	3	4	5	6	7	8	9	10	11	12	13	14
Number of Units and Description*	Year Acquired	Lessee or Location	Amount of Encumbrances	Cost to Company	Book Value at December 31, Less Encumbrances	Statement Value at December 31	Market or Investment Value at December 31, Less Encumbrances	Additions to or (Reductions) in Investment	(Decrease) or Increase by Adjustment in Book Value During Year‡	Gross Income Received During Year	Net Income Received During Year §	Amounts Accrued at December 31, §§	Amounts Past Due at December 31 §§

07999X   Totals

*Give detail description of investment and underlying security (Footnotes may be used to describe leases for each class in the aggregate). Indicate statutory category of investment; i.e. real estate, mortgage, security, or other. Include in this Schedule, showing subtotals by class and grand total for all classes: (1) All loans on or investments in oil and gas production payments except those listed in Schedule D, Part 1 or Schedule DA; (2) All Transportation Equipment; (3) Timber Deeds; (4) Mineral Rights earned as admitted assets; (5) Motor Vehicle Trust Certificates; (6) Any other class of admitted investment not clearly includable in other statement schedules.

‡Include additional investments made, or portion of investment repaid.

‡Include depreciation on real estate and transportation equipment, etc. amortization of premium and accrual of discount if applicable.

§After appropriate reduction for interest paid to manufacturer during year and depletion and amortization of mineral rights.

§§After appropriate reduction for due and accrued interest payable to manufacturers.

SCHEDULE B A—VERIFICATION BETWEEN YEARS

1 Book value of other invested assets (Exhibit 1, Item 7, prior year annual statement) ....

2 Cost of acquisitions during year:
  (a) Column 5, Part 2 ....
  (b) Column 9, Part 1 ....
  (c) Column 7, Part 3 ....

3 Increase by adjustment during year:
  (a) Column 10, Part 1 ....
  (b) Column 8, Part 3 ....

4 Profit on disposition. Column 9, Part 3 ....

5 Total ....

6 Deduct consideration on disposition. Column 5, Part 3 ....

7 Reductions in investment during year:⊙
  (a) Column 9, Part 1 ....
  (b) Column 7, Part 3 ....

8 Decrease by adjustment during year:
  (a) Column 10, Part 1 ....
  (b) Column 8, Part 3 ....

9 Loss on disposition. Column 10, Part 3 ....

10 Book value of other invested assets. Exhibit 1, Item 7, current year ....

⊙Cash payments on account of capital, e.g. depletion and amortization of Mineral Rights.

Form 2

ANNUAL STATEMENT FOR THE YEAR 19 89 OF THE .... (Name)

SCHEDULE B A—PART 2

Showing Other Long-Term Invested Assets ACQUIRED During Current Year

1	2	3	4	5	6
Number of Units and Description*	Date Acquired	Lessee or Location	Cost to Company	Consideration Paid During Current Year	Name of Vendor

TOTALS

0799999   XXX

SCHEDULE B A—PART 3

Showing Other Long-Term Invested Assets DISPOSED of During Current Year

1	2	3	4	5	6	7	8	9	10	11
Number of Units and Description*	Date Disposed of	Lessee or Location	Name of Purchaser or Nature of Disposition	Consideration	Book Value at Date of Sale	Additions to or (Reductions) in Investment	(Decrease) or Increase by Adjustment in Book Value During Year	Profit on Sale	Loss on Sale	Net Income

TOTALS

0799999

*Include in this Schedule, showing subtotals by class and grand total for all classes: (1) All loans on or investments in oil and gas production payments except those listed in Schedule D, Part 1, or Schedule DA. (2) All Transportation Equipment. (3) Timber Deeds. (4) Mineral Rights earned as admitted assets. (5) Motor Vehicle Trust Certificate. (6) Any other class of admitted investment not clearly includable in other statement schedules.

27

20

ANNUAL STATEMENT FOR THE YEAR 1969 OF THE ....

(Name)

SCHEDULE C—PART 1

Showing all Long-Term Collateral Loans IN FORCE December 31 of Current Year

1 No	2 Description of Securities Held as Collateral December 31 of Current Year (Give in this column the number of shares of each block of stock and rate of interest and year of maturity of each bond held as collateral)	3 Par Value	4 Rate Used to Obtain Market Value	5 Market Value Dec. 31 of Current Year	6 Amount Loaned Thereon	7 Date of Loan	8 Maturity of Loan	Interest				13 Name of Actual Borrower (State if the borrower is a parent, subsidiary, affiliate, officer or director)
								9 Rate on Loan	10 Amount Past Due Dec. 31 of Current Year	11 Amount Accrued Dec. 31 of Current Year	12 Amount Received During Year	
999999	TOTALS					XXXX	XXXX	XXXX		XXXX		XXXX

SCHEDULE C—PART 2

Showing all Long-Term Collateral Loans MADE During the Year

1 No	2 Description of Security Accepted as Collateral When Loan was Made	3 Par Value	4 Rate Used to Obtain Market Value	5 Market Value at Date of Loan	6 Amount Loaned Thereon	7 Date of Loan	8 Maturity of Loan	9 Rate of Interest on Loan	10 Name of Actual Borrower (State if the borrower is a parent, subsidiary, affiliate, officer or director)
999999	TOTALS					XXXX	XXXX	XXXX	XXXX

Form 2

ANNUAL STATEMENT FOR THE YEAR 1989 OF THE _____ (Name)

SCHEDULE C — PART 3

Showing all Long-Term Collateral Loans DISCHARGED in Whole or in Part During the Year

1 Indicate Partial Payments by the Letter "P"	2 Description of Collateral Released When Loan Was Discharged (In case of partial payments enter collateral release only)	3 Par Value	4 Rate Used to Obtain Market Value	5 Market Value at Date of Discharge	6 Amount of Loan Repaid	7 Date of Loan	8 Date of Repayment	Interest		11 Name of Actual Borrower (State if the Borrower is a Parent, Subsidiary, Affiliate, Officer or Director)
								9 Rate on Loan	10 Amount Received During Year	
999999 Totals						XXXX	XXXX	XXXX	XXXX	XXXX

SCHEDULE C — PART 4

Showing All Substitutions of Collateral During the Year

1 No. (To Correspond with No. Shown in Parts 1, 2 and 3)	2 Amount of Loan Col. 6 of Parts 1, 2 or 3	Collateral Substituted				Collateral Released			
		3 Description	4 Date	5 Par Value	6 Market Value	7 Description	8 Date	9 Par Value	10 Market Value
999999 TOTALS		XXXX	XXXX	XXXX		XXXX	XXXX	XXXX	XXXX

29

ANNUAL STATEMENT FOR THE YEAR 1989 OF THE

SCHEDULE D — SUMMARY BY COUNTRY

Long-Term Bonds and Stocks **OWNED** December 31 of Current Year

1 Description		2 Book Value	3 †Market Value (Excluding accrued interest)	4 Actual Cost (Excluding accrued interest)	5 Par Value of Bonds	6 *Amortized or Investment Value
BONDS	1 United States					
Governments (Including all obligations guaranteed by governments)	2 Canada					
	3 Other Countries					
	4 Totals					
States, Territories and Possessions (Direct and guaranteed)	5 United States					
	6 Canada					
	7 Other Countries					
	8 Totals					
Political Subdivisions of States, Territories and Possessions (Direct and guaranteed)	9 United States					
	10 Canada					
	11 Other Countries					
	12 Totals					
Special revenue and special assessment obligations and all non-guaranteed obligations of agencies and authorities of governments and their political subdivisions	13 United States					
	14 Canada					
	15 Other Countries					
	16 Totals					
Railroads (unaffiliated)	17 United States					
	18 Canada					
	19 Other Countries					
	20 Totals					
Public Utilities (unaffiliated)	21 United States					
	22 Canada					
	23 Other Countries					
	24 Totals					
Industrial and Miscellaneous (unaffiliated)	25 United States					
	26 Canada					
	27 Other Countries					
	28 Totals					
Parent, Subsidiaries, and Affiliates	29 Totals					
	30. Total Bonds					
PREFERRED STOCKS	31 United States					
Railroads (unaffiliated)	32 Canada					
	33 Other Countries					
	34 Totals					
Public Utilities (unaffiliated)	35 United States					
	36 Canada					
	37 Other Countries					
	38 Totals					
Banks, Trust and Insurance Companies (unaffiliated)	39 United States					
	40 Canada					
	41 Other Countries					
	42 Totals					
Industrial and Miscellaneous (unaffiliated)	43 United States					
	44 Canada					
	45 Other Countries					
	46 Totals					
Parent, Subsidiaries, and Affiliates	47 Totals					
	48. Total Preferred Stocks					
COMMON STOCKS	49 United States					
Railroads (unaffiliated)	50 Canada					
	51 Other Countries					
	52 Totals					
Public Utilities (unaffiliated)	53 United States					
	54 Canada					
	55 Other Countries					
	56 Totals					
Banks, Trust and Insurance Companies (unaffiliated)	57 United States					
	58 Canada					
	59 Other Countries					
	60 Totals					
Industrial and Miscellaneous (unaffiliated)	61 United States					
	62 Canada					
	63 Other Countries					
	64 Totals					
Parent, Subsidiaries, and Affiliates	65 Totals					
	66. Total Common Stocks					
	67 Total Stocks					
	68 Total Bonds and Stocks					

†Statement value for preferred stocks. For certain bonds, values other than actual market may appear in this column (See Schedule D, Part 1, for details).
The aggregate value of bonds which are valued at other than actual market is $_____.
*Companies, societies, and associations which do not amortize their bonds should leave this column blank.

SCHEDULE D — VERIFICATION BETWEEN YEARS

1. Book value of bonds and stocks, per Items 1 and 2, Col. 1. Exhibit 1, previous year _____

2. Cost of bonds and stocks acquired, Col. 5, Part 3 _____

3. Increase by adjustment in book value
    (a) Col. 10, Part 1 _____
    (b) Col. 9, Part 2, Sec. 1 _____
    (c) Col. 8, Part 2, Sec. 2 _____
    (d) Col. 9, Part 4 _____

4. Profit on disposal of bonds and stocks, Col. 11, Part 4 _____

5. Total _____

6. Deduct consideration for bonds and stocks disposed of, Col. 5, Part 4 _____

7. Decrease by adjustment in book value
    (a) Col. 11, Part 1 _____
    (b) Col. 10, Part 2, Sec. 1 _____
    (c) Col. 9, Part 2, Sec. 2 _____
    (d) Col. 10, Part 4 _____

8. Loss on disposal of bonds and stocks, Col. 12, Part 4 _____

9. Book value of bonds and stocks, per Items 1 and 2, Col. 1, Exhibit 1, current year _____

Form 2

ANNUAL STATEMENT FOR THE YEAR 1989 OF THE .... (Name) ....

SCHEDULE D—PART 1A

Quality Distribution of All Bonds Owned December 31, Current Yearat Statement Values and By Major Types of Issues

Quality Rating Per The NAIC Designation (1)	1 Year or Less (2)	Over 1 Year Through 5 Years (3)	Over 5 Years through 10 Years (4)	Over 10 Years Through 20 Years (5)	Over 20 Years (6)	Total Current Year (7)	Col. 7 as A % of Line 5.5 Col. 7 (8)	Totals From Col. 7 Prior Year (9)	% From Col. 8 Prior Year (10)
Section 1 Governments Schedule D (Group 1)									
1.1 YES X YES C									
1.2 NO* NO* C									
1.3 NO** NO** C									
1.4 NO									
1.5 TOTAL									
Section 2 Political Subdivisions, Governmental Agencies and Authorities (Groups 2, 3 and 4)									
2.1 YES YES X YES C									
2.2 NO* NO* C									
2.3 NO** NO** C									
2.4 NO									
2.5 TOTAL									
Section 3 Other (Unaffiliated) (Groups 5, 6 and 7)									
3.1 YES YES X YES C									
3.2 NO* NO* C									
3.3 NO** NO** C									
3.4 NO									
3.5 TOTAL									
Section 4 Parent, Subsidiaries and Affiliates (Group 8)									
4.1 YES YES X YES C									
4.2 NO* NO* C									
4.3 NO** NO** C									
4.4 NO									
4.5 TOTAL									
Section 5 Total Bonds									
5.1 YES YES X YES C									
5.2 NO* NO* C									
5.3 NO** NO** C									
5.4 NO									
5.5 TOTAL									

* Includes aggregate statement value of all bonds shown in Schedules D and DA .... prior year of bonds with ; designation:
* Includes $ .... current year $ ....

NAIC Designation Definitions
YES — Investment Grade
NO* — Non Investment Grade — Average Quality
NO** — Non Investment Grade — Below Average Quality
NO — Bonds on or near default on principal or interest payments.

NOTE: The letter "C" following a designation indicates a demand or perpetual obligation valued at original cost. The letter "X" following a designation indicates the obligation is rated in the top four categories by a recognized rating organization. The letter "Z" indicates an obligation whose NAIC designation was not approved by the Securities Valuation Office of the date of statement.

Form 2

ANNUAL STATEMENT FOR THE YEAR 1989 OF THE ....

SCHEDULE D — PART 1

Showing all Long-Term **BONDS** Owned December 31 of Current Year

Bonds to be grouped in the following manner and each group arranged alphabetically (The listing in Groups 2, 3 and 4 should be alphabetical by State.) Show sub-totals for each group.
1. Governments (including all obligations guaranteed by governments)
2. States, Territories and Possessions (direct and guaranteed)
3. Political Subdivisions of States, Territories and Possessions (direct and guaranteed)
4. Special revenue and special assessment obligations and all non-guaranteed obligations of agencies and authorities of governments and their political subdivisions.
5. Railroads (unaffiliated)
6. Public Utilities (unaffiliated)
7. Industrial and Miscellaneous (unaffiliated)
8. Parent, Subsidiaries and Affiliates.

1		2		3					4	5	6	7	8	Interest				Supplemental columns for data concerning Amortization							See Note		
		Interest		Date of										9.1	9.2	10	11	12	13	14	15	16	17	18
**Description		Rate of	*How Paid	Maturity			††Option		Book Value	Par Value	Rate Used to Obtain Market Value	§§Market Value (including accrued interest)	Actual Cost (including accrued interest)	Amount Due and Accrued Dec 31 of Current Year on Bonds not in default	Gross Am't Received During Year	Increase by Adjustment in Book Value During Year	Decrease by Adjustment in Book Value During Year	Amount of interest due and accrued Dec. 31, current year, on bonds in default as to principal or interest	NAIC Desig- nation	Year Ac- quired	Effective Rate of Interest at Which Purchase Was Made	‡Amortized or Investment Value Dec. 31 of Current Year	Increase Amortized Value During Year	(Decrease) Amortized Value During Year
CUSIP Identi- fication***	Give complete and accurate description of all bonds owned, including the location of all street railway and miscellaneous companies. In bonds are "serial" issues give amount maturing each year			Year	Month	Day	Year	Call Price																	
099999	TOTALS										X X X								X X X	X X X	X X X			

*Insert initial letters of months in which interest is payable.

**Where a bond is payable in a foreign currency the par value and purchase price in that currency should be excluded as part of the description.

†Perpetual bonds; bonds in default as to principal or interest and bonds not amply secured, are to be entered in this column at market value.

‡Companies which use "Amortized Values" as "Book Values" may omit entering figures in these columns, and provide the following footnote: "The increases and decreases as amortized values are the same as those shown in the columns for 'Increase and Decrease by Adjustment in Book Value' excepting as elsewhere indicated."

§Insert the NAIC designation for such security printed in the NAIC Valuations of Securities manual.

NOTE: This supplemental information required of all Companies which amortize their bonds, is not to be used as a substitute for the information required or providing columns, but is additional thereto.

††Show year and call price pertaining to option if any on which amortization is based. On bonds purchased at a premium, the maturity date or call feature producing lowest amortized value should be used.

§§Where a market value is published in the NAIC Valuation of Securities Manual, it must be entered in Column 7. Where amortized value is any other value is used, insert a symbol and give code of the amount reported.

***CUSIP numbers entered are to conform to those provided and published by the Securities Valuation Office. See Annual Statement instructions.

ANNUAL STATEMENT FOR THE YEAR 1989 OF THE ....

SCHEDULE D—PART 2—SECTION 1

Showing all PREFERRED STOCKS Owned December 31 of Current Year

Stocks to be grouped in following order and each group arranged alphabetically, showing sub-totals for each group

Railroads (unaffiliated)   Industrial and Miscellaneous (unaffiliated)
Public Utilities (unaffiliated)   Parent, Subsidiaries and Affiliates.
Banks, Trust and Insurance Companies (unaffiliated)

CUSIP Identification***	1 Description	2 No. of Shares	3 Par Value Per Share	4 Book Value	5 *Rate Per Share	5 Statement Value	5A Rate Per Share Used to Obtain Market Value	6B Market Value	7 Actual Cost	Dividends 8.1 Declared but Unpaid	Dividends 8.2 Amount Received During Year	9 Increase by Adjustment in Book Value During Year	10 Decrease by Adjustment in Book Value During Year	11 §NAIC Designation	12 Year Acquired
	Give complete and accurate description of all preferred stocks owned including redeemable options, if any, and location of all street railway, bank, trust and miscellaneous companies.														
0689999	Total Preferred Stocks			X X X		X X X	X X X X							X X X	X X X X

*Insert the word "cost" for all preferred stocks eligible for amortization under Section 1 (3) (e) of the N.A.I.C. Valuation Procedures. Insert the market value rate for preferred stocks not eligible for stabilization.

***CUSIP numbers entered are to conform to those as provided and published by the Securities Valuation Office. See Annual Statement instructions.

§ Insert the NAIC Designation for such securities priced on the NAIC Valuation of Securities manual.

33

Form 2

ANNUAL STATEMENT FOR THE YEAR 1989 OF THE

Name

SCHEDULE D — PART 2 — SECTION 2

Showing all **COMMON STOCKS** Owned December 31 of Current Year

Stocks to be grouped in following order and each group arranged alphabetically showing sub-totals for each group
Railroads (unaffiliated)
Public Utilities (unaffiliated)   Industrial and Miscellaneous (unaffiliated)
Banks, Trust and Insurance Companies (unaffiliated)   Parent, Subsidiaries, and Affiliates

| 1 | | 2 | 3 | 4 | 5 | 6 | Dividends | | 8 | 9 | 10 | 11 |
CUSIP Identification***	Description	No. of Shares	Book Value	Rate Per Share Used to Obtain Market Value	Market Value	Actual Cost	7.1 Declared but Unpaid	7.2 Amount Received During Year	Increase by Adjustment in Book Value During Year	Decrease by Adjustment in Book Value During Year	NAIC Designation	Year Acquired
	Give complete and accurate description of all common stocks owned, including redeemable options, if any and addresses (City and State) of all street railway, banks, trust and insurance companies, savings and loan or building and loan associations and miscellaneous companies											
069999	**Total Common Stocks**			XXXX							XXX	XXXX
079999	**Total Preferred and Common Stocks**			XXXX							XXX	XXXX

NOTES: Complete information must be furnished in connection with any holding of preferred or common stock on the statement date which is optioned or restricted in any way as to its sale by the insurer

Identify all such securities by the symbol 'R' to be inserted beside the figure shown as the rate per share to obtain market value

Transferable shares only of Savings and Loan or Building and Loan Associations to be reported herein

***CUSIP numbers entered are to conform to those as provided and published by the Securities Valuation Office. See Annual Statement instructions.

Insert the NAIC designation for such security printed in the NAIC Valuations of Securities manual. For all common stocks bearing the NAIC designation 'U' provide the number of such issues .... the total $ value of all such issues ....

ANNUAL STATEMENT FOR THE YEAR 1989 OF THE

(Name)

SCHEDULE D—PART 3

Showing all Long-Term Bonds and Stocks ACQUIRED During Year

Bonds, preferred stocks and common stocks to be grouped separately
showing sub-totals for each group.

1 Description		2 Date Acquired*	3 Name of Vendor*	4 No. of Shares of Stock	5 Actual Cost (Excluding Accrued Interest and Dividends)	6 Par Value of Bonds	7 Paid for Accrued Interest and Dividends
CUSIP Identification***	Give complete and accurate description of each bond and stock††						

TOTALS

*Enter as separate summary items the totals of Columns 5, 7 and 15 of Part 1 for bonds, preferred stocks and common stocks. All bonds and stocks acquired and fully disposed of during the year are not to be detailed in this Part.
**The items with reference to cash value of bonds and stocks acquired in public offerings may be totaled in one line and the word "Various" inserted in Columns 2 and 3.
***CUSIP numbers entered are to conform to those as provided and published by the Securities Valuation Office. See Annual Statement instructions.
†If bonds are serial issues, give amounts maturing each year. Securities acquired under a reverse repurchase agreement must be identified.

269999
TOTALS

Form 2

ANNUAL STATEMENT FOR THE YEAR 1989 OF THE ....

....
(Name)

SCHEDULE D—PART 4

Showing all Long-Term Bonds and Stocks SOLD, REDEEMED or otherwise DISPOSED OF During Year

Bonds, preferred stocks and common stocks to be grouped separately
showing sub-totals for each group

CUSIP Identification***	Description† Give complete and accurate description of each bond and stock, including location of all street railway, bank, trust and miscellaneous companies.††	2 Disposal Date**	3 Name of Purchaser (If matured or called under redemption option, so state and give price at which called)	4 No. of Shares of Stock	5 Consideration (Excluding Accrued Interest and Dividends)	6 Par Value of Bonds	7 Actual Cost (Excluding Accrued Interest and Dividends)	8 Book Value at Disposal Date	9 Increase by Adjustment in Book Value During Year	10 Decrease by Adjustment in Book Value During Year	11 Profit on Disposal	12 Loss on Disposal	13 Interest on Bonds Received During Year†	14 Dividends on Stocks Received During Year†
269999	TOTALS													

†Enter as separate summary items the totals of Columns 5 to 14 of Part 5 for bonds, preferred stocks and common stocks. All bonds and stocks acquired and fully disposed of during the year are not to be itemized in this Part.

**Companies may at their option summarize all bonds of the same issue called, matured or redeemed during the year and omit disposal dates.

***CUSIP numbers entered are to conform to those as provided by the Securities Valuation Office. See Annual Statement instructions.

****From entry in the previous year's Annual Statement if owned at that time, from the purchase confirmation (or certificate) if purchased subsequently. Leave blank for private placements.

†Including accrued interest and dividends on bonds and stocks disposed of.

††If bonds are serial issues give amounts maturing each year. Securities sold under a reverse repurchase agreement must be identified.

Form 2

Name

SCHEDULE D—PART 5

Showing all Long-Term Bonds and Stocks **ACQUIRED** During the Current Year and Those **DISPOSED OF** During the Current Year

Bonds, preferred stocks and common stocks to be grouped separately showing sub-totals for each group.

CUSIP Identification***	Description Give complete and accurate description of each bond and stock, including location of all street railway, bank, trust and miscellaneous companies.††	2 Date Acquired**	3 Name of Vendor*	4 Disposal Date**	5 Name of Purchaser (If matured or called under redemption option, so state and give price at which called.)	6 Par Value (Bonds) or Number of Shares (Stocks)	7 Cost to Company (Excluding Accrued Interest and Dividends)	8 Consideration (Excluding Accrued Interest and Dividends)	9 Book Value at Disposal Date	10 Increase by Adjustment in Book Value During Year	11 Decrease by Adjustment in Book Value During Year	12 Profit on Disposal	13 Loss on Disposal	14 Interest and Dividends Received During Year	15 Paid for Accrued Interest and Dividends
BONDS															
099999	Sub-totals — Bonds														
STOCKS															
229999	Sub-totals — Stocks														
239999	GRAND TOTALS														

*The items with reference to each issue of bonds and stocks acquired at public offerings may be totaled in one line and the word "Various" inserted in Columns 2 and 3

**Companies may at their option summarize all bonds of the same issue called, matured or redeemed during the year and omit disposal dates.

***CUSIP numbers entered are to conform to those as provided and published by the Securities Valuation Office. See Annual Statement Instructions

†Including accrued interest and dividends on bonds and stocks disposed of

††If bonds are serial issues give amounts maturing each year. Securities acquired or disposed of under a reverse repurchase agreement must be identified

37

SCHEDULE D — PART 6 — SECTION 1

Questionnaire Relating to the Valuation of Shares of Certain Subsidiary, Controlled or Affiliated Companies

1 Name of Subsidiary Controlled or Affiliated Company	2 Do Insurer's Admitted Assets Include Intangible Assets Connected with Holding of Such Company's Stock?	3 If Yes, Amount of Such Intangible Assets	Common Stock of Such Company Owned by Insurer on Statement Date		6 NAIC Valuation Method
			4 No. of Shares	5 % of Outstanding	
999999		TOTAL	XXXX	XXXX	XXXX

Amount of Insurer's Capital and Surplus (Page 3, Item 26 of previous year's statement filed by the insurer with its domiciliary insurance department): $ ....

SCHEDULE D — PART 6 — SECTION 2

1 Name of Lower-tier Company	2 Name of Company Listed in Section 1 which controls Lower-tier Company	3 Amount of Intangible Assets Included in Amount Shown in Column 3, Section 1	Common Stock of Lower-tier Company Owned Indirectly by Insurer on Statement Date	
			4 No. of Shares	5 % of Outstanding
999999		TOTAL	XXXX	XXXX

ANNUAL STATEMENT FOR THE YEAR 19.. OF THE ....

SCHEDULE DA — PART 1

Showing All **SHORT-TERM INVESTMENTS** Current December 31 of Current Year

CUSIP Identi-fication***	1 Description** Give complete and accurate description of all investments owned including identifying the kind of investment vehicle if other than short-term bond	2 § Date Acquired	3 § Name of Vendor	4 § Interest		5 §Date of Maturity		6 Book Value	7 Increase or (Decrease) by Adjustment in Book Value During Year	8 Par Value	9 Rate Used To Obtain Statement Value	10 Statement Value (Excluding Accrued Interest)	11 Actual Cost (Excluding Accrued Interest)	12 Interest		13 Paid for Accrued Interest	14 NAIC Designation††	15 Effective Rate of Interest at Which Purchase Was Made §
				Rate Of	*How Paid	Yr.	Mo.							12 1 Amount Due and Accrued Dec. 31 of Current Year not in default	12 2 Gross Amount Received			

| Totals | | | | | | | | †† | | | XXX | | | | | | XXX | XXX |

*Insert initial Letters of months in which interest is payable

§Where an investment is payable in a foreign currency, the par value and the purchase price in that currency should be included as part of the description

***CUSIP numbers entered are to conform to those as provided and published by the Securities Valuation Office. See Annual Statement instructions.

†Include all investments whose maturities for repurchase rates under Repurchase Agreements, at time of acquisition were one year or less. Identify Repos. and certificates of deposit in Column and for Repos, show repurchase date

††Insert the NAIC Designation for such security printed in the NAIC Valuation of Securities Manual

††Includes $ .... either that accrual of discount and amortization of premium

§Purchases of various issues of the same issue of short-term investments may be totalled on one line and the word various inserted in the columns

179999

39

Form 2

ANNUAL STATEMENT FOR THE YEAR 1989 OF THE .... Name

SCHEDULE DA—PART 2

Verification of SHORT-TERM INVESTMENTS Between Years

	1 Total*	2 Bonds	3 Collateral Loans	4 Mortgage Loans	5 Other Short-term Investment Assets**	6 Investments in Parent Subsidiaries and Affiliates
1. Book value, previous year						
2. Cost of short-term investments acquired						
3. Increase by adjustment in book value						
4. Profit on disposal of short-term investments						
5. Subtotals (Total of items 2 to 4)						
6. Consideration received on disposal of short-term investments						
7. Decrease by adjustment in book value						
8. Loss on disposal of short-term investments						
9. Subtotals (Total of items 6 to 8)						
10. Book value, current year						
11. Income collected during year (Part 1, Line 6.2, Column 3)						
12. Income earned during year (Part 1, Line 6.2, Column 8)						

* Column 1 amounts equal the sum of Columns 2 through 6. Column 1, Line 10 equals Part 1, Column 6, total.

** Indicate the category of such assets, for example, joint ventures, transportation equipment.

Form 2

ANNUAL STATEMENT FOR THE YEAR 1989 OF THE .... (Name)

SCHEDULE DB — PART A — SECTION 1

Showing All Financial Options/Owned December 31 of Current Year

Separate financial options into 2 group, put options and call options, within each group. Show separately fixed income, equity and other financial options. Show subtotals for each group and category

1 Description of all financial options owned, including description of underlying security(s) or contract(s)	2 Expiration Date	3 Exercise Price	4 Indication of Existence of Hedge*	5 Date Acquired	6 Actual Cost	7 Increase/(Decrease) by Adjustment or Book Value	8 Book Value	9 Market Value	10 Statement Value	11 Gain (Loss) (a) Recognized	11 Gain (Loss) (b) Deferred

459999   Grand Totals

SCHEDULE DB — PART A — SECTION 2

Showing All Financial Options Acquired During Current Year

1 Description of all financial options acquired, including description of underlying security(s) or contract(s). Summary amounts by group may be shown for non-affiliated entities.	2 Expiration Date	3 Exercise Price	4 Indication of Existence of Hedge*	5 Name of Vendor	6 Date Acquired	7 Actual Cost

459999   Grand Total

*Has a comprehensive description of the hedge program been made available to the domiciliary state? _____ If not, attach a description with this statement.

Form 2

ANNUAL STATEMENT FOR THE YEAR 1989 OF THE ....

Name ....

Separate financial options into 2 groups, put options and
call options, within each group, show separately held in
income equals and other financial options. Show subtotals for
each group and category

SCHEDULE DB — PART A — SECTION 3

Showing All Financial Options Terminated During Current Year

1	2	3	4	5	6	7	8	9	10	11	12 Gain/(Loss) on Termination		
Description of financial options terminated including description of underlying security(s) or contract(s)	Expiration Date	Exercise Price	Indicate Exercise Expiration or Sale	Date Acquired	Date Terminated	Actual Cost	Increase/(Decrease) by Adjustment in Book Value During Year	Book Value at Termination Date	Consideration Received on Termination	Premiums Allocated to Purchase Cost or Sale Proceeds on Exercise	(a) Deferred	(b) Recognized	(c) Used to Adjust Basis of Hedge

| 459999 | Grand Totals | | | | | | | | | | | | | |

SCHEDULE DB—PART A—SECTION 4

Verification Between Years of Book Value of Financial Options Owned

1. Book value, December 31, previous year (Sec. 4, Line 7, previous year) ....
2. Cost of options acquired (Section 2, Column 7) ....
3. Increase/(decrease) by adjustment in book value of options (Sum of Section 1, Column 7 and Section 3, Column 8) ....
4. Deduct (gain)/loss on termination of options

    (a) deferred (Sec. 3, Col. 12a) ....

    (b) recognized (Sec. 3, Col. 12b) ....

    (c) used to adjust basis of hedge (Sec. 3, Col. 12c) ....

5. Deduct consideration received on termination of options (Section 3, Column 10) ....
6. Deduct premiums allocated to purchase cost or sale proceeds on exercise (Section 3, Column 11) ....
7. Book value of options owned, December 31, current year (Section 1, Column 8, current year) ....

ANNUAL STATEMENT FOR THE YEAR 19th OF THE ....

Name

SCHEDULE DB — PART B — SECTION 1

Showing All Financial Options Written and In-Force December 31 of Current Year

Separate financial options into 2 groups, put options and call options, within each group. Show separately fixed income, equity and other financial options. Show subtotals for each group and category.

1 Description of financial options written and in-force including description or underlying security(s) or contract(s)	2 XX	3 Expiration Date	4 Exercise Price	5 Indication of Existence of Hedge*	6 Date Issued	7 Consideration Received	8 Market Value	9 Statement Value	10 Gain/(Loss) (a) Recognized	10 Gain/(Loss) (b) Deferred
459999 Grand Totals										

SCHEDULE DB — PART B — SECTION 2

Showing All Financial Options Written During Current Year

1 Description of all financial options issued, including description of underlying security(s) or contract(s). Summary amount by group may be shown for non-affiliated entities.	2 XX	3 Expiration Date	4 Exercise Price	5 Indication of Existence of Hedge*	6 Date Issued	7 Consideration Received
459999 Grand Total						

* Was a comprehensive description of the hedge program been made available to the domiciliary state?   If not attach a description with this statement.
XX If a call option, indicate 'no' if the underlying investment was not owned at the time option was written; otherwise leave blank.

Form 2

ANNUAL STATEMENT FOR THE YEAR 1989 OF THE ....

Separate financial options into 2 groups: put options and
call options within each group show separately fixed income, equity and other financial options. Show subtotals for
each group and category

SCHEDULE DB — PART B — SECTION 3

Showing All Financial Options Written That Were Terminated During Current Year

1	2	3	4	5	6	7	8	9	10		
										Gain (Loss) on Termination	
Description of all financial options terminated including description of underlying security(s) or contract(s)	Expiration Date	Exercise Price	Date Issued	Date Terminated	Indication of Exercise Expiration or Closing Purchase Transaction	Consideration Received	Cost of Termination	Premiums Allocated to Purchase Cost or Sale Proceeds on Exercise	(a) Deferred	(b) Recognized	(c) Used to Adjust Basis of Hedge

Grand Totals

459999

SCHEDULE DB—PART B—SECTION 4

Verification Between Years of Consideration Received For Financial Options Written

1. Consideration received for financial options written and outstanding, previous year (Sec. 4, Line 6, previous year) ....
2. Consideration received for options written during year (Sec. 2, Col 7) ....
3. Deduct cost of terminating options by closing purchase transaction during year (Sec. 3, Col 8) ....
4. Deduct gain/(loss) on termination:
   (a) deferred (Sec. 3, Col 10a) ....
   (b) recognized (Sec. 3, Col 10b) ....
   (c) used to adjust basis of hedge (Sec. 3, Col 10c) ....
5. Deduct premiums allocated to purchase cost or sale proceeds on exercise (Sec. 3, Col 9) ....
6. Consideration received for financial options written and outstanding, current year (Sec. 1, Col 7 current year) ....

Form 2

ANNUAL STATEMENT FOR THE YEAR 1989 OF THE ....

.... (Name)

SCHEDULE DB—PART C—SECTION 1
Showing All Financial Futures Contracts Open December 31 of Current Year

Separate financial futures contracts into 2 groups, long positions and short positions, within each group. Show separately interest rate futures and other financial futures contracts. Show subtotals for each group and category.

1	2	3	4	5	6 Futures Contracts			7 Margin Information			
										Variance Margin	
Description of all financial futures contracts open	Number of Contracts	Date of Maturity	Indication of Existence of Hedge*		(a) Original Price	(b) Current Price	(c) Difference	(a) Initial Deposit Requirement	(b) Deferred Gain (Loss)	(c) Recognized Gain (Loss)	
			XX								
299999 Grand Totals											

SCHEDULE DB—PART C—SECTION 2
Showing All Financial Futures Contracts Opened During the Current Year

Description of each financial futures contract executed. Summary amounts by group may be shown for non-affiliated entities.

1	2	3	4	5	5	7	8	9
	Number of Contracts	Name of Vendor	Date of Opening Position	Date of Maturity	XX	Indication of Existence of Hedge*	Original Price of Futures Contracts	Initial Margin Deposit Requirement
299999 Grand Total								

* Has a comprehensive description of the hedge program been made available to the domiciliary state? .... If not, attach a description with this statement.
XX If contract requires the company to deliver securities at the contract maturity date, indicate "no" if the underlying instruments were not owned at the time the futures contract was opened; otherwise leave blank.

45

Form 2

ANNUAL STATEMENT FOR THE YEAR 1989 OF THE .... (Name)

SCHEDULE DB—PART C—SECTION 3

Showing All Financial Futures Contracts That Were Terminated During Current Year

Separate financial futures contracts into 2 groups: long positions and short positions, within each group, show separately interest rate futures and other financial futures contracts. Show subtotals for each group and category.

1	2	3	4	5 Futures Contracts			6 Margin Information		
Description of each financial futures contract terminated	Number of Contracts	Date of Termination	Indication of Existence of Hedge*	(a) Original Price	(b) Closing Transaction Price	(c) Gain (Loss) on Termination	(a) Gain (Loss) Utilized to Adjust Basis of Hedge	(b) Gain (Loss) Recognized in Current Year	(c) Gain (Loss) Deferred Over Year End

299999 Grand Totals

*Has a comprehensive description of the hedge program been made available to the domiciliary state? .... If not, attach a description with this statement.

SCHEDULE DB—PART C—SECTION 4

Verification Between Years of Deferred Gain/(Loss) on Financial Futures Contracts

1. Deferred gain/(loss), December 31, previous year (Sec. 4, Line 6, previous year) ....

2. Change in deferred gain/(loss) on open contracts (Difference between years—Sec. 1, Col. 7a) ....

3. a. Gain/(loss) on contracts terminated during the year (Sec. 3, Col. 5c) ....
   b. Less:
      (i) Gain/(loss) used to adjust basis of hedge (Sec. 3, Col. 6a) ....
      (ii) Gain/(loss) recognized in current year (Sec. 3, Col. 6b) ....
      (iii) Subtotal (Line 3b(i) plus 3b(ii)) ....
   c. Subtotal (Line 3a minus 3b(iii)) ....

4. Subtotal (Line 1 + Line 2 + Line 3c) ....

5. Less:
   Disposition of gain/(loss) on contracts terminated in prior years:
      (a) recognized ....
      (b) used to adjust basis of hedge ....

6. Deferred gain/(loss), December 31, current year (Line 4 minus Line 5) ....

ANNUAL STATEMENT FOR THE YEAR 1989 OF THE ....
(Name)

SCHEDULE F — PART 1A — SECTION 1

Ceded Reinsurance as of December 31, Current Year

Federal ID Number	Name of Reinsurer*	Location**	Reinsurance/Recoverable on Paid Losses Days Overdue					Reinsurance Recoverable on Unpaid Losses	Unearned Premiums (Estimated)	Reinsurance Premiums Ceded
			1					2	3	4
			(a) Current and 1-29	(b) 30-90	(c) 91-180	(d) Over 180	(e) Total			
0599999	Totals									

* All companies should be listed in straight alphabetical order within the following groups with subtotals shown for each group Affiliates; U.S. insurers; U.S. branches of alien insurers; pools, associations and similar underwriting facilities; and all other insurers

** Show the precise location of the reinsurance company

† Insert in this column, if applicable, the following letter designation: (I) Reinsurer in conservation, rehabilitation or liquidation, or in the case of an alien reinsurer, equivalent proceedings.

47

ANNUAL STATEMENT FOR THE YEAR 1989 OF THE ....
(Name)

SCHEDULE F — PART 1A — SECTION 2

Assumed Reinsurance as of December 31, Current Year (To be filed not later than April 1)

Federal ID Number	Name of Reinsured*	Location**	1 Reinsurance Payable on Paid Losses	2 Reinsurance Payable on Unpaid Losses	3 Unearned Premiums (Estimated)
059999 Grand Totals					

*All companies should be listed in straight alphabetical order within the following groups with subtotals shown for each group: Affiliates, U.S. insurers and U.S. branches of alien insurers; pools, associations and similar underwriting facilities, and all other insurers.
**Show the precise location of the reinsurance company.

ANNUAL STATEMENT FOR THE YEAR 1989 OF THE ....

SCHEDULE F — PART 1B

Portfolio Reinsurance Effected or (Cancelled) during Current Year

Federal ID Number	Name of Company	1 Date of Contract	2 Amount of Original Premiums	3 Amount of Reinsurance Premiums
	(a) Reinsurance Ceded			
019999	Total Reinsurance Ceded by Portfolio			
	(b) Reinsurance Assumed			
029999	Total Reinsurance Assumed by Portfolio			

Form 2

ANNUAL STATEMENT FOR THE YEAR 1989 OF THE ....

SCHEDULE F — PART 2A

Funds Withheld on Account of Reinsurance in Unauthorized Companies as of December 31, Current Year

Federal ID Number	Name of Reinsurer	1 Unearned Premiums (Debit)	2 (a) Paid and Unpaid Losses Recoverable (Total of amounts in Cols. 1 + 2 of Schedule F Part 1A, Section I for unauthorized companies) (Debit)	2 (b) Incurred But Not Reported Losses Recoverable (Estimates of amounts recoverable from unauthorized companies) (Debit)	2 (c) Paid and Unpaid Allocated Loss Adjustment Expenses Recoverable (Debit)	3 Total 1 + 2a + 2b + 2c	4 Deposits by and Funds Withheld from Reinsurers (Credit)	5 Miscellaneous Balances (Credit)	6 Sum of 4 + 5 but not or excess of 3

999999   TOTALS

NOTES: Total of Column 6 to agree with deduction taken in Item 13d, Page 3

Securities held on deposit or held in a trust account should be valued at their fair market value.

NAIC published market values must be used when available.

Amounts included in Column 4 should be identified separately as letters of credit (LL), trust agreements (T), funds deposited by and withheld from reinsurer (F), or other (O).

Letters of credit and trust agreements are not to be included in assets or liabilities on Pages 2 or 3 or supporting pages or exhibits.

ANNUAL STATEMENT FOR THE YEAR 1989 OF THE ....
(Name)

SCHEDULE F — PART 2B — SECTION 1

Provision for overdue authorized reinsurance as of December 31, Current Year

Federal ID Number	Name of Reinsurer	1 Amounts 90 Days Overdue	2 Reinsurance Recoverable on Paid Losses	3 Amounts Received Prior 90 Days	4 Col 1 divided by (Col 2 + Col 3)	5 Amounts in Column 1 for Companies Reporting Less than 20% in Column 4
	TOTALS					

NOTES (1) Amounts in dispute should be excluded from Columns 1 and 2
(2) If the results of the calculation in Column 4 exceeds 20%, complete Schedule F, Part 2B, Section 2
(3) Carry Column 5 total to Schedule F, Part 2B, Section 2 for calculation of Provisions for Overdue Authorized Reinsurance

SCHEDULE F — PART 2B — SECTION 2

Provision for overdue authorized reinsurance as of December 31, Current Year

Federal ID Number	Name of Reinsurer	1 Unearned Premiums (Debit)	2 (a) Paid and Unpaid Losses Recoverable (Amounts in Cols (?) + 7 of Sch F, Part 1A, Section 1 for authorized companies) (Debit)	2 (b) Incurred But Not Reported Losses Recoverable (Estimates of amounts recoverable from authorized companies (Debit)	2 (c) Paid and Unpaid Allocated Loss Adjustment Expenses Recoverable (Debit)	3 Total 1 + 2a + 2b + 2c	4 Deposits by and Funds Withheld from Reinsurers (Credit)	5 Miscellaneous Balances (Credit)	6 Sum of [illegible] but not in excess [illegible]
	TOTALS								

CALCULATION OF PROVISION FOR OVERDUE AUTHORIZED REINSURANCE
(1) Total from Column 5 of Schedule F, Part 2B, Section 1
(2) Total from Column 3 of Schedule F, Part 2B, Section 2
(3) Total from Column 6 of Schedule F, Part 2B, Section 2
(4) (1) + (2) (3)
(5) Total Provision for Overdue Authorized Reinsurance (20 + (4))
Enter this amount on Page 3, Item 13e

NOTES: Securities held on deposit or held in a trust account should be valued at their fair market value
NAIC published market values must be used when available
Amounts included in Column 4 should be identified separately as letters of credit (1), trust agreements (1), funds deposited by and withheld from [illegible]
Letters of credit and trust agreements are not to be included in assets or liabilities on Pages 2 or 3 or supporting pages or exhibits

Form 2

ANNUAL STATEMENT FOR THE YEAR 1989 OF THE ....

SCHEDULE H—ACCIDENT AND HEALTH EXHIBIT

(To be filed not later than April 1)

PART 1.—ANALYSIS OF UNDERWRITING OPERATIONS

	1 Total		2 Group Accident and Health		3 Credit[a] (Group and Individual)		4 Collectively Renewable		5 Non Cancellable		6 Guaranteed Renewable		Other Individual Policies			
													Non Cancellable for Stated Reasons Only		Other	
	Amount	%	Amount	%	Amount	%	Amount	%	Amount	%	Amount	%	Amount	%	Amount	%
1 Premiums written																
2 Premiums earned (see note b)																
3 Incurred claims																
4 Increase in policy reserves																
5 Commissions*																
6 General insurance expenses																
7 Taxes, licenses and fees																
8 Total expenses incurred																
8A Aggregate write-ins for deductions																
9 Gain from underwriting before dividends to policyholders																
10 Dividends to policyholders																
11 Gain from underwriting after dividends to policyholders																

DETAILS OF WRITE-INS AGGREGATED AT ITEM 8A FOR DEDUCTIONS

08A01																
08A02																
08A03																
08A04																
08A05 Summary of remaining write-ins for Item 8A from overflow page																
08A98																
08A99 Total (Items 8A01 thru 8A05 plus 8A98 (Schedule H, Part 1 Item 8A)																

* In each column of Part 1, show the percentages of Line 2 for Lines 3 through 11 inclusive
* Includes $ .... reported as "Policy membership and other fees retained by agents.
(a) Business not exceeding 120 months duration
(b) Premiums earned are before adjustment for the increase in policy reserves which has been treated as a separate deduction

ANNUAL STATEMENT FOR THE YEAR 1989 OF THE ....

(Name)

SCHEDULE H—ACCIDENT AND HEALTH EXHIBIT (Continued)

(To be filed not later than April 1)

	1 Total	2 Group Accident and Health	3 Credit[b] (Group and Individual)	4 (Effectively) Renewable	5 Non-Cancellable	6 Guaranteed Renewable	7 Non-Renewable for Stated Reasons Only	8 Other Accident Only	9 All Other

PART 2.—RESERVES AND LIABILITIES

A. Premium Reserves:
  1. Unearned premiums
  2. Advance premiums
  3. Reserve for rate credits
  4. Total premium reserves, current year
  5. Total premium reserves, previous year
  6. Increase in total premium reserves

B. Policy Reserves:
  1. Additional reserves
  2. Reserve for future contingent benefit. (deferred maternity and other similar benefits)**
  3. Total policy reserves, current year
  4. Total policy reserves, previous year
  5. Increase in policy reserves

C. Claim Reserves and Liabilities:
  1. Total current year
  2. Total previous year
  3. Increase

PART 3.—TEST OF PREVIOUS YEAR'S CLAIM RESERVES AND LIABILITIES

1. Claims paid during the year:
  a. On claims incurred prior to current year
  b. On claims incurred during current year
2. Claim reserves and liabilities, December 31, current year:
  a. On claims incurred prior to current year
  b. On claims incurred during current year
3. Test:
  a. Line 1a and 2a
  b. Claim reserves and liabilities, December 31, previous year
  c. Line a minus line b

PART 4.—REINSURANCE

A. Reinsurance assumed
  1. Premiums written
  2. Premiums earned (see note b)
  3. Incurred claims
  4. Commissions

B. Reinsurance Ceded
  1. Premiums written
  2. Premiums earned (see note b)
  3. Incurred claims
  4. Commissions

a Business not exceeding 120 months duration
** If not included in claim reserves
(b) Premiums earned are before adjustment for the increase in policy reserves which has been treated as a separate deduction.

53

ANNUAL STATEMENT FOR THE YEAR 1989 OF THE ....
(Name)

SCHEDULE M—PART 1

Showing all direct or indirect payments of more than $100 (exclusive of expenses paid in connection with settlement of losses, claims and salvage
under policy contracts) in connection with any matter, measure or proceeding before legislative bodies, officers or departments of government
during the year, excluding company's share of such expenditures made by organizations listed in Part 4 below.

1 Payee		2	3
Name	Address	Amount Paid	Matter, Measure or Proceeding

SCHEDULE M—PART 2

Showing all payments (other than salary, compensation, emoluments and dividends) to or on behalf of any officer, director or employee which exceeded
$1,000 or amounted in the aggregate to more than $10,000 during the year. (Excluding reimbursement of expenditures for transportation, board and
lodging of Company Auditors, Inspectors, Claims Investigators and Adjusters, and Special Agents, and excluding payments listed in Part 1.)

1 Name of Payee	2 Amount Paid	3 Occasion of Expense

ANNUAL STATEMENT FOR THE YEAR 1989 OF THE ....
(Name)

SCHEDULE M—PART 3

Showing all payments for legal expenses which exceeded $500 or aggregated more than $5,000 during the year, exclusive of
payments in connection with settlement of losses, claims and salvage under policy contracts. (Excluding payments listed in Part 1.)

1 Payee		2	3
Name	Address	Amount Paid	Occasion of Expense

SCHEDULE M—PART 4

Showing all payments in excess of $1,000 to each Trade Association, Service Organization, Statistical, Actuarial or Rating Bureau during the year.
(A service organization is defined as every person, partnership, association or corporation who or which formulates rules, establishes standards
or assists in the making of rates, rules, or standards for the information or benefit of insurers or rating organizations.)

1 Payee		2	3
Name	Address	Amount Paid	Occasion of Expense

ANNUAL STATEMENT FOR THE YEAR 1989 OF THE ....
(Name)

SCHEDULE N

Showing all Banks, Trust Companies, Savings and Loan and Building and Loan Associations in which deposits were maintained by the company at any time during the year and the balances, if any (according to Company's records) on December 31, of the current year. Exclude balances represented by a negotiable instrument.

1 Depository* (Give Full Name and Location. State if depository is a parent, subsidiary or affiliate.) Show rate of interest and maturity date in the case of certificates of deposit or time deposits	2 Amount of Interest Received During Year	3 Amount of Interest Accrued December 31 of Current Year	4 Balance
OPEN DEPOSITORIES			
019999 TOTALS—Open Depositories			
SUSPENDED DEPOSITORIES			
029999 TOTALS—Suspended Depositories			
039999 GRAND TOTALS—All Depositories			

TOTALS OF DEPOSITORY BALANCES ON THE LAST DAY OF EACH MONTH DURING THE CURRENT YEAR

January		April		July		October	
February		May		August		November	
March		June		September		December	

* In each case where the depository is not incorporated and subject to governmental supervision, the word "PRIVATE" in capitals and in parentheses, thus — (PRIVATE), should be inserted to the left of the name of the depository. Any deposit in a suspended depository which is taken credit for should have a star placed opposite the amount in the schedule.

Deposits in federally insured depositories not exceeding $40,000 may be combined and reported opposite the caption "Deposits in (insert number) depositories which do not exceed the $40,000 amount in any one depository."

Short-Term Negotiable Certificates of Deposit to be reported in Schedule DA. Long-Term Negotiable Certificates of Deposit to be reported in Schedule D.

ANNUAL STATEMENT FOR THE YEAR 1989 OF THE

SCHEDULE P — ANALYSIS OF LOSSES AND LOSS EXPENSES

Notes to Schedule P

(1) The Parts of Schedule P
   Part 1   detailed information on losses and loss expenses
   Part 2   history of incurred losses and allocated expenses
   Part 3   history of loss and allocated expense payments
   Part 4   derated discount information now in Part 1 and Notes to Financial Statements. Reserved for future use
   Part 5   schedule for claims-made policies
   Part 6   history of bulk and incurred but not reported reserves
   Schedule P interrogatories

(2) Lines of business A through M are groupings of the lines of business used on page 14 the state page

(3) Reinsurance A, B, C and D (lines N to Q) are
   Reinsurance A   nonproportional property (1988 and subsequent)
   Reinsurance B   nonproportional liability (1988 and subsequent)
   Reinsurance C   financial lines (1988 and subsequent)
   Reinsurance D   old Schedule O line 30 (1987 and prior)

(4) The instructions to Schedule P contain directions necessary for filling out Schedule P

SCHEDULE P—PART 1—SUMMARY
(000 omitted)

1	Premiums Earned			Loss and Loss Expense Payments								
Years In Which Premiums Were Earned and Losses Were Incurred				Loss Payments		Allocated Loss Expense Payments		9	10	11	12	
	2 Direct and Assumed	3 Ceded	4 Net (2 3)	5 Direct and Assumed	6 Ceded	7 Direct and Assumed	8 Ceded	Salvage and Subrogation Received	Uncollected Loss Expense Payments	Total Net Paid (5 6 7 8 10)	Number of Claims Reported Direct and Assumed	
1. Prior	XXXX	XXXX	XXXX								XXXX	
2. 1980											XXXX	
3. 1981											XXXX	
4. 1982											XXXX	
5. 1983											XXXX	
6. 1984											XXXX	
7. 1985											XXXX	
8. 1986											XXXX	
9. 1987											XXXX	
10. 1988											XXXX	
11. 1989											XXXX	
12. Totals	XXXX	XXXX	XXXX								XXXX	

Note. For "prior" report amounts paid or received in current year only. Report cumulative amounts paid or received for specific years.
Report loss payments net of salvage and subrogation received

Years In Which Premiums Were Earned and Losses Were Incurred	Losses Unpaid				Allocated Loss Expenses Unpaid				21	22	23
	Case Basis		Bulk + IBNR		Case Basis		Bulk IBNR		Unallocated Loss Expenses Unpaid	Total Net Losses and Expenses Unpaid	Number of Claims Outstanding— Direct and Assumed
	13 Direct and Assumed	14 Ceded	15 Direct and Assumed	16 Ceded	17 Direct and Assumed	18 Ceded	19 Direct and Assumed	20 Ceded			
1. Prior											XXXX
2. 1980											XXXX
3. 1981											XXXX
4. 1982											XXXX
5. 1983											XXXX
6. 1984											XXXX
7. 1985											XXXX
8. 1986											XXXX
9. 1987											XXXX
10. 1988											XXXX
11. 1989											XXXX
12. Totals											XXXX

Years In Which Premiums Were Earned and Losses Were Incurred	Total Losses and Loss Expenses Incurred			Loss and Loss Expense Percentage (Incurred/Premiums Earned)			Discount for Time Value of Money		32	Net Balance Sheet Reserves After Discount	
	24 Direct and Assumed	25 Ceded	26 Net*	27 Direct and Assumed	28 Ceded	29 Net	30 Loss	31 Loss Expense	Inter-Company Pooling Participation Percentage	33 Losses Unpaid	34 Loss Expenses Unpaid
1. Prior	XXXX	XXXX	XXXX	XXXX	XXXX	XXXX			XXXX		
2. 1980											
3. 1981											
4. 1982											
5. 1983											
6. 1984											
7. 1985											
8. 1986											
9. 1987											
10. 1988											
11. 1989											
12. Totals	XXXX	XXXX	XXXX	XXXX	XXXX	XXXX			XXXX		

*Net = (24 − 25) = (11 + 22)

ANNUAL STATEMENT FOR THE YEAR 1989 OF THE

(Name)

SCHEDULE P — PART 2 — SUMMARY

Years in Which Losses Were Incurred	INCURRED LOSSES AND ALLOCATED EXPENSES REPORTED AT YEAR END (000 OMITTED)										DEVELOPMENT**	
	2 1980	3 1981	4 1982	5 1983	6 1984	7 1985	8 1986	9 1987	10 1988	11 1989	12 One Year	13 Two Year
1 Prior												
2 1980	XXXX											
3 1981	XXXX	XXXX										
4 1982	XXXX	XXXX	XXXX									
5 1983	XXXX	XXXX	XXXX	XXXX								
6 1984	XXXX	XXXX	XXXX	XXXX	XXXX							
7 1985	XXXX	XXXX	XXXX	XXXX	XXXX	XXXX						
8 1986	XXXX	XXXX	XXXX	XXXX	XXXX	XXXX	XXXX					
9 1987	XXXX	XXXX	XXXX	XXXX	XXXX	XXXX	XXXX	XXXX				
10 1988	XXXX	XXXX	XXXX	XXXX	XXXX	XXXX	XXXX	XXXX	XXXX			XXXX
11 1989	XXXX	XXXX	XXXX	XXXX	XXXX	XXXX	XXXX	XXXX	XXXX	XXXX	XXXX	XXXX

*Reported reserves only. Subsequent development relates only to subsequent payments and reserves.
**Current year less first or second prior year showing (redundant) or adverse

12 Totals

SCHEDULE P — PART 3 — SUMMARY

1 Years in Which Losses Were Incurred	CUMULATIVE PAID LOSSES AND ALLOCATED EXPENSES REPORTED AT YEAR END (000 OMITTED)										12 Number of Claims Closed With Loss Payment	13 Number of Claims Closed Without Loss Payment
	2 1980	3 1981	4 1982	5 1983	6 1984	7 1985	8 1986	9 1987	10 1988	11 1989		
1 Prior	000										XXXX	XXXX
2 1980											XXXX	XXXX
3 1981	XXXX										XXXX	XXXX
4 1982	XXXX	XXXX									XXXX	XXXX
5 1983	XXXX	XXXX	XXXX								XXXX	XXXX
6 1984	XXXX	XXXX	XXXX	XXXX							XXXX	XXXX
7 1985	XXXX	XXXX	XXXX	XXXX	XXXX						XXXX	XXXX
8 1986	XXXX	XXXX	XXXX	XXXX	XXXX	XXXX					XXXX	XXXX
9 1987	XXXX	XXXX	XXXX	XXXX	XXXX	XXXX	XXXX				XXXX	XXXX
10 1988	XXXX	XXXX	XXXX	XXXX	XXXX	XXXX	XXXX	XXXX			XXXX	XXXX
11 1989	XXXX	XXXX	XXXX	XXXX	XXXX	XXXX	XXXX	XXXX	XXXX		XXXX	XXXX

Note: Net of salvage and subrogation received.

SCHEDULE P — PART 6 — SUMMARY

1 Years in Which Losses Were Incurred	BULK AND INCURRED BUT NOT REPORTED RESERVES ON LOSSES AND ALLOCATED EXPENSES AT YEAR END (000 OMITTED)									
	2 1980	3 1981	4 1982	5 1983	6 1984	7 1985	8 1986	9 1987	10 1988	11 1989
1 Prior										
2 1980										
3 1981	XXXX									
4 1982	XXXX	XXXX								
5 1983	XXXX	XXXX	XXXX							
6 1984	XXXX	XXXX	XXXX	XXXX						
7 1985	XXXX	XXXX	XXXX	XXXX	XXXX					
8 1986	XXXX	XXXX	XXXX	XXXX	XXXX	XXXX				
9 1987	XXXX	XXXX	XXXX	XXXX	XXXX	XXXX	XXXX			
10 1988	XXXX	XXXX	XXXX	XXXX	XXXX	XXXX	XXXX	XXXX		
11 1989	XXXX	XXXX	XXXX	XXXX	XXXX	XXXX	XXXX	XXXX	XXXX	

ANNUAL STATEMENT FOR THE YEAR 1989 OF THE   Name

SCHEDULE P—PART 1A—HOMEOWNERS/FARMOWNERS
(000 omitted)

Years In Which Premiums Were Earned and Losses Were Incurred	Premiums Earned			Loss and Loss Expense Payments								
	2 Direct and Assumed	3 Ceded	4 Net (2 - 3)	Loss Payments		Allocated Loss Expense Payments		9 Salvage and Subrogation Received	10 Unallocated Loss Expense Payments	11 Total Net Paid (5 - 6 - 7 - 8 - 10)	12 Number of Claims Reported Direct and Assumed
				5 Direct and Assumed	6 Ceded	7 Direct and Assumed	8 Ceded				
1 Prior	XXXX	XXXX	XXXX								XXXX
2 1980											XXXX
3 1981											XXXX
4 1982											XXXX
5 1983											XXXX
6 1984											XXXX
7 1985											XXXX
8 1986											XXXX
9 1987											XXXX
10 1988											XXXX
11 1989											XXXX
12 Totals	XXXX	XXXX	XXXX								XXXX

Note For "prior" report amounts paid or received in current year only. Report cumulative amounts paid or received for specific years.
Report loss payments net of salvage and subrogation received

Years In Which Premiums Were Earned and Losses Were Incurred	Losses Unpaid				Allocated Loss Expenses Unpaid				21 Unallocated Loss Expenses Unpaid	22 Total Net Losses and Expenses Unpaid	23 Number of Claims Outstanding Direct and Assumed
	Case Basis		Bulk - IBNR		Case Basis		Bulk - IBNR				
	13 Direct and Assumed	14 Ceded	15 Direct and Assumed	16 Ceded	17 Direct and Assumed	18 Ceded	19 Direct and Assumed	20 Ceded			
1 Prior											
2 1980											
3 1981											
4 1982											
5 1983											
6 1984											
7 1985											
8 1986											
9 1987											
10 1988											
11 1989											
12 Totals											

Years In Which Premiums Were Earned and Losses Were Incurred	Total Losses and Loss Expenses Incurred			Loss and Loss Expense Percentage (Incurred Premiums Earned)			Discount for Time Value of Money		32 Inter-Company Pooling Participation Percentage	Net Balance Sheet Reserves After Discount	
	24 Direct and Assumed	25 Ceded	26 Net*	27 Direct and Assumed	28 Ceded	29 Net	30 Loss	31 Loss Expense		33 Losses Unpaid	34 Loss Expenses Unpaid
1 Prior	XXXX	XXXX	XXXX	XXXX	XXXX	XXXX			XXXX		
2 1980											
3 1981											
4 1982											
5 1983											
6 1984											
7 1985											
8 1986											
9 1987											
10 1988											
11 1989											
12 Totals	XXXX	XXXX	XXXX	XXX	XXXX	XXXX			XXXX		

*Net = (24 - 25)² = (11 + 22)

ANNUAL STATEMENT FOR THE YEAR 1989 OF THE

SCHEDULE P—PART 1B—PRIVATE PASSENGER AUTO LIABILITY/MEDICAL

Years in Which Premiums Were Earned and Losses Were Incurred	Premiums Earned			Loss and Loss Expense Payments							Number of Claims Reported Direct and Assumed
				Loss Payments		Allocated Loss Expense Payments		9	10	11	12
	1 Direct and Assumed	2 Ceded	3 Net (1 - 2)	4 Direct and Assumed	5 Ceded	6 Direct and Assumed	8 Ceded	Salvage and Subrogation Received	Unallocated Loss Expense Payments	Total Net Paid (5 - 6 - 7 - 8 - 10)	
1. Prior	X X X X	X X X X	X X X X								X X X X
2. 1980											
3. 1981											
4. 1982											
5. 1983											
6. 1984											
7. 1985											
8. 1986											
9. 1987											
10. 1988											
11. 1989											
12 Totals	X X X X	X X X X	X X X X								X X X X

Note: For prior report amounts paid or received in current year only. Report cumulative amounts paid or received for specific years.
Report loss payments net of salvage and subrogation received.

Years in Which Premiums Were Earned and Losses Were Incurred	Losses Unpaid				Allocated Loss Expenses Unpaid				21	22	23
	Case Basis		Bulk - IBNR		Case Basis		Bulk - IBNR		Unallocated Loss Expenses Unpaid	Total Net Losses and Expenses Unpaid	Number of Claims Outstanding Direct and Assumed
	13 Direct and Assumed	14 Ceded	15 Direct and Assumed	16 Ceded	17 Direct and Assumed	18 Ceded	19 Direct and Assumed	20 Ceded			
1 Prior											
2 1980											
3 1981											
4 1982											
5 1983											
6 1984											
7 1985											
8 1986											
9 1987											
10 1988											
11 1989											
12 Totals											

Years in Which Premiums Were Earned and Losses Were Incurred	Total Losses and Loss Expenses Incurred			Loss and Loss Expense Percentage (Incurred Premiums Earned)			Discount for Time Value of Money		32	Net Balance Sheet Reserves After Discount	
	24 Direct and Assumed	25 Ceded	26 Net*	27 Direct and Assumed	28 Ceded	29 Net	30 Loss	31 Loss Expense	Inter Company Pooling Participation Percentage	33 Losses Unpaid	34 Loss Expenses Unpaid
1 Prior	X X X X	X X X X	X X X X	X X X X	X X X X	X X X X			X X X X		
2 1980											
3 1981											
4 1982											
5 1983											
6 1984											
7 1985											
8 1986											
9 1987											
10 1988											
11 1989											
12 Totals	X X X X	X X X X	X X X X	X X X	X X X X	X X X X			X X X X		

*Net (24 - 25) (21 - 22)

ANNUAL STATEMENT FOR THE YEAR 1989 OF THE ....
(Name)

SCHEDULE P—PART 1C—COMMERCIAL AUTO/TRUCK LIABILITY/MEDICAL
(000 omitted)

1 Years In Which Premiums Were Earned and Losses Were Incurred	Premiums Earned			Loss and Loss Expense Payments								12 Number of Claims Reported Direct and Assumed
	2 Direct and Assumed	3 Ceded	4 Net (2 - 3)	Loss Payments		Allocated Loss Expense Payments		9 Salvage and Subrogation Received	10 Unallocated Loss Expense Payments	11 Total Net Paid (5 - 6 - 7 8 - 10)		
				5 Direct and Assumed	6 Ceded	7 Direct and Assumed	8 Ceded					
1 Prior	X X X X	X X X X	X X X X									X X X X
2 1980												
3 1981												
4 1982												
5 1983												
6 1984												
7 1985												
8 1986												
9 1987												
10 1988												
11 1989												
12 Totals	X X X X	X X X X	X X X X									X X X X

Note For "prior" report amounts paid or received in current year only. Report cumulative amounts paid or received for specific years.
Report loss payments net of salvage and subrogation received

Years In Which Premiums Were Earned and Losses Were Incurred	Losses Unpaid				Allocated Loss Expenses Unpaid				21 Unallocated Loss Expenses Unpaid	22 Total Net Losses and Expenses Unpaid	23 Number of Claims Outstanding Direct and Assumed
	Case Basis		Bulk - IBNR		Case Basis		Bulk - IBNR				
	13 Direct and Assumed	14 Ceded	15 Direct and Assumed	16 Ceded	17 Direct and Assumed	18 Ceded	19 Direct and Assumed	20 Ceded			
1 Prior											
2 1980											
3 1981											
4 1982											
5 1983											
6 1984											
7 1985											
8 1986											
9 1987											
10 1988											
11 1989											
12 Totals											

Years In Which Premiums Were Earned and Losses Were Incurred	Total Losses and Loss Expenses Incurred			Loss and Loss Expense Percentage (Incurred Premiums Earned)			Discount for Time Value of Money		32 Inter-Company Pooling Participation Percentage	Net Balance Sheet Reserves After Discount	
	24 Direct and Assumed	25 Ceded	26 Net*	27 Direct and Assumed	28 Ceded	29 Net	30 Loss	31 Loss Expense		33 Losses Unpaid	34 Loss Expenses Unpaid
1 Prior	X X X X	X X X X	X X X X	X X X X	X X X X	X X X X			X X X X		
2 1980											
3 1981											
4 1982											
5 1983											
6 1984											
7 1985											
8 1986											
9 1987											
10 1988											
11 1989											
12 Totals	X X X X	X X X X	X X X X	X X X X	X X X X	X X X X			X X X X		

*Net - (24 - 25) - (11 + 22)

ANNUAL STATEMENT FOR THE YEAR 1989 OF THE ....
(Name)

SCHEDULE P—PART 1D—WORKERS' COMPENSATION
(000 omitted)

Years In Which Premiums Were Earned and Losses Were Incurred	Premiums Earned			Loss and Loss Expense Payments								Number of Claims Reported— Direct and Assumed
				Loss Payments		Allocated Loss Expense Payments		9	10	11	12	
	2 Direct and Assumed	3 Ceded	4 Net (2 - 3)	5 Direct and Assumed	6 Ceded	7 Direct and Assumed	8 Ceded	Salvage and Subrogation Received	Unallocated Loss Expense Payments	Total Net Paid (5 - 6 - 7 - 8 - 10)		
1 Prior	XXXX	XXXX	XXXX									XXXX
2 1980												
3 1981												
4 1982												
5 1983												
6 1984												
7 1985												
8 1986												
9 1987												
10 1988												
11 1989												
12 Totals	XXXX	XXXX	XXXX									XXXX

Note For "prior" report amounts paid or received in current year only. Report cumulative amounts paid or received for specific years.
Report loss payments net of salvage and subrogation received

Years In Which Premiums Were Earned and Losses Were Incurred	Losses Unpaid				Allocated Loss Expenses Unpaid				21	22	23
	Case Basis		Bulk - IBNR		Case Basis		Bulk - IBNR		Unallocated Loss Expenses Unpaid	Total Net Losses and Expenses Unpaid	Number of Claims Outstanding — Direct and Assumed
	13 Direct and Assumed	14 Ceded	15 Direct and Assumed	16 Ceded	17 Direct and Assumed	18 Ceded	19 Direct and Assumed	20 Ceded			
1 Prior											
2 1980											
3 1981											
4 1982											
5 1983											
6 1984											
7 1985											
8 1986											
9 1987											
10 1988											
11 1989											
12 Totals											

Years In Which Premiums Were Earned and Losses Were Incurred	Total Losses and Loss Expenses Incurred			Loss and Loss Expense Percentage (Incurred Premiums Earned)			Discount for Time Value of Money		32	Net Balance Sheet Reserves After Discount	
	24 Direct and Assumed	25 Ceded	26 Net	27 Direct and Assumed	28 Ceded	29 Net	30 Loss	31 Loss Expense	Inter-Company Pooling Participation Percentage	33 Losses Unpaid	34 Loss Expenses Unpaid
1 Prior	XXXX	XXXX	XXXX	XXXX	XXXX	XXXX			XXXX		
2 1980											
3 1981											
4 1982											
5 1983											
6 1984											
7 1985											
8 1986											
9 1987											
10 1988											
11 1989											
12 Totals	XXXX	XXXX	XXXX	XXXX	XXXX	XXXX			XXXX		

*Net (24 - 25) (21 - 22)

ANNUAL STATEMENT FOR THE YEAR 1989 OF THE ....
(Name)

SCHEDULE P—PART 1E—COMMERCIAL MULTIPLE PERIL
(000 omitted)

1 Years In Which Premiums Were Earned and Losses Were Incurred	Premiums Earned			Loss and Loss Expense Payments							12 Number of Claims Reported Direct and Assumed
	2 Direct and Assumed	3 Ceded	4 Net (2 3)	Loss Payments		Allocated Loss Expense Payments		9 Salvage and Subrogation Received	10 Unallocated Loss Expense Payments	11 Total Net Paid (5 6 7 8 10)	
				5 Direct and Assumed	6 Ceded	7 Direct and Assumed	8 Ceded				
1 Prior	XXXX	XXXX	XXXX								XXXX
2 1980											
3 1981											
4 1982											
5 1983											
6 1984											
7 1985											
8 1986											
9 1987											
10 1988											
11 1989											
12 Totals	XXXX	XXXX	XXXX								XXXX

Note For "prior" report amounts paid or received in current year only Report cumulative amounts paid or received for specific years
Report loss payments net of salvage and subrogation received

Years In Which Premiums Were Earned and Losses Were Incurred	Losses Unpaid				Allocated Loss Expenses Unpaid				21 Unallocated Loss Expenses Unpaid	22 Total Net Losses and Expenses Unpaid	23 Number of Claims Outstanding— Direct and Assumed
	Case Basis		Bulk - IBNR		Case Basis		Bulk - IBNR				
	13 Direct and Assumed	14 Ceded	15 Direct and Assumed	16 Ceded	17 Direct and Assumed	18 Ceded	19 Direct and Assumed	20 Ceded			
1 Prior											
2 1980											
3 1981											
4 1982											
5 1983											
6 1984											
7 1985											
8 1986											
9 1987											
10 1988											
11 1989											
12 Totals											

Years In Which Premiums Were Earned and Losses Were Incurred	Total Losses and Loss Expenses Incurred			Loss and Loss Expense Percentage (Incurred Premiums Earned)			Discount for Time Value of Money		32 Inter-Company Pooling Participation Percentage	Net Balance Sheet Reserves After Discount	
	24 Direct and Assumed	25 Ceded	26 Net*	27 Direct and Assumed	28 Ceded	29 Net	30 Loss	31 Loss Expense		33 Losses Unpaid	34 Loss Expenses Unpaid
1 Prior	XXXX	XXXX	XXXX	XXXX	XXXX	XXXX			XXXX		
2 1980											
3 1981											
4 1982											
5 1983											
6 1984											
7 1985											
8 1986											
9 1987											
10 1988											
11 1989											
12 Totals	XXXX	XXXX	XXXX	XXXX	XXXX	XXXX			XXXX		

*Net (24 25) (11 22)

ANNUAL STATEMENT FOR THE YEAR 1989 OF THE ....
(Name)

SCHEDULE P—PART 1F—MEDICAL MALPRACTICE
(000 omitted)

Years In Which Premiums Were Earned and Losses Were Incurred	Premiums Earned			Loss and Loss Expense Payments							Number of Claims Reported—Direct and Assumed
				Loss Payments		Allocated Loss Expense Payments		9	10	11	12
	2 Direct and Assumed	3 Ceded	4 Net (2 - 3)	5 Direct and Assumed	6 Ceded	7 Direct and Assumed	8 Ceded	Salvage and Subrogation Received	Unallocated Loss Expense Payments	Total Net Paid (5 - 6 + 7 - 8 - 10)	
1 Prior	XXXX	XXXX	XXXX								XXXX
2 1980											
3 1981											
4 1982											
5 1983											
6 1984											
7 1985											
8 1986											
9 1987											
10 1988											
11 1989											
12 Totals	XXXX	XXXX	XXXX								XXXX

Note: For "prior" report amounts paid or received in current year only. Report cumulative amounts paid or received for specific years.
Report loss payments net of salvage and subrogation received

Years In Which Premiums Were Earned and Losses Were Incurred	Losses Unpaid				Allocated Loss Expenses Unpaid				21 Unallocated Loss Expenses Unpaid	22 Total Net Losses and Expenses Unpaid	23 Number of Claims Outstanding—Direct and Assumed
	Case Basis		Bulk - IBNR		Case Basis		Bulk - IBNR				
	13 Direct and Assumed	14 Ceded	15 Direct and Assumed	16 Ceded	17 Direct and Assumed	18 Ceded	19 Direct and Assumed	20 Ceded			
1 Prior											
2 1980											
3 1981											
4 1982											
5 1983											
6 1984											
7 1985											
8 1986											
9 1987											
10 1988											
11 1989											
12 Totals											

Years In Which Premiums Were Earned and Losses Were Incurred	Total Losses and Loss Expenses Incurred			Loss and Loss Expense Percentage (Incurred Premiums Earned)			Discount for Time Value of Money		32 Inter-Company Pooling Participation Percentage	Net Balance Sheet Reserves After Discount	
	24 Direct and Assumed	25 Ceded	26 Net	27 Direct and Assumed	28 Ceded	29 Net	30 Loss	31 Loss Expense		33 Losses Unpaid	34 Loss Expenses Unpaid
1 Prior	XXXX	XXXX	XXXX	XXXX	XXXX	XXXX			XXXX		
2 1980											
3 1981											
4 1982											
5 1983											
6 1984											
7 1985											
8 1986											
9 1987											
10 1988											
11 1989											
12 Totals	XXXX	XXXX	XXXX	XXX	XXXX	XXXX			XXXX		

*Net (24 - 25) (11 - 22)

Form 2   ANNUAL STATEMENT FOR THE YEAR 1989 OF THE

SCHEDULE P—PART 1G—SPECIAL LIABILITY (OCEAN MARINE, AIRCRAFT (ALL PERILS), BOILER AND MACHINERY)
(000 omitted)

Years In Which Premiums Were Earned and Losses Were Incurred	Premiums Earned			Loss and Loss Expense Payments							Number of Claims Reported Direct and Assumed
	2 Direct and Assumed	3 Ceded	4 Net (2 - 3)	Loss Payments		Allocated Loss Expense Payments		9 Salvage and Subrogation Received	10 Unallocated Loss Expense Payments	11 Total Net Paid (5 - 6 + 7 - 8 + 10)	12
				5 Direct and Assumed	6 Ceded	7 Direct and Assumed	8 Ceded				
1 Prior	X X X X	X X X X	X X X X								X X X X
2 1980											X X X X
3 1981											X X X X
4 1982											X X X X
5 1983											X X X X
6 1984											X X X X
7 1985											X X X X
8 1986											X X X X
9 1987											X X X X
10 1988											X X X X
11 1989											X X X X
12 Totals	X X X X	X X X X	X X X X								X X X X

Note: For "prior" report amounts paid or received in current year only. Report cumulative amounts paid or received for specific years.
Report loss payments net of salvage and subrogation received

Years In Which Premiums Were Earned and Losses Were Incurred	Losses Unpaid				Allocated Loss Expenses Unpaid				21 Unallocated Loss Expenses Unpaid	22 Total Net Losses and Expenses Unpaid	23 Number of Claims Outstanding Direct and Assumed
	Case Basis		Bulk + IBNR		Case Basis		Bulk + IBNR				
	13 Direct and Assumed	14 Ceded	15 Direct and Assumed	16 Ceded	17 Direct and Assumed	18 Ceded	19 Direct and Assumed	20 Ceded			
1 Prior											
2 1980											
3 1981											
4 1982											
5 1983											
6 1984											
7 1985											
8 1986											
9 1987											
10 1988											
11 1989											
12 Totals											

Years In Which Premiums Were Earned and Losses Were Incurred	Total Losses and Loss Expenses Incurred			Loss and Loss Expense Percentage (Incurred/Premiums Earned)			Discount for Time Value of Money		32 Inter-Company Pooling Participation Percentage	Net Balance Sheet Reserves After Discount	
	24 Direct and Assumed	25 Ceded	26 Net*	27 Direct and Assumed	28 Ceded	29 Net	30 Loss	31 Loss Expense		33 Losses Unpaid	34 Loss Expenses Unpaid
1 Prior	X X X X	X X X X	X X X X	X X X X	X X X X	X X X X			X X X X		
2 1980											
3 1981											
4 1982											
5 1983											
6 1984											
7 1985											
8 1986											
9 1987											
10 1988											
11 1989											
12 Totals	X X X X	X X X X	X X X X	X X X	X X X X	X X X X			X X X X		

*Net = (24 - 25) = (11 - 22)

ANNUAL STATEMENT FOR THE YEAR 1989 OF THE

SCHEDULE P—PART 1H—OTHER LIABILITY

Years in Which Premiums Were Earned and Losses Were Incurred	Premiums Earned			Loss and Loss Expense Payments								Number of Claims Reported Direct and Assumed
	Direct and Assumed	Ceded	Net	Payment		Allocated Loss Expense Payments		Salvage and Subrogation Received	Unallocated Loss Expense Payments	Total Net Paid (4 - 5 + 7 - 8 + 10)		
				Direct and Assumed	Ceded	Direct and Assumed	Ceded					
1. Prior	x x x x	x x x x	x x x x									x x x x
2. 1980												
3. 1981												
4. 1982												
5. 1983												
6. 1984												
7. 1985												
8. 1986												
9. 1987												
10. 1988												
11. 1989												
12. Totals	x x x x	x x x x	x x x x									x x x x

Note: For prior report amounts paid or received in current year only. Report cumulative amounts paid or received for specific years.
Report loss payments net of salvage and subrogation received.

Years in Which Premiums Were Earned and Losses Were Incurred	Losses Unpaid				Allocated Loss Expenses Unpaid				21 Unallocated Loss Expenses Unpaid	22 Total Net Losses and Expenses Unpaid	23 Number of Claims Outstanding Direct and Assumed
	Case Basis		Bulk + IBNR		Case Basis		Bulk + IBNR				
	Direct and Assumed	Ceded	Direct and Assumed	Ceded	Direct and Assumed	Ceded	Direct and Assumed	Ceded			
1. Prior											
2. 1980											
3. 1981											
4. 1982											
5. 1983											
6. 1984											
7. 1985											
8. 1986											
9. 1987											
10. 1988											
11. 1989											
12. Totals											

Years in Which Premiums Were Earned and Losses Were Incurred	Total Losses and Loss Expenses Incurred			Loss and Loss Expense Percentage (Incurred/Premiums Earned)			Discount for Time Value of Money		32 Inter-Company Pooling Participation Percentage	Net Balance Sheet Reserves After Discount	
	24 Direct and Assumed	25 Ceded	26 Net*	27 Direct and Assumed	28 Ceded	29 Net	30 Loss	31 Loss Expense		33 Losses Unpaid	34 Loss Expenses Unpaid
1. Prior	x x x x	x x x x	x x x x	x x x x	x x x x	x x x x				x x x x	
2. 1980											
3. 1981											
4. 1982											
5. 1983											
6. 1984											
7. 1985											
8. 1986											
9. 1987											
10. 1988											
11. 1989											
12. Totals	x x x x	x x x x	x x x x	x x x x	x x x x	x x x x				x x x x	

*Net (24 - 25) (21 - 22)

ANNUAL STATEMENT FOR THE YEAR 1989 OF THE .... Name

SCHEDULE P—PART 1I—SPECIAL PROPERTY (FIRE, ALLIED LINES, INLAND MARINE, EARTHQUAKE, GLASS, BURGLARY AND THEFT)
(000 omitted)

Years In Which Premiums Were Earned and Losses Were Incurred	Premiums Earned			Loss and Loss Expense Payments								Number of Claims Reported Direct and Assumed
	2 Direct and Assumed	3 Ceded	4 Net (2 - 3)	Loss Payments		Allocated Loss Expense Payments		9 Salvage and Subrogation Received	10 Uncollected Loss Expense Payments	11 Total Net Paid (5 - 6 + 7 - 8 - 10)		
				5 Direct and Assumed	6 Ceded	7 Direct and Assumed	8 Ceded					
1 Prior	X X X X	X X X X	X X X X									X X X X
2 1988												X X X X
3 1989												X X X X
4 Totals	X X X X	X X X X	X X X X									X X X X

Note: For "prior" report amounts paid or received in current year only. Report cumulative amounts paid or received for specific years.
Report loss payment net of salvage and subrogation received.

Years In Which Premiums Were Earned and Losses Were Incurred	Losses Unpaid				Allocated Loss Expenses Unpaid				21 Unallocated Loss Expenses Unpaid	22 Total Net Losses and Expenses Unpaid	23 Number of Claims Outstanding Direct and Assumed
	Case Basis		Bulk - IBNR		Case Basis		Bulk - IBNR				
	13 Direct and Assumed	14 Ceded	15 Direct and Assumed	16 Ceded	17 Direct and Assumed	18 Ceded	19 Direct and Assumed	20 Ceded			
1 Prior											
2 1988											
3 1989											
4 Totals											

Years In Which Premiums Were Earned and Losses Were Incurred	Total Losses and Loss Expenses Incurred			Loss and Loss Expense Percentage (Incurred Premiums Earned)			Discount for Time Value of Money		32 Inter-Company Pooling Participation Percentage	Net Balance Sheet Reserves After Discount	
	24 Direct and Assumed	25 Ceded	26 Net*	27 Direct and Assumed	28 Ceded	29 Net	30 Loss	31 Loss Expense		33 Losses Unpaid	34 Loss Expenses Unpaid
1 Prior	X X X X	X X X X	X X X X	X X X X	X X X X	X X X X			X X X X		
2 1988											
3 1989											
4 Totals	X X X X	X X X X	X X X X	X X X	X X X X	X X X X			X X X X		

*Net = (24 - 25) = (11 + 22)

SCHEDULE P—PART 1J—AUTO PHYSICAL DAMAGE
(000 omitted)

Years In Which Premiums Were Earned and Losses Were Incurred	Premiums Earned			Loss and Loss Expense Payments								Number of Claims Reported— Direct and Assumed
	2 Direct and Assumed	3 Ceded	4 Net (2 - 3)	Loss Payments		Allocated Loss Expense Payments		9 Salvage and Subrogation Received	10 Uncollected Loss Expense Payments	11 Total Net Paid (5 - 6 + 7 - 8 - 10)		
				5 Direct and Assumed	6 Ceded	7 Direct and Assumed	8 Ceded					
1 Prior	X X X X	X X X X	X X X X									Y Y Y Y
2 1988												
3 1989												
4 Totals	X X X X	X X X X	X X X X									X X X X

Note: For "prior" report amounts paid or received in current year only. Report cumulative amounts paid or received for specific years.
Report loss payments net of salvage and subrogation received.

Years In Which Premiums Were Earned and Losses Were Incurred	Losses Unpaid				Allocated Loss Expenses Unpaid				21 Unallocated Loss Expenses Unpaid	22 Total Net Losses and Expenses Unpaid	23 Number of Claims Outstanding Direct and Assumed
	Case Basis		Bulk - IBNR		Case Basis		Bulk - IBNR				
	13 Direct and Assumed	14 Ceded	15 Direct and Assumed	16 Ceded	17 Direct and Assumed	18 Ceded	19 Direct and Assumed	20 Ceded			
1 Prior											
2 1988											
3 1989											
4 Totals											

Years In Which Premiums Were Earned and Losses Were Incurred	Total Losses and Loss Expenses Incurred			Loss and Loss Expense Percentage (Incurred Premiums Earned)			Discount for Time Value of Money		32 Inter-Company Pooling Participation Percentage	Net Balance Sheet Reserves After Discount	
	24 Direct and Assumed	25 Ceded	26 Net*	27 Direct and Assumed	28 Ceded	29 Net	30 Loss	31 Loss Expense		33 Losses Unpaid	34 Loss Expenses Unpaid
1 Prior	X X X X	X X X X	X X X X	X X X X	X X X X	X X X X			X X X X		
2 1988											
3 1989											
4 Totals	X X X X	X X X X	X X X X	X X X X	X X X X	X X X X			X X X X		

*Net = (24 - 25) = (11 + 22)

SCHEDULE P—PART 1K—FIDELITY, SURETY, FINANCIAL GUARANTY, MORTGAGE GUARANTY
(000 omitted)

Years In Which Premiums Were Earned and Losses Were Incurred	Premiums Earned			Loss and Loss Expense Payments								
				Loss Payments		Allocated Loss Expense Payments		9	10	11	12
	2 Direct and Assumed	3 Ceded	4 Net (2 - 3)	5 Direct and Assumed	6 Ceded	7 Direct and Assumed	8 Ceded	Salvage and Subrogation Received	Unallocated Loss Expense Payments	Total Net Paid (5 - 6 + 7 - 8 - 10)	Number of Claims Reported Direct and Assumed
1 Prior	XXXX	XXXX	XXXX								XXXX
2 1988											XXXX
3 1989											XXXX
4 Totals	XXXX	XXXX	XXXX								XXXX

Note For "prior" report amounts paid or received in current year only. Report cumulative amounts paid or received for specific years
Report loss payments net of salvage and subrogation received

Years In Which Premiums Were Earned and Losses Were Incurred	Losses Unpaid				Allocated Loss Expenses Unpaid				21	22	23
	Case Basis		Bulk - IBNR		Case Basis		Bulk - IBNR		Unallocated Loss Expenses Unpaid	Total Net Losses and Expenses Unpaid	Number of Claims Outstanding Direct and Assumed
	13 Direct and Assumed	14 Ceded	15 Direct and Assumed	16 Ceded	17 Direct and Assumed	18 Ceded	19 Direct and Assumed	20 Ceded			
1 Prior											
2 1988											
3 1989											
4 Totals											

Years In Which Premiums Were Earned and Losses Were Incurred	Total Losses and Loss Expenses Incurred			Loss and Loss Expense Percentage (Incurred/Premiums Earned)			Discount for Time Value of Money		32	Net Balance Sheet Reserves After Discount	
	24 Direct and Assumed	25 Ceded	26 Net*	27 Direct and Assumed	28 Ceded	29 Net	30 Loss	31 Loss Expense	Inter-Company Pooling Participation Percentage	33 Losses Unpaid	34 Loss Expenses Unpaid
1 Prior	XXXX	XXXX	XXXX	XXXX	XXXX	XXXX			XXXX		
2 1988											
3 1989											
4 Totals	XXXX	XXXX	XXXX	XXX	XXXX	XXXX			XXXX		

*Net = (24 - 25) (11 - 22)

SCHEDULE P—PART 1L—OTHER (INCLUDING CREDIT, ACCIDENT AND HEALTH)
(000 omitted)

1 Years In Which Premiums Were Earned and Losses Were Incurred	Premiums Earned			Loss and Loss Expense Payments								
	2	3	4	Loss Payments		Allocated Loss Expense Payments		9	10	11	12
	Direct and Assumed	Ceded	Net (2 - 3)	5 Direct and Assumed	6 Ceded	7 Direct and Assumed	8 Ceded	Salvage and Subrogation Received	Unallocated Loss Expense Payments	Total Net Paid (5 - 6 + 7 - 8 - 10)	Number of Claims Reported Direct and Assumed
1 Prior	XXXX	XXXX	XXXX								XXXX
2 1988											XXXX
3 1989											XXXX
4 Totals	XXXX	XXXX	XXXX								XXXX

Note For "prior" report amounts paid or received in current year only. Report cumulative amounts paid or received for specific years
Report loss payments net of salvage and subrogation received

Years In Which Premiums Were Earned and Losses Were Incurred	Losses Unpaid				Allocated Loss Expenses Unpaid				21	22	23
	Case Basis		Bulk - IBNR		Case Basis		Bulk - IBNR		Unallocated Loss Expenses Unpaid	Total Net Losses and Expenses Unpaid	Number of Claims Outstanding Direct and Assumed
	13 Direct and Assumed	14 Ceded	15 Direct and Assumed	16 Ceded	17 Direct and Assumed	18 Ceded	19 Direct and Assumed	20 Ceded			
1 Prior											
2 1988											
3 1989											
4 Totals											

Years In Which Premiums Were Earned and Losses Were Incurred	Total Losses and Loss Expenses Incurred			Loss and Loss Expense Percentage (Incurred/Premiums Earned)			Discount for Time Value of Money		32	Net Balance Sheet Reserves After Discount	
	24 Direct and Assumed	25 Ceded	26 Net*	27 Direct and Assumed	28 Ceded	29 Net	30 Loss	31 Loss Expense	Inter-Company Pooling Participation Percentage	33 Losses Unpaid	34 Loss Expenses Unpaid
1 Prior	XXXX	XXXX	XXXX	XXXX	XXXX	XXXX			XXXX		
2 1988											
3 1989											
4 Totals	XXXX	XXXX	XXXX	XXX	XXXX	XXXX			XXXX		

*Net = (24 - 25) (11 - 22)

SCHEDULE P—PART 1M—INTERNATIONAL
(000 omitted)

1	Premiums Earned			Loss and Loss Expense Payments								12
Years In Which Premiums Were Earned and Losses Were Incurred	2	3	4	Loss Payments		Allocated Loss Expense Payments		9	10	11		Number of Claims Reported Direct and Assumed
	Direct and Assumed	Ceded	Net (2 - 3)	5 Direct and Assumed	6 Ceded	7 Direct and Assumed	8 Ceded	Salvage and Subrogation Received	Unallocated Loss Expense Payments	Total Net Paid (5 - 6 + 7 - 8 - 10)		
1 Prior	XXXX	XXXX	XXXX									XXXX
2 1980												XXXX
3 1981												XXXX
4 1982												XXXX
5 1983												XXXX
6 1984												XXXX
7 1985												XXXX
8 1986												XXXX
9 1987												XXXX
10 1988												XXXX
11 1989												XXXX
12 Totals	XXXX	XXXX	XXXX									XXXX

Note For "prior" report amounts paid or received in current year only. Report cumulative amounts paid or received for specific years
Report loss payments net of salvage and subrogation received

Years In Which Premiums Were Earned and Losses Were Incurred	Losses Unpaid				Allocated Loss Expenses Unpaid				21	22	23
	Case Basis		Bulk - IBNR		Case Basis		Bulk - IBNR		Unallocated Loss Expenses Unpaid	Total Net Losses and Expenses Unpaid	Number of Claims Outstanding— Direct and Assumed
	13 Direct and Assumed	14 Ceded	15 Direct and Assumed	16 Ceded	17 Direct and Assumed	18 Ceded	19 Direct and Assumed	20 Ceded			
1 Prior											
2 1980											
3 1981											
4 1982											
5 1983											
6 1984											
7 1985											
8 1986											
9 1987											
10 1988											
11 1989											
12 Totals											

Years In Which Premiums Were Earned and Losses Were Incurred	Total Losses and Loss Expenses Incurred			Loss and Loss Expense Percentage (Incurred Premiums Earned)			Discount for Time Value of Money		32	Net Balance Sheet Reserves After Discount	
	24 Direct and Assumed	25 Ceded	26 Net*	27 Direct and Assumed	28 Ceded	29 Net	30 Loss	31 Loss Expense	Inter-Company Pooling Participation Percentage	33 Losses Unpaid	34 Loss Expenses Unpaid
1 Prior	XXXX	XXXX	XXXX	XXXX	XXXX	XXXX			XXXX		
2 1980											
3 1981											
4 1982											
5 1983											
6 1984											
7 1985											
8 1986											
9 1987											
10 1988											
11 1989											
12 Totals	XXXX	XXXX	XXXX	XXX	XXXX	XXXX			XXXX		

Net (24 - 25) - (11 + 22)

70 ANNUAL STATEMENT FOR THE YEAR 1989 OF THE .... Form 2

(Name)

SCHEDULE P—PART 1N—REINSURANCE A

(000 omitted)

Years In Which Premiums Were Earned and Losses Were Incurred	Premiums Earned			Loss and Loss Expense Payments							Number of Claims Reported Direct and Assumed
	2 Direct and Assumed	3 Ceded	4 Net (2 - 3)	Loss Payments		Allocated Loss Expense Payments		9 Salvage and Subrogation Received	10 Unallocated Loss Expense Payments	11 Total Net Paid (5 - 6 - 7 - 8 - 10)	12
				5 Direct and Assumed	6 Ceded	7 Direct and Assumed	8 Ceded				
1 1988											X X X X
2 1989											X X X X
3 Totals	X X X X	X X X X	X X X X								X X X X

Years In Which Premiums Were Earned and Losses Were Incurred	Losses Unpaid				Allocated Loss Expenses Unpaid				21 Unallocated Loss Expenses Unpaid	22 Total Net Losses and Expenses Unpaid	23 Number of Claims Outstanding Direct and Assumed
	Case Basis		Bulk - IBNR		Case Basis		Bulk - IBNR				
	13 Direct and Assumed	14 Ceded	15 Direct and Assumed	16 Ceded	17 Direct and Assumed	18 Ceded	19 Direct and Assumed	20 Ceded			
1 1988											X X X X
2 1989											X X X X
3 Totals											X X X X

Years In Which Premiums Were Earned and Losses Were Incurred	Total Losses and Loss Expenses Incurred			Loss and Loss Expense Percentage (Incurred Premiums Earned)			Discount for Time Value of Money		32 Inter-Company Pooling Participation Percentage	Net Balance Sheet Reserves After Discount	
	24 Direct and Assumed	25 Ceded	26 Net*	27 Direct and Assumed	28 Ceded	29 Net	30 Loss	31 Loss Expense		33 Losses Unpaid	34 Loss Expenses Unpaid
1 1988											
2 1989											
3 Totals	X X X X	X X X X	X X X X	X X X X	X X X X	X X X X			X X X X		

*Net (24 - 25) - (11 - 22)

SCHEDULE P—PART 1O—REINSURANCE B

(000 omitted)

Years In Which Premiums Were Earned and Losses Were Incurred	Premiums Earned			Loss and Loss Expense Payments							Number of Claims Reported Direct and Assumed
1	2 Direct and Assumed	3 Ceded	4 Net (2 - 3)	Loss Payments		Allocated Loss Expense Payments		9 Salvage and Subrogation Received	10 Unallocated Loss Expense Payments	11 Total Net Paid (5 - 6 - 7 - 8 - 10)	12
				5 Direct and Assumed	6 Ceded	7 Direct and Assumed	8 Ceded				
1 1988											X X X X
2 1989											X X X X
3 Totals	X X X X	X X X X	X X X X								X X X X

Years In Which Premiums Were Earned and Losses Were Incurred	Losses Unpaid				Allocated Loss Expenses Unpaid				21 Unallocated Loss Expenses Unpaid	22 Total Net Losses and Expenses Unpaid	23 Number of Claims Outstanding Direct and Assumed
	Case Basis		Bulk - IBNR		Case Basis		Bulk - IBNR				
	13 Direct and Assumed	14 Ceded	15 Direct and Assumed	16 Ceded	17 Direct and Assumed	18 Ceded	19 Direct and Assumed	20 Ceded			
1 1988											X X X X
2 1989											X X X X
3 Totals											X X X X

Years In Which Premiums Were Earned and Losses Were Incurred	Total Losses and Loss Expenses Incurred			Loss and Loss Expense Percentage (Incurred Premiums Earned)			Discount for Time Value of Money		32 Inter-Company Pooling Participation Percentage	Net Balance Sheet Reserves After Discount	
	24 Direct and Assumed	25 Ceded	26 Net*	27 Direct and Assumed	28 Ceded	29 Net	30 Loss	31 Loss Expense		33 Losses Unpaid	34 Loss Expenses Unpaid
1 1988											
2 1989											
3 Totals	X X X X	X X X X	X X X X	X X X X	X X X X	X X X X			X X X X		

*Net (24 - 25) - (11 - 22)

SCHEDULE P—PART 1P—REINSURANCE C
(000 omitted)

1	Premiums Earned			Loss and Loss Expense Payments								12
Years In Which Premiums Were Earned and Losses Were Incurred	2 Direct and Assumed	3 Ceded	4 Net (2-3)	Loss Payments		Allocated Loss Expense Payments		9 Salvage and Subrogation Received	10 Unallocated Loss Expense Payments	11 Total Net Paid (5-6-7 8-10)		Number of Claims Reported Direct and Assumed
				5 Direct and Assumed	6 Ceded	7 Direct and Assumed	8 Ceded					
1 1988												X X X X
2 1989												X X X X
3 Totals	X X X X	X X X X	X X X X									X X X X

1	Losses Unpaid				Allocated Loss Expenses Unpaid				21	22	23
Years In Which Premiums Were Earned and Losses Were Incurred	Case Basis		Bulk - IBNR		Case Basis		Bulk - IBNR		Unallocated Loss Expenses Unpaid	Total Net Losses and Expenses Unpaid	Number of Claims Outstanding Direct and Assumed
	13 Direct and Assumed	14 Ceded	15 Direct and Assumed	16 Ceded	17 Direct and Assumed	18 Ceded	19 Direct and Assumed	20 Ceded			
1 1988											X X X X
2 1989											X X X X
3 Totals											X X X X

1	Total Losses and Loss Expenses Incurred			Loss and Loss Expense Percentage (Incurred Premiums Earned)			Discount for Time Value of Money		32	Net Balance Sheet Reserves After Discount	
Years In Which Premiums Were Earned and Losses Were Incurred	24 Direct and Assumed	25 Ceded	26 Net*	27 Direct and Assumed	28 Ceded	29 Net	30 Loss	31 Loss Expense	Inter-Company Pooling Participation Percentage	33 Losses Unpaid	34 Loss Expenses Unpaid
1 1988											
2 1989											
3 Totals	X X X X	X X X X	X X X X	X X X X	X X X X	X X X X			X X X X		

*Net = (24 - 25) + (11 - 22)

SCHEDULE P—PART 1Q—REINSURANCE D
(000 omitted)

1	Premiums Earned			Loss and Loss Expense Payments								12
Years In Which Premiums Were Earned and Losses Were Incurred	2 Direct and Assumed	3 Ceded	4 Net (2-3)	Loss Payments		Allocated Loss Expense Payments		9 Salvage and Subrogation Received	10 Unallocated Loss Expense Payments	11 Total Net Paid (5-6-7 8-10)		Number of Claims Reported Direct and Assumed
				5 Direct and Assumed	6 Ceded	7 Direct and Assumed	8 Ceded					
1 Prior	X X X X	X X X X	X X X X									X X X X
2 1980												X X X X
3 1981												X X X X
4 1982												X X X X
5 1983												X X X X
6 1984												X X X X
7 1985												X X X X
8 1986												X X X X
9 1987												X X X X
10 Totals	X X X X	X X X X	X X X X									X X X X

Note: For "prior" report amounts paid or received in current year only. Report cumulative amounts paid or received for specific years.
Report loss payments net of salvage and subrogation received.

1	Losses Unpaid				Allocated Loss Expenses Unpaid				21	22	23
Years In Which Premiums Were Earned and Losses Were Incurred	Case Basis		Bulk - IBNR		Case Basis		Bulk - IBNR		Unallocated Loss Expenses Unpaid	Total Net Losses and Expenses Unpaid	Number of Claims Outstanding Direct and Assumed
	13 Direct and Assumed	14 Ceded	15 Direct and Assumed	16 Ceded	17 Direct and Assumed	18 Ceded	19 Direct and Assumed	20 Ceded			
1 Prior											X X X X
2 1980											X X X X
3 1981											X X X X
4 1982											X X X X
5 1983											X X X X
6 1984											X X X X
7 1985											X X X X
8 1986											X X X X
9 1987											X X X X
10 Totals											X X X X

1	Total Losses and Loss Expenses Incurred			Loss and Loss Expense Percentage (Incurred Premiums Earned)			Discount for Time Value of Money		37	Net Balance Sheet Reserves After Discount	
Years In Which Premiums Were Earned and Losses Were Incurred	24 Direct and Assumed	25 Ceded	26 Net*	27 Direct and Assumed	28 Ceded	29 Net	30 Loss	31 Loss Expense	Inter-Company Pooling Participation Percentage	33 Losses Unpaid	34 Loss Expenses Unpaid
1 Prior	X X X X	X X X X	X X X X	X X X X	X X X X	X X X X			X X X X		
2 1980											
3 1981											
4 1982											
5 1983											
6 1984											
7 1985											
8 1986											
9 1987											
10 Totals	X X X X	X X X X	X X X X	X X X X	X X X X	X X X X			X X X X		

*Net = (24 - 25) + (11 - 22)

SCHEDULE P — PART 2A — HOMEOWNERS/FARMOWNERS

Years in Which Losses Were Incurred	INCURRED LOSSES AND ALLOCATED EXPENSES REPORTED AT YEAR END (000 OMITTED)										DEVELOPMENT**	
	2 1980	3 1981	4 1982	5 1983	6 1984	7 1985	8 1986	9 1987	10 1988	11 1989	12 One Year	13 Two Year
1 Prior	*											
2 1980												
3 1981	x x x x											
4 1982	x x x x	x x x x										
5 1983	x x x x	x x x x	x x x x									
6 1984	x x x x	x x x x	x x x x	x x x x								
7 1985	x x x x	x x x x	x x x x	x x x x	x x x x							
8 1986	x x x x	x x x x	x x x x	x x x x	x x x x	x x x x						
9 1987	x x x x	x x x x	x x x x	x x x x	x x x x	x x x x	x x x x					
10 1988	x x x x	x x x x	x x x x	x x x x	x x x x	x x x x	x x x x	x x x x				x x x x
11 1989	x x x x	x x x x	x x x x	x x x x	x x x x	x x x x	x x x x	x x x x	x x x x		x x x x	x x x x
12 Totals												

SCHEDULE P — PART 2B — PRIVATE PASSENGER AUTO LIABILITY/MEDICAL

Years	2 1980	3 1981	4 1982	5 1983	6 1984	7 1985	8 1986	9 1987	10 1988	11 1989	12 One Year	13 Two Year
1 Prior	*											
2 1980												
3 1981	x x x x											
4 1982	x x x x	x x x x										
5 1983	x x x x	x x x x	x x x x									
6 1984	x x x x	x x x x	x x x x	x x x x								
7 1985	x x x x	x x x x	x x x x	x x x x	x x x x							
8 1986	x x x x	x x x x	x x x x	x x x x	x x x x	x x x x						
9 1987	x x x x	x x x x	x x x x	x x x x	x x x x	x x x x	x x x x					
10 1988	x x x x	x x x x	x x x x	x x x x	x x x x	x x x x	x x x x	x x x x				x x x x
11 1989	x x x x	x x x x	x x x x	x x x x	x x x x	x x x x	x x x x	x x x x	x x x x		x x x x	x x x x
12 Totals												

SCHEDULE P — PART 2C — COMMERCIAL AUTO/TRUCK LIABILITY/MEDICAL

Years	2 1980	3 1981	4 1982	5 1983	6 1984	7 1985	8 1986	9 1987	10 1988	11 1989	12 One Year	13 Two Year
1 Prior	*											
2 1980												
3 1981	x x x x											
4 1982	x x x x	x x x x										
5 1983	x x x x	x x x x	x x x x									
6 1984	x x x x	x x x x	x x x x	x x x x								
7 1985	x x x x	x x x x	x x x x	x x x x	x x x x							
8 1986	x x x x	x x x x	x x x x	x x x x	x x x x	x x x x						
9 1987	x x x x	x x x x	x x x x	x x x x	x x x x	x x x x	x x x x					
10 1988	x x x x	x x x x	x x x x	x x x x	x x x x	x x x x	x x x x	x x x x				x x x x
11 1989	x x x x	x x x x	x x x x	x x x x	x x x x	x x x x	x x x x	x x x x	x x x x		x x x x	x x x x
12 Totals												

SCHEDULE P — PART 2D — WORKERS' COMPENSATION

Years	2 1980	3 1981	4 1982	5 1983	6 1984	7 1985	8 1986	9 1987	10 1988	11 1989	12 One Year	13 Two Year
1 Prior	*											
2 1980												
3 1981	x x x x											
4 1982	x x x x	x x x x										
5 1983	x x x x	x x x x	x x x x									
6 1984	x x x x	x x x x	x x x x	x x x x								
7 1985	x x x x	x x x x	x x x x	x x x x	x x x x							
8 1986	x x x x	x x x x	x x x x	x x x x	x x x x	x x x x						
9 1987	x x x x	x x x x	x x x x	x x x x	x x x x	x x x x	x x x x					
10 1988	x x x x	x x x x	x x x x	x x x x	x x x x	x x x x	x x x x	x x x x				x x x x
11 1989	x x x x	x x x x	x x x x	x x x x	x x x x	x x x x	x x x x	x x x x	x x x x		x x x x	x x x x
12 Totals												

SCHEDULE P — PART 2E — COMMERCIAL MULTIPLE PERIL

Years	2 1980	3 1981	4 1982	5 1983	6 1984	7 1985	8 1986	9 1987	10 1988	11 1989	12 One Year	13 Two Year
1 Prior	*											
2 1980												
3 1981	x x x x											
4 1982	x x x x	x x x x										
5 1983	x x x x	x x x x	x x x x									
6 1984	x x x x	x x x x	x x x x	x x x x								
7 1985	x x x x	x x x x	x x x x	x x x x	x x x x							
8 1986	x x x x	x x x x	x x x x	x x x x	x x x x	x x x x						
9 1987	x x x x	x x x x	x x x x	x x x x	x x x x	x x x x	x x x x					
10 1988	x x x x	x x x x	x x x x	x x x x	x x x x	x x x x	x x x x	x x x x				x x x x
11 1989	x x x x	x x x x	x x x x	x x x x	x x x x	x x x x	x x x x	x x x x	x x x x		x x x x	x x x x
12 Totals												

*Reported reserves only. Subsequent development relates only to subsequent payments and reserves
**Current year less first or second prior year showing redundant or adverse

SCHEDULE P — PART 2F — MEDICAL MALPRACTICE

Years in Which Losses Were Incurred	INCURRED LOSSES AND ALLOCATED EXPENSES REPORTED AT YEAR END (000 OMITTED)											DEVELOPMENT**	
	1 1980	2 1981	3 1982	4 1983	5 1984	6 1985	7 1986	8 1987	9 1988	10 1989	11	12 One Year	13 Two Year
1 Prior	•												
2 1980													
3 1981	XXXX												
4 1982	XXXX	XXXX											
5 1983	XXXX	XXXX	XXXX										
6 1984	XXXX	XXXX	XXXX	XXXX									
7 1985	XXXX	XXXX	XXXX	XXXX	XXXX								
8 1986	XXXX	XXXX	XXXX	XXXX	XXXX	XXXX							
9 1987	XXXX	XXXX	XXXX	XXXX	XXXX	XXXX	XXXX						
10 1988	XXXX	XXXX	XXXX	XXXX	XXXX	XXXX	XXXX	XXXX					XXXX
11 1989	XXXX	XXXX	XXXX	XXXX	XXXX	XXXX	XXXX	XXXX	XXXX			XXXX	XXXX

12 Totals

SCHEDULE P — PART 2G — SPECIAL LIABILITY (OCEAN MARINE, AIRCRAFT (ALL PERILS), BOILER AND MACHINERY)

	1980	1981	1982	1983	1984	1985	1986	1987	1988	1989		One Year	Two Year
1 Prior	•												
2 1980													
3 1981	XXXX												
4 1982	XXXX	XXXX											
5 1983	XXXX	XXXX	XXXX										
6 1984	XXXX	XXXX	XXXX	XXXX									
7 1985	XXXX	XXXX	XXXX	XXXX	XXXX								
8 1986	XXXX	XXXX	XXXX	XXXX	XXXX	XXXX							
9 1987	XXXX	XXXX	XXXX	XXXX	XXXX	XXXX	XXXX						
10 1988	XXXX	XXXX	XXXX	XXXX	XXXX	XXXX	XXXX	XXXX					XXXX
11 1989	XXXX	XXXX	XXXX	XXXX	XXXX	XXXX	XXXX	XXXX	XXXX			XXXX	XXXX

12 Totals

SCHEDULE P — PART 2H — OTHER LIABILITY

	1980	1981	1982	1983	1984	1985	1986	1987	1988	1989		One Year	Two Year
1 Prior	•												
2 1980													
3 1981	XXXX												
4 1982	XXXX	XXXX											
5 1983	XXXX	XXXX	XXXX										
6 1984	XXXX	XXXX	XXXX	XXXX									
7 1985	XXXX	XXXX	XXXX	XXXX	XXXX								
8 1986	XXXX	XXXX	XXXX	XXXX	XXXX	XXXX							
9 1987	XXXX	XXXX	XXXX	XXXX	XXXX	XXXX	XXXX						
10 1988	XXXX	XXXX	XXXX	XXXX	XXXX	XXXX	XXXX	XXXX					XXXX
11 1989	XXXX	XXXX	XXXX	XXXX	XXXX	XXXX	XXXX	XXXX	XXXX			XXXX	XXXX

12 Totals

SCHEDULE P — PART 2I — SPECIAL PROPERTY (FIRE, ALLIED LINES, INLAND MARINE, EARTHQUAKE, GLASS, BURGLARY AND THEFT)

	1980	1981	1982	1983	1984	1985	1986	1987	1988	1989		One Year	Two Year
1 Prior	XXXX	XXXX	XXXX	XXXX	XXXX	XXXX	XXXX	•					
2 1988	XXXX	XXXX	XXXX	XXXX	XXXX	XXXX	XXXX	XXXX					XXXX
3 1989	XXXX	XXXX	XXXX	XXXX	XXXX	XXXX	XXXX	XXXX	XXXX			XXXX	XXXX

4 Totals

SCHEDULE P — PART 2J — AUTO PHYSICAL DAMAGE

	1980	1981	1982	1983	1984	1985	1986	1987	1988	1989		One Year	Two Year
1 Prior	XXXX	XXXX	XXXX	XXXX	XXXX	XXXX	XXXX	•					
2 1988	XXXX	XXXX	XXXX	XXXX	XXXX	XXXX	XXXX	XXXX					XXXX
3 1989	XXXX	XXXX	XXXX	XXXX	XXXX	XXXX	XXXX	XXXX	XXXX			XXXX	XXXX

4 Totals

SCHEDULE P — PART 2K — FIDELITY, SURETY, FINANCIAL GUARANTY, MORTGAGE GUARANTY

	1980	1981	1982	1983	1984	1985	1986	1987	1988	1989		One Year	Two Year
1 Prior	XXXX	XXXX	XXXX	XXXX	XXXX	XXXX	XXXX	•					
2 1988	XXXX	XXXX	XXXX	XXXX	XXXX	XXXX	XXXX	XXXX					XXXX
3 1989	XXXX	XXXX	XXXX	XXXX	XXXX	XXXX	XXXX	XXXX	XXXX			XXXX	XXXX

*Reported reserves only. Subsequent development relates only to subsequent payments and reserves.
**Current year less first or second prior year, showing (redundant) or adverse.

4 Totals

SCHEDULE P — PART 2L — OTHER (INCLUDING CREDIT, ACCIDENT AND HEALTH)

Years in Which Losses Were Incurred	INCURRED LOSSES AND ALLOCATED EXPENSES REPORTED AT YEAR END (000 OMITTED)										DEVELOPMENT**	
	1	2	3	4	5	6	8	9	10	11	12 One Year	13 Two Year
	1980	1981	1982	1983	1984	1985	1986	1987	1988	1989		
1 Prior	XXXX	XXXX	XXXX	XXXX	XXXX	XXXX	XXXX					
2 1988	XXXX	XXXX	XXXX	XXXX	XXXX	XXXX	XXXX	XXXX				XXXX
3 1989	XXXX	XXXX	XXXX	XXXX	XXXX	XXXX	XXXX	XXXX	XXXX		XXXX	XXXX

1 Totals

SCHEDULE P — PART 2M — INTERNATIONAL

1 Prior												
2 1980												
3 1981	XXXX											
4 1982	XXXX	XXXX										
5 1983	XXXX	XXXX	XXXX									
6 1984	XXXX	XXXX	XXXX	XXXX								
7 1985	XXXX	XXXX	XXXX	XXXX	XXXX							
8 1986	XXXX	XXXX	XXXX	XXXX	XXXX	XXXX						
9 1987	XXXX	XXXX	XXXX	XXXX	XXXX	XXXX	XXXX					
10 1988	XXXX	XXXX	XXXX	XXXX	XXXX	XXXX	XXXX	XXXX				XXXX
11 1989	XXXX	XXXX	XXXX	XXXX	XXXX	XXXX	XXXX	XXXX	XXXX		XXXX	XXXX

12 Totals

SCHEDULE P — PART 2N — REINSURANCE A

1 1988	XXXX	XXXX	XXXX	XXXX	XXXX	XXXX	XXXX	XXXX				XXXX
2 1989	XXXX	XXXX	XXXX	XXXX	XXXX	XXXX	XXXX	XXXX	XXXX		XXXX	XXXX

3 Totals

SCHEDULE P — PART 2O — REINSURANCE B

1 1988	XXXX	XXXX	XXXX	XXXX	XXXX	XXXX	XXXX	XXXX				XXXX
2 1989	XXXX	XXXX	XXXX	XXXX	XXXX	XXXX	XXXX	XXXX	XXXX		XXXX	XXXX

3 Totals

SCHEDULE P — PART 2P — REINSURANCE C

1 1988	XXXX	XXXX	XXXX	XXXX	XXXX	XXXX	XXXX	XXXX				XXXX
2 1989	XXXX	XXXX	XXXX	XXXX	XXXX	XXXX	XXXX	XXXX	XXXX		XXXX	XXXX

3 Totals

SCHEDULE P — PART 2Q — REINSURANCE D

1 Prior												
2 1980												
3 1981	XXXX											
4 1982	XXXX	XXXX										
5 1983	XXXX	XXXX	XXXX									
6 1984	XXXX	XXXX	XXXX	XXXX								
7 1985	XXXX	XXXX	XXXX	XXXX	XXXX							
8 1986	XXXX	XXXX	XXXX	XXXX	XXXX	XXXX						
9 1987	XXXX	XXXX	XXXX	XXXX	XXXX	XXXX	XXXX					

10 Totals

*Reported reserves only Subsequent development relates only to subsequent payments and reserves
**Current year less first or second prior year showing (redundant) or adverse

ANNUAL STATEMENT FOR THE YEAR 1989 OF THE

(Name)

SCHEDULE P — PART 3A — HOMEOWNERS/FARMOWNERS

Years in Which Losses Were Incurred	CUMULATIVE PAID LOSSES AND ALLOCATED EXPENSES AT YEAR END (000 OMITTED)										Number of Claims Closed With Loss Payment	Number of Claims Closed Without Loss Payment
	2 1980	3 1981	4 1982	5 1983	6 1984	7 1985	8 1986	9 1987	10 1988	11 1989		
1 Prior	000										XXXX	XXXX
2 1980											XXXX	XXXX
3 1981	XXXX										XXXX	XXXX
4 1982	XXXX	XXXX									XXXX	XXXX
5 1983	XXXX	XXXX	XXXX								XXXX	XXXX
6 1984	XXXX	XXXX	XXXX	XXXX							XXXX	XXXX
7 1985	XXXX	XXXX	XXXX	XXXX	XXXX						XXXX	XXXX
8 1986	XXXX	XXXX	XXXX	XXXX	XXXX	XXXX					XXXX	XXXX
9 1987	XXXX	XXXX	XXXX	XXXX	XXXX	XXXX	XXXX				XXXX	XXXX
10 1988	XXXX	XXXX	XXXX	XXXX	XXXX	XXXX	XXXX	XXXX			XXXX	XXXX
11 1989	XXXX	XXXX	XXXX	XXXX	XXXX	XXXX	XXXX	XXXX	XXXX		XXXX	XXXX

SCHEDULE P — PART 3B — PRIVATE PASSENGER AUTO LIABILITY/MEDICAL

1 Prior	000											
2 1980												
3 1981	XXXX											
4 1982	XXXX	XXXX										
5 1983	XXXX	XXXX	XXXX									
6 1984	XXXX	XXXX	XXXX	XXXX								
7 1985	XXXX	XXXX	XXXX	XXXX	XXXX							
8 1986	XXXX	XXXX	XXXX	XXXX	XXXX	XXXX						
9 1987	XXXX	XXXX	XXXX	XXXX	XXXX	XXXX	XXXX					
10 1988	XXXX	XXXX	XXXX	XXXX	XXXX	XXXX	XXXX	XXXX				
11 1989	XXXX	XXXX	XXXX	XXXX	XXXX	XXXX	XXXX	XXXX	XXXX			

SCHEDULE P — PART 3C — COMMERCIAL AUTO/TRUCK LIABILITY/MEDICAL

1 Prior	000											
2 1980												
3 1981	XXXX											
4 1982	XXXX	XXXX										
5 1983	XXXX	XXXX	XXXX									
6 1984	XXXX	XXXX	XXXX	XXXX								
7 1985	XXXX	XXXX	XXXX	XXXX	XXXX							
8 1986	XXXX	XXXX	XXXX	XXXX	XXXX	XXXX						
9 1987	XXXX	XXXX	XXXX	XXXX	XXXX	XXXX	XXXX					
10 1988	XXXX	XXXX	XXXX	XXXX	XXXX	XXXX	XXXX	XXXX				
11 1989	XXXX	XXXX	XXXX	XXXX	XXXX	XXXX	XXXX	XXXX	XXXX			

SCHEDULE P — PART 3D — WORKERS' COMPENSATION

1 Prior	000											
2 1980												
3 1981	XXXX											
4 1982	XXXX	XXXX										
5 1983	XXXX	XXXX	XXXX									
6 1984	XXXX	XXXX	XXXX	XXXX								
7 1985	XXXX	XXXX	XXXX	XXXX	XXXX							
8 1986	XXXX	XXXX	XXXX	XXXX	XXXX	XXXX						
9 1987	XXXX	XXXX	XXXX	XXXX	XXXX	XXXX	XXXX					
10 1988	XXXX	XXXX	XXXX	XXXX	XXXX	XXXX	XXXX	XXXX				
11 1989	XXXX	XXXX	XXXX	XXXX	XXXX	XXXX	XXXX	XXXX	XXXX			

SCHEDULE P — PART 3E — COMMERCIAL MULTIPLE PERIL

1 Prior	000											
2 1980												
3 1981	XXXX											
4 1982	XXXX	XXXX										
5 1983	XXXX	XXXX	XXXX									
6 1984	XXXX	XXXX	XXXX	XXXX								
7 1985	XXXX	XXXX	XXXX	XXXX	XXXX							
8 1986	XXXX	XXXX	XXXX	XXXX	XXXX	XXXX						
9 1987	XXXX	XXXX	XXXX	XXXX	XXXX	XXXX	XXXX					
10 1988	XXXX	XXXX	XXXX	XXXX	XXXX	XXXX	XXXX	XXXX				
11 1989	XXXX	XXXX	XXXX	XXXX	XXXX	XXXX	XXXX	XXXX	XXXX			

Note: Net of salvage and subrogation received.

ANNUAL STATEMENT FOR THE YEAR 1989 OF THE

(Name)

SCHEDULE P — PART 3F — MEDICAL MALPRACTICE

Years in Which Losses Were Incurred	CUMULATIVE PAID LOSSES AND ALLOCATED EXPENSES AT YEAR END (000 OMITTED)										12 Number of Claims Closed With Loss Payment	13 Number of Claims Closed Without Loss Payment
	1 1980	2 1981	3 1982	4 1983	5 1984	6 1985	7 1986	8 1987	9 1988	10 1989		
1 Prior	000											
2 1980												
3 1981	x x x x											
4 1982	x x x x	x x x x										
5 1983	x x x x	x x x x	x x x x									
6 1984	x x x x	x x x x	x x x x	x x x x								
7 1985	x x x x	x x x x	x x x x	x x x x	x x x x							
8 1986	x x x x	x x x x	x x x x	x x x x	x x x x	x x x x						
9 1987	x x x x	x x x x	x x x x	x x x x	x x x x	x x x x	x x x x					
10 1988	x x x x	x x x x	x x x x	x x x x	x x x x	x x x x	x x x x	x x x x				
11 1989	x x x x	x x x x	x x x x	x x x x	x x x x	x x x x	x x x x	x x x x	x x x x			

SCHEDULE P — PART 3G — SPECIAL LIABILITY (OCEAN MARINE, AIRCRAFT (ALL PERILS), BOILER AND MACHINERY)

1 Prior	000										x x x x	x x x x
2 1980											x x x x	x x x x
3 1981	x x x x										x x x x	x x x x
4 1982	x x x x	x x x x									x x x x	x x x x
5 1983	x x x x	x x x x	x x x x								x x x x	x x x x
6 1984	x x x x	x x x x	x x x x	x x x x							x x x x	x x x x
7 1985	x x x x	x x x x	x x x x	x x x x	x x x x						x x x x	x x x x
8 1986	x x x x	x x x x	x x x x	x x x x	x x x x	x x x x					x x x x	x x x x
9 1987	x x x x	x x x x	x x x x	x x x x	x x x x	x x x x	x x x x				x x x x	x x x x
10 1988	x x x x	x x x x	x x x x	x x x x	x x x x	x x x x	x x x x	x x x x			x x x x	x x x x
11 1989	x x x x	x x x x	x x x x	x x x x	x x x x	x x x x	x x x x	x x x x	x x x x		x x x x	x x x x

SCHEDULE P — PART 3H — OTHER LIABILITY

1 Prior	000											
2 1980												
3 1981	x x x x											
4 1982	x x x x	x x x x										
5 1983	x x x x	x x x x	x x x x									
6 1984	x x x x	x x x x	x x x x	x x x x								
7 1985	x x x x	x x x x	x x x x	x x x x	x x x x							
8 1986	x x x x	x x x x	x x x x	x x x x	x x x x	x x x x						
9 1987	x x x x	x x x x	x x x x	x x x x	x x x x	x x x x	x x x x					
10 1988	x x x x	x x x x	x x x x	x x x x	x x x x	x x x x	x x x x	x x x x				
11 1989	x x x x	x x x x	x x x x	x x x x	x x x x	x x x x	x x x x	x x x x	x x x x			

SCHEDULE P — PART 3I — SPECIAL PROPERTY (FIRE, ALLIED LINES, INLAND MARINE, EARTHQUAKE, GLASS, BURGLARY AND THEFT)

1 Prior	x x x x	x x x x	x x x x	x x x x	x x x x	x x x x x	x x x x	000			x x x x	x x x x
2 1988	x x x x	x x x x	x x x x	x x x x	x x x x	x x x x	x x x x	x x x x			x x x x	x x x x
3 1989	x x x x	x x x x	x x x x	x x x x	x x x x	x x x x	x x x x	x x x x	x x x x		x x x x	x x x x

SCHEDULE P — PART 3J — AUTO PHYSICAL DAMAGE

1 Prior	x x x x	x x x x	x x x x	x x x x	x x x x	x x x x x	x x x x	000				
2 1988	x x x x	x x x x	x x x x	x x x x	x x x x	x x x x	x x x x	x x x x				
3 1989	x x x x	x x x x	x x x x	x x x x	x x x x	x x x x	x x x x	x x x x	x x x x			

SCHEDULE P — PART 3K — FIDELITY, SURETY, FINANCIAL GUARANTY, MORTGAGE GUARANTY

1 Prior	x x x x	x x x x	x x x x	x x x x	x x x x	x x x x x	x x x x	000			x x x x	x x x x
2 1988	x x x x	x x x x	x x x x	x x x x	x x x x	x x x x	x x x x	x x x x			x x x x	x x x x
3 1989	x x x x	x x x x	x x x x	x x x x	x x x x	x x x x	x x x x	x x x x	x x x x		x x x x	x x x x

Note: Net of salvage and subrogation received

ANNUAL STATEMENT FOR THE YEAR 1989 OF THE ....
(Name)

SCHEDULE P — PART 3L — OTHER (INCLUDING CREDIT, ACCIDENT AND HEALTH)

1 Years in Which Losses Were Incurred	CUMULATIVE PAID LOSSES AND ALLOCATED EXPENSES AT YEAR END (000 OMITTED)										12 Number of Claims Closed With Loss Payment	13 Number of Claims Closed Without Loss Payment
	2 1980	3 1981	4 1982	5 1983	6 1984	7 1985	8 1986	9 1987	10 1988	11 1989		
1 Prior	XXXX	XXXX	XXXX	XXXX	XXXX	XXXX	XXXX	000			XXXX	XXXX
2 1988	XXXX	XXXX	XXXX	XXXX	XXXX	XXXX	XXXX	XXXX			XXXX	XXXX
3 1989	XXXX	XXXX	XXXX	XXXX	XXXX	XXXX	XXXX	XXXX	XXXX		XXXX	XXXX

SCHEDULE P — PART 3M — INTERNATIONAL

1 Prior	000										XXXX	XXXX
2 1980											XXXX	XXXX
3 1981	XXXX										XXXX	XXXX
4 1982	XXXX	XXXX									XXXX	XXXX
5 1983	XXXX	XXXX	AAAA								XXXX	XXXX
6 1984	XXXX	XXXX	XXXX	XXXX							XXXX	XXXX
7 1985	XXXX	XXXX	XXXX	XXXX	XXXX						XXXX	XXXX
8 1986	XXXX	XXXX	XXXX	XXXX	XXXX	XXXX					XXXX	AAAA
9 1987	XXXX	XXXX	XXXX	XXXX	XXXX	XXXX	XXXX				XXXX	XXXX
10 1988	XXXX	XXXX	XXXX	XXXX	XXXX	XXXX	XXXX	XXXX			XXXX	XXXX
11 1989	XXXX	XXXX	XXXX	XXXX	XXXX	XXXX	XXXX	XXXX	XXXX		XXXX	YYYY

SCHEDULE P — PART 3N — REINSURANCE A

1 1988	XXXX	XXXX	XXXX	XXXX	XXXX	XXXX	XXXX	XXXX			XXXX	XXXX
2 1989	AAAA	XXXX	XXXX	XXXX	XXXX	XXXX	XXXX	XXXX	XXXX		XXXX	XXXX

SCHEDULE P — PART 3O — REINSURANCE B

1 1988	XXXX	XXXX	XXXX	XXXX	XXXX	XXXX	AAAA	XXXX			XXXX	XXXX
2 1989	YYYY	XXXX	XXXX	XXXX	XXXX	XXXX	AAAA	XXXX	XXXX		XXXX	XXXX

SCHEDULE P — PART 3P — REINSURANCE C

1 1988	YYYY	XXXX	XXXX	XXXX	XXXX	XXXX	AAAA	AAAA			XXXX	XXXX
2 1989	XXXX	XXXX	YYYY	XXXX	XXXX	XXXX	YYYY	YYYY	XXXX		XXXX	XXXX

SCHEDULE P — PART 3Q — REINSURANCE D

1 Prior	UUU										XXXX	XXXX
2 1980											XXXX	XXXX
3 1981	XXXX										XXXX	XXXX
4 1982	XXXX	XXXX									XXXX	XXXX
5 1983	XXXX	XXXX	XXXX								XXXX	XXXX
6 1984	XXXX	XXXX	XXXX	XXXX							XXXX	XXXX
7 1985	XXXX	XXXX	XXXX	XXXX	XXXX						XXXX	XXXX
8 1986	XXXX	XXXX	XXXX	XXXX	XXXX	XXXX					XXXX	XXXX
9 1987	XXXX	XXXX	XXXX	XXXX	XXXX	XXXX	XXXX				XXXX	XXXX

Note Net of salvage and subrogation received

Form 2

(Name)

SCHEDULE P—PART 5—CLAIMS - MADE
(000 omitted)

PART 5E — COMMERCIAL MULTIPLE PERIL

| 1
Years in Which Premiums Were Earned and Losses Were Incurred | 2
Premiums Earned | 3
Loss Payments | 3.1
Cumulative Number of Claims Closed with Payments | 3.2
Cumulative Number of Claims Closed without Payment | (d) Loss Expense Payments | | | | 6
Loss and Loss Expense Payments (3 + 4 + 5) | 7
Percent 6 ÷ 2 | 8
Number of Claims Outstanding | 9
Losses Unpaid | 10
Loss Expense Unpaid | 11
Total Losses and Loss Expense Incurred (6 + 9 + 10) | 12
Percent 11 ÷ 2 |
					4 Allocated	4a Percent 4 ÷ 3	5 Unallocated	5a Percent 5 ÷ 3							
1. 1987															
2. 1988															
3. 1989															
4. Totals															

PART 5F — MEDICAL MALPRACTICE

1. 1987															
2. 1988															
3. 1989															
4. Totals															

PART 5H — OTHER LIABILITY

1. 1987															
2. 1988															
3. 1989															
4. Totals															

SCHEDULE P — PART 6A — HOMEOWNERS/FARMOWNERS

1 Years in Which Losses Were Incurred	BULK AND INCURRED BUT NOT REPORTED RESERVES ON LOSSES AND ALLOCATED EXPENSES AT YEAR END (000 OMITTED)									
	2 1980	3 1981	4 1982	5 1983	6 1984	7 1985	8 1986	9 1987	10 1988	11 1989
1 Prior										
2 1980										
3 1981	XXXX									
4 1982	XXXX	XXXX								
5 1983	XXXX	XXXX	XXXX							
6 1984	XXXX	XXXX	XXXX	XXXX						
7 1985	XXXX	XXXX	XXXX	XXXX	XXXX					
8 1986	XXXX	XXXX	XXXX	XXXX	XXXX	XXXX				
9 1987	XXXX	XXXX	XXXX	XXXX	XXXX	XXXX	XXXX			
10 1988	XXXX	XXXX	XXXX	XXXX	XXXX	XXXX	XXXX	XXXX		
11 1989	XXXX	XXXX	XXXX	XXXX	XXXX	XXXX	XXXX	XXXX	XXXX	

SCHEDULE P — PART 6B — PRIVATE PASSENGER AUTO LIABILITY/MEDICAL

1 Prior										
2 1980										
3 1981	XXXX									
4 1982	XXXX	XXXX								
5 1983	XXXX	XXXX	XXXX							
6 1984	XXXX	XXXX	XXXX	XXXX						
7 1985	XXXX	XXXX	XXXX	XXXX	XXXX					
8 1986	XXXX	XXXX	XXXX	XXXX	XXXX	XXXX				
9 1987	XXXX	XXXX	XXXX	XXXX	XXXX	XXXX	XXXX			
10 1988	XXXX	XXXX	XXXX	XXXX	XXXX	XXXX	XXXX	XXXX		
11 1989	XXXX	XXXX	XXXX	XXXX	XXXX	XXXX	XXXX	XXXX	XXXX	

SCHEDULE P — PART 6C — COMMERCIAL AUTO/TRUCK LIABILITY/MEDICAL

1 Prior										
2 1980										
3 1981	XXXX									
4 1982	XXXX	XXXX								
5 1983	XXXX	XXXX	XXXX							
6 1984	XXXX	XXXX	XXXX	XXXX						
7 1985	XXXX	XXXX	XXXX	XXXX	XXXX					
8 1986	XXXX	XXXX	XXXX	XXXX	XXXX	XXXX				
9 1987	XXXX	XXXX	XXXX	XXXX	XXXX	XXXX	XXXX			
10 1988	XXXX	XXXX	XXXX	XXXX	XXXX	XXXX	XXXX	XXXX		
11 1989	XXXX	XXXX	XXXX	XXXX	XXXX	XXXX	XXXX	XXXX	XXXX	

SCHEDULE P — PART 6D — WORKERS' COMPENSATION

1 Prior										
2 1980										
3 1981	XXXX									
4 1982	XXXX	XXXX								
5 1983	XXXX	XXXX	XXXX							
6 1984	XXXX	XXXX	XXXX	XXXX						
7 1985	XXXX	XXXX	XXXX	XXXX	XXXX					
8 1986	XXXX	XXXX	XXXX	XXXX	XXXX	XXXX				
9 1987	XXXX	XXXX	XXXX	XXXX	XXXX	XXXX	XXXX			
10 1988	XXXX	XXXX	XXXX	XXXX	XXXX	XXXX	XXXX	XXXX		
11 1989	XXXX	XXXX	XXXX	XXXX	XXXX	XXXX	XXXX	XXXX	XXXX	

SCHEDULE P — PART 6E — COMMERCIAL MULTIPLE PERIL

1 Prior										
2 1980										
3 1981	XXXX									
4 1982	XXXX	XXXX								
5 1983	XXXX	XXXX	XXXX							
6 1984	XXXX	XXXX	XXXX	XXXX						
7 1985	XXXX	XXXX	XXXX	XXXX	XXXX					
8 1986	XXXX	XXXX	XXXX	XXXX	XXXX	XXXX				
9 1987	XXXX	XXXX	XXXX	XXXX	XXXX	XXXX	XXXX			
10 1988	XXXX	XXXX	XXXX	XXXX	XXXX	XXXX	XXXX	XXXX		
11 1989	XXXX	XXXX	XXXX	XXXX	XXXX	XXXX	XXXX	XXXX	XXXX	

SCHEDULE P — PART 6F — MEDICAL MALPRACTICE

1 Years in Which Losses Were Incurred	BULK AND INCURRED BUT NOT REPORTED RESERVES ON LOSSES AND ALLOCATED EXPENSES AT YEAR END (000 OMITTED)									
	2 1980	3 1981	4 1982	5 1983	6 1984	7 1985	8 1986	9 1987	10 1988	11 1989
1 Prior										
2 1980										
3 1981	XXXX									
4 1982	XXXX	XXXX								
5 1983	XXXX	XXXX	XXXX							
6 1984	XXXX	XXXX	XXXX	XXXX						
7 1985	XXXX	XXXX	XXXX	XXXX	XXXX					
8 1986	XXXX	XXXX	XXXX	XXXX	XXXX	XXXX				
9 1987	XXXX	XXXX	XXXX	XXXX	XXXX	XXXX	XXXX			
10 1988	XXXX	XXXX	XXXX	XXXX	XXXX	XXXX	XXXX	XXXX		
11 1989	XXXX	XXXX	XXXX	XXXX	XXXX	XXXX	XXXX	XXXX	XXXX	

SCHEDULE P — PART 6G — SPECIAL LIABILITY (OCEAN MARINE, AIRCRAFT (ALL PERILS), BOILER AND MACHINERY)

1 Prior										
2 1980										
3 1981	XXXX									
4 1982	XXXX	XXXX								
5 1983	XXXX	XXXX	XXXX							
6 1984	XXXX	XXXX	XXXX	XXXX						
7 1985	XXXX	XXXX	XXXX	XXXX	XXXX					
8 1986	XXXX	XXXX	XXXX	XXXX	XXXX	XXXX				
9 1987	XXXX	XXXX	XXXX	XXXX	XXXX	XXXX	XXXX			
10 1988	XXXX	XXXX	XXXX	XXXX	XXXX	XXXX	XXXX	XXXX		
11 1989	XXXX	XXXX	XXXX	XXXX	XXXX	XXXX	XXXX	XXXX	XXXX	

SCHEDULE P — PART 6H — OTHER LIABILITY

1 Prior										
2 1980										
3 1981	XXXX									
4 1982	XXXX	XXXX								
5 1983	XXXX	XXXX	XXXX							
6 1984	XXXX	XXXX	XXXX	XXXX						
7 1985	XXXX	XXXX	XXXX	XXXX	XXXX					
8 1986	XXXX	XXXX	XXXX	XXXX	XXXX	XXXX				
9 1987	XXXX	XXXX	XXXX	XXXX	XXXX	XXXX	XXXX			
10 1988	XXXX	XXXX	XXXX	XXXX	XXXX	XXXX	XXXX	XXXX		
11 1989	XXXX	XXXX	XXXX	XXXX	XXXX	XXXX	XXXX	XXXX	XXXX	

SCHEDULE P — PART 6I — SPECIAL PROPERTY (FIRE, ALLIED LINES, INLAND MARINE, EARTHQUAKE, GLASS, BURGLARY AND THEFT)

1 Prior	XXXX	XXXX	XXXX	XXXX	XXXX	XXXX	XXXX			
2 1988	XXXX	XXXX	XXXX	XXXX	XXXX	XXXX	XXXX	XXXX		
3 1989	XXXX	XXXX	XXXX	XXXX	XXXX	XXXX	XXXX	XXXX	XXXX	

SCHEDULE P — PART 6J — AUTO PHYSICAL DAMAGE

1 Prior	XXXX	XXXX	XXXX	XXXX	XXXX	XXXX	XXXX			
2 1988	XXXX	XXXX	XXXX	XXXX	XXXX	XXXX	XXXX	XXXX		
3 1989	XXXX	XXXX	XXXX	XXXX	XXXX	XXXX	XXXX	XXXX	XXXX	

SCHEDULE P — PART 6K — FIDELITY, SURETY, FINANCIAL GUARANTY, MORTGAGE GUARANTY

1 Prior	XXXX	XXXX	XXXX	XXXX	XXXX	XXXX	XXXX			
2 1988	XXXX	XXXX	XXXX	XXXX	XXXX	XXXX	XXXX	XXXX		
3 1989	XXXX	XXXX	XXXX	XXXX	XXXX	XXXX	XXXX	XXXX	XXXX	

SCHEDULE P — PART 6L — OTHER (INCLUDING CREDIT, ACCIDENT AND HEALTH)

1 Years in Which Losses Were Incurred	BULK AND INCURRED BUT NOT REPORTED RESERVES ON LOSSES AND ALLOCATED EXPENSES AT YEAR END (000 OMITTED)									
	2 1980	3 1981	4 1982	5 1983	6 1984	7 1985	8 1986	9 1987	10 1988	11 1989
1. Prior	XXXX	XXXX	XXXX	XXXX	XXXX	XXXX	XXXX			
2. 1988	XXXX	XXXX	XXXX	XXXX	XXXX	XXXX	XXXX	XXXX		
3. 1989	XXXX	XXXX	XXXX	XXXX	XXXX	XXXX	XXXX	XXXX	XXXX	

SCHEDULE P — PART 6M — INTERNATIONAL

1. Prior										
2. 1980										
3. 1981	XXXX									
4. 1982	XXXX	XXXX								
5. 1983	XXXX	XXXX	XXXX							
6. 1984	XXXX	XXXX	XXXX	XXXX						
7. 1985	XXXX	XXXX	XXXX	XXXX	XXXX					
8. 1986	XXXX	XXXX	XXXX	XXXX	XXXX	XXXX				
9. 1987	XXXX	XXXX	XXXX	XXXX	XXXX	XXXX	XXXX			
10. 1988	XXXX	XXXX	XXXX	XXXX	XXXX	XXXX	XXXX	XXXX		
11. 1989	XXXX	XXXX	XXXX	XXXX	XXXX	XXXX	XXXX	XXXX	XXXX	

SCHEDULE P — PART 6N — REINSURANCE A

1. 1988	XXXX	XXXX	XXXX	XXXX	XXXX	XXXX	XXXX	XXXX		
2. 1989	XXXX	XXXX	XXXX	XXXX	XXXX	XXXX	XXXX	XXXX	XXXX	

SCHEDULE P — PART 6O — REINSURANCE B

1. 1988	XXXX	XXXX	XXXX	XXXX	XXXX	XXXX	XXXX	XXXX		
2. 1989	XXXX	XXXX	XXXX	XXXX	XXXX	XXXX	XXXX	XXXX	XXXX	

SCHEDULE P — PART 6P — REINSURANCE C

1. 1988	XXXX	XXXX	XXXX	XXXX	XXXX	XXXX	XXXX	XXXX		
2. 1989	XXXX	XXXX	XXXX	XXXX	XXXX	XXXX	XXXX	XXXX	XXXX	

SCHEDULE P — PART 6Q — REINSURANCE D

1. Prior										
2. 1980										
3. 1981	XXXX									
4. 1982	XXXX	XXXX								
5. 1983	XXXX	XXXX	XXXX							
6. 1984	XXXX	XXXX	XXXX	XXXX						
7. 1985	XXXX	XXXX	XXXX	XXXX	XXXX					
8. 1986	XXXX	XXXX	XXXX	XXXX	XXXX	XXXX				
9. 1987	XXXX	XXXX	XXXX	XXXX	XXXX	XXXX	XXXX			

ANNUAL STATEMENT FOR THE YEAR 1989 OF THE

(Name)

SCHEDULE P INTERROGATORIES

1   Computation of excess statutory reserves over statement reserves See Instructions for explanation and formulas

  (a) Auto Liability (private passenger and commercial)

     1989 $ _____ (_____ %)   1988 $ _____ (_____ %)

     1987 $ _____ (_____ %)   Total $ _____

  (b) Other Liability

     1989 $ _____ (_____ %)   1988 $ _____ (_____ %)

     1987 $ _____ (_____ %)   Total $ _____

  (c) Medical Malpractice

     1989 $ _____ (_____ %)   1988 $ _____ (_____ %)

     1987 $ _____ (_____ %)   Total $ _____

  (d) Workers Compensation

     1989 $ _____ (_____ %)   1988 $ _____ (_____ %)

     1987 $ _____ (_____ %)   Total $ _____

  (e) Credit   Total $ _____

  (f) All Lines Total (Report here and Page 3)   Total $ _____

2   Claims-made policies. Schedule P — Part 5
   State the amount of current year premiums earned on claims-made policies. If this amount is more than $100,000 and greater than 15% of current year premiums earned in that line,
   then you must submit a Supplemental Schedule P — Part 5; see instructions.

  (a) Commercial Multiple Peril
        (i) claims-made premiums $ _____
        (ii) Part 5 required   Yes ( )   No ( )

  (b) Medical Malpractice
        (i) claims-made premiums $ _____
        (ii) Part 5 required   Yes ( )   No ( )

  (c) Other Liability
        (i) claims-made premiums $ _____
        (ii) Part 5 required   Yes ( )   No ( )

3.   The term "Loss expense" includes all payments for legal expenses, including attorney's and witness fees and court costs, salaries and expenses of investigators, adjustors and field
   men, rents, stationery, telegraph and telephone charges, postage, salaries and expenses of office employees, home office expenses and all other payments under or on account of such
   injuries, whether the payments are allocated to specific claims or are unallocated. Are they so reported in this statement?
                                                                    Answer: Yes ( )   No ( )

4.   The unallocated loss expense payments paid during the most recent calendar year should be distributed to the various years in which losses were incurred as follows: (1) 45% to the
   most recent year, (2) 5% to the next most recent year, and (3) the balance to all years, including the most recent, in proportion to the amount of loss payments paid for each year
   during the most recent calendar year. If the distribution in (1) or (2) produces an accumulated distribution to such year in excess of 10% of the premiums earned for such year,
   disregarding all distributions made under (3), such accumulated distribution should be limited to 10% of premiums earned and the balance distributed in accordance with (3). Are
   they so reported in this Statement?
                                                                    Answer: Yes ( )   No ( )

5.   Do any lines in Schedule P include reserves which are reported gross of any discount to present value of future payments, but are reported net of such discounts on page 10?
                                                                    Yes ( )   No ( )

   If Yes, proper reporting must be made in the Notes to Financial Statements, as specified in the Instructions. Also, the discounts must be reported in Schedule P — Part 1, columns 30
   and 31.

   Schedule P must be completed gross of non-tabular discounting. Work papers relating to discount calculations must be available for examination upon request.

   Discounting is allowed only if expressly permitted by the state insurance department to which this Annual Statement is being filed.

6.   What were the net premiums in force at the end of the year for:
   (in thousands of dollars)   (a) Fidelity _____
                                                                (b) Surety _____

7.   Claim count information is reported (check one)   (a) per claim _____
   If not the same in all years, explain in question 8.   (b) per claimant _____

8.   The information provided in Schedule P will be used by many persons to estimate the adequacy of the current loss and expense reserves, among other things. Are there any especially significant events, coverage,
   retention or accounting changes which have occurred which must be considered when making such analyses (An extended statement may be attached)?

   _____

   _____

   _____

   _____

   _____

   _____

ANNUAL STATEMENT FOR THE YEAR 1985 OF THE ....

(Name)

SCHEDULE X — PART 1 — UNLISTED ASSETS

*Showing all property owned by the Company or in which it had any interest, on December 31 of current year, which is not entered on any other schedule and which is not included in the financial statement for the current year

1 Description	2 From Whom Acquired	3 Date When Acquired	4 Date When Charged Off from Statement	5 Par Value	6 Actual Cost	7 Book Value When Charged Off	8 Market Value December 31 of Current Year	9 Gross Income Therefrom During Year	10 Outlays Made During Year	11 Reasons For Not Carrying Property on Books
999999 TOTALS										XXXX

SCHEDULE X — PART 2

Showing all property acquired or transferred to Schedule X, Part 1, during the year except that shown in invested asset schedules and except furniture, fixtures and supplies

1 Description	2 Date of Acquisition	3 From Whom Acquired	4 Par Value	5 Actual Cost
999999 TOTALS				

SCHEDULE X — PART 3

Showing all property sold or transferred from Schedule X, Part 1, during the year except that shown in invested asset schedules

1 Description	2 Date of Acquisition	3 From Whom Acquired	4 Par Value	5 Actual Cost	6 Date of Sale	7 To Whom Sold	8 Consideration	9 Gross Income Therefrom During Year	10 Outlay Thereon During Year Other Than Cost
999999 TOTALS					XXXX		XXXXXXXXXXXX		

*Companies should limit entries in this schedule to items transferred from asset accounts.
NOTE: Interest, dividends and real estate income should be reported in Part 1, Line 6, Page 4. Capital gains on investments should be reported in Part 1A, Line 9, Page 6. Any other receipts should be reported in Item 12, Page 4.

Form 2

ANNUAL STATEMENT FOR THE YEAR 1989 OF THE ....

(Name)

SCHEDULE Y — INFORMATION CONCERNING ACTIVITIES OF INSURER MEMBERS OF A HOLDING COMPANY GROUP

NOTE: All insurer members of a Holding Company Group shall prepare a common Schedule for inclusion in each of the individual annual statements and the consolidated Fire and Casualty Annual Statement of the Group

PART 1 — ORGANIZATIONAL CHART

Attach a chart or listing presenting the identities of interrelationships between the parent, all affiliated insurers and other affiliates, identifying all insurers as such and listing the Federal Employers Identification Number for each. The relationship of the Holding Company Group to the ultimate parent (if such parent is outside the reported holding company) should be shown. No non-insurer need be shown if it does not have any activities reported in Part 2 and its total assets are less than one-half of one percent of the total assets of the largest affiliated insurer.

ANNUAL STATEMENT FOR THE YEAR 1989 OF THE ....

....
(Name)

SCHEDULE Y — (Continued)

NOTE: All insurer members of a Holding Company Group shall prepare a common Schedule for inclusion in each of the individual annual statements and the consolidated Fire and Casualty Annual Statement of the Group

PART 2 — SUMMARY OF THE INSURER'S TRANSACTIONS WITH ANY AFFILIATES

Include the aggregate of transactions, for the reporting period, within each category involving the parent company (companies), all insurance companies in the Holding Company System, and all other companies in the system with which an insurance company member has a transaction. Exclude: transactions of a non-insurer with an insurance company that are of a routine nature (i.e., the purchase of insurance coverage) and cost allocation transactions that are based upon generally accepted principles of accounting.

1	2	3	4	5	6	7	8	9	10
Name of Insurer and Parent, Subsidiary or Affiliate	Shareholder Dividends	Capital Contributions	Purchases, Sales or Exchanges of Loans, Securities, Real Estate, Mortgage Loans or Other Investments	Receipts/ (Payments) in Connection with Guarantees or Undertakings for the Benefit of an Affiliate	Management Agreements, Service Contracts (including Contracts for Services Provided by the Insurer or Purchased by the Insurer from Other Affiliates) and Non-GAAP Cost Sharing Agreements	Receipts/ (Payments) Made Under Reinsurance Agreements	Any Other Material Activity not in the Ordinary Course of the Insurer's Business	Totals	Reinsurance Reserve Credits
Control Totals									

NOTE: If the nature of the transactions reported in Part 2 requires explanation with this Schedule report such in an explanatory note immediately following Part 2

86

ANNUAL STATEMENT FOR THE YEAR 1989 OF THE ....
(Name)

Form 2

SCHEDULE T — EXHIBIT OF PREMIUMS WRITTEN
Allocated by States and Territories

1 States, Etc	1a Is Insurer Licensed? (Yes or No)	Gross Premiums, Including Policy and Membership Fees, Less Return Premiums and Premiums on Policies Not Taken 2 Direct Premiums Written	3 Direct Premiums Earned	4 Dividends Paid or Credited to Policyholders on Direct Business	5 Direct Losses Paid (Deducting Salvage)	6 Direct Losses Incurred	7 Direct Losses Unpaid	8 Finance and Service Charges Not Included in Premiums	9 Direct Premiums Written for Federal Purchasing Groups (Included in Column 2)
1. Alabama .... AL									
2. Alaska .... AK									
3. Arizona .... AZ									
4. Arkansas .... AR									
5. California .... CA									
6. Colorado .... CO									
7. Connecticut .... CT									
8. Delaware .... DE									
9. Dist. Columbia .... DC									
10. Florida .... FL									
11. Georgia .... GA									
12. Hawaii .... HI									
13. Idaho .... ID									
14. Illinois IL									
15. Indiana .... IN									
16. Iowa .... IA									
17. Kansas .... KS									
18. Kentucky .... KY									
19. Louisiana .... LA									
20. Maine .... ME									
21. Maryland .... MD									
22. Massachusetts .... MA									
23. Michigan .... MI									
24. Minnesota .... MN									
25. Mississippi .... MS									
26. Missouri .... MO									
27. Montana .... MT									
28. Nebraska .... NE									
29. Nevada .... NV									
30. New Hampshire .... NH									
31. New Jersey .... NJ									
32. New Mexico .... NM									
33. New York .... NY									
34. North Carolina .... NC									
35. North Dakota .... ND									
36. Ohio .... OH									
37. Oklahoma .... OK									
38. Oregon .... OR									
39. Pennsylvania .... PA									
40. Rhode Island .... RI									
41. South Carolina .... SC									
42. South Dakota .... SD									
43. Tennessee .... TN									
44. Texas .... TX									
45. Utah .... UT									
46. Vermont .... VT									
47. Virginia .... VA									
48. Washington .... WA									
49. West Virginia .... WV									
50. Wisconsin .... WI									
51. Wyoming .... WY									
52. American Samoa .... AS									
53. Guam .... GU									
54. Puerto Rico .... PR									
55. U.S. Virgin Is. VI									
56. Canada .... CN									
57. Aggregate Other Alien .... OT**									
98. *Totals	††								

DETAILS OF WRITE-INS AGGREGATED AT LINE 57 FOR OTHER ALIEN

5701									
5702									
5703									
5704									
5705									
5798 Summary of remaining write-ins for line 57 from overflow page									
5799 Totals (Items 5701 thru 5705 plus 5798) (Schedule T, Line 57)									

Explanation of basis of allocation of premiums by states, etc.

*Total for Column 2 to agree with the total of Column 1 in Part 2B, Page 8. Total for Column 5 to agree with the total of Column 1 in Part 3, Page 9.
Total for Column 6 to agree with the sum of totals for Columns 5 and 7 less the total for Column 7 in the previous annual statement.
Total for Column 7 to equal Part 3A, Page 10, totals for Columns 1a and 4a. Total for Column 8 to agree with Item 11, Page 4.
**All U.S. business must be allocated by state regardless of license status.
††Insert the number of yes responses except for Canada and Other alien.

ANNUAL STATEMENT FOR THE YEAR 1989 OF THE ....
(Name)

SUPPLEMENTAL EXHIBITS AND SCHEDULES
INTERROGATORIES

The following supplemental reports are required to be filed as part of your annual statement filing. However, in the event that your company does not transact the type of business for which the special report must be filed, your response to the specific interrogatory will be accepted in lieu of filing a "NONE" report.

1. Will Supplement A to Schedule T (Medical Malpractice Supplement) be filed with this Department by March 1?   Yes [ ]   No [ ]
   If answer is no, please explain: ....

2. Will Schedule SIS (Stockholder Information Supplement) be filed with this Department by March 1?   Yes [ ]   No [ ]
   If answer is no, please explain: ....

3. Will the Financial Guaranty Insurance Exhibit be filed with this Department by March 1?   Yes [ ]   No [ ]
   If answer is no, please explain: ....

4. Will the Insurance Expense Exhibit be filed with this Department by April 1?   Yes [ ]   No [ ]
   If answer is no, please explain: ....

5. Will Schedule H be filed with this Department by April 1?   Yes [ ]   No [ ]
   If answer is no, please explain: ....

6. Will Schedule F, Part 1A, Section 2 be filed with this Department by April 1?   Yes [ ]   No [ ]
   If answer is no, please explain: ....

7. Will the Statement of Opinion relating to loss and loss adjustment expense reserves be filed with this Department by April 1?   Yes [ ]   No [ ]
   If answer is no, please explain: ....

8. Will the Products Liability Supplement be filed with this Department by May 1?   Yes [ ]   No [ ]
   If answer is no, please explain: ....

9. Will the Credit Life and Accident & Health Experience Exhibit be filed with this Department by May 1?   Yes [ ]   No [ ]
   If answer is no, please explain: ....

10. Will the Accident and Health Policy Experience Exhibit be filed with this Department by June 30?   Yes [ ]   No [ ]
    If answer is no, please explain: ....

11. Will the Medicare Supplement Insurance Experience Exhibit be filed with this Department by June 30?   Yes [ ]   No [ ]
    If answer is no, please explain: ....

ANNUAL STATEMENT FOR THE YEAR 1989 OF THE ....
(Name)

OVERFLOW PAGE FOR WRITE-INS